Luther in Light of Recent Research

BY

HEINRICH BÖHMER
Marburg University

TRANSLATED BY

CARL F. HUTH, JR.
University of Chicago

1916
THE CHRISTIAN HERALD
NEW YORK

FOREWORD.

By Prof. James Harvey Robinson,

Columbia University.

IT is a great pleasure to introduce this book to the
intelligent American reader. Everyone who has
even a modicum of historical interest finds his curiosity
aroused by Luther, and welcomes more information
in regard to this German national hero whose influence has spread so far beyond the bounds of his own
land. We may be attracted or repelled by what we
know of his teachings and personality, but he can
hardly leave anyone indifferent and neutral. The
volume of which this is a translation appears in one of
those excellent series designed for the cultivated German public, similar to our "Home University
Library." The author seems to me particularly well
qualified by knowledge, temperament and style to
give us a fresh and stimulating conception of Luther.
He is broadly sympathetic but no hero worshiper.
There is no trace of religious partisanship in him. He
feels that he can afford to tell all the varied truth
without suppression or distortion. He is well aware
of the widely divergent judgments that have been
passed upon Luther by Protestant, Catholic and so-
called "rationalistic" writers during the four centuries which have elapsed since Luther began to criti-

i

cize the existing order, and no small part of the interest of his book lies in the dexterous manner in which he gives the reader an idea of the conflicting interpretations which have been placed upon the Reformer's deeds and sayings. <u>His consistent aim is to place himself in the milieu in which Luther lived and worked</u>. <u>He judges</u> him not from the standpoint of to-day but <u>from that of the first half of the sixteenth century</u>. He is critical without any tendency to lapse into mere negativity. To him and his readers Luther is always the livest man possible. <u>His style is clear and cogent, with a certain familiar homeliness, suggesting that of Luther himself</u>. No matter how wide or how narrow has been one's reading in regard to Luther, <u>Professor Böhmer will give the reader new facts, new judgments and new points of view</u>. He is able to take the beginner in hand and at the same time to instruct the historical student who may think that he already knows as much about Luther as he cares to.

Professor Huth's translation seems to me not only correct and intelligent, <u>but it reproduces with skill the spirit of the original style</u>. If he now and then permits the German idiom to show through, that will not disturb the reader but will serve rather to strengthen his confidence in the fidelity of the rendering.

JAMES HARVEY ROBINSON.

CHAPTER I.

The Old Portrait of Luther and the Development of Research on Luther.

Open your eyes and see me as I am.—DANTE.

MARTIN LUTHER voluntarily sat for a portrait perhaps only once in his life—at the time
of his wedding. Nevertheless, even to-day every halfway educated person is quite familiar with his features. In Germany the school children know his face
so well that they can point to it without difficulty in
paintings representing many characters. Indeed,
little girls need sometimes only to determine with a
rapid glance "what the man in the picture is wearing"
to know: that is Doctor Luther. This knowledge and
acuteness, especially on the part of the female portion
of our offspring, certainly is quite pleasing, though
it surely is partially due to the fact that the pictures of
the Reformer which they see in school and at home
are all so much alike. Almost every one of them
shows a man in the portliness of advanced years, with
a broad peasant countenance, unusually well developed jaws, peculiarly full brown, curly hair, small
gentle eyes and on the whole rather pudgy features.

But is the Luther of these pictures really the
Reformer Luther? Without doubt it is the Luther
one expects to see in approaching a monument or
portrait of him, the Luther whom Rietschel after some
hesitation chose as model when he created his famous
statue, though he knew very well that the real Luther

1

in 1521 looked very different. It is the Luther whom even the most extravagantly modern artists with astonishing consistency ever again portray, and from whose skull formation physiognomists and race theorists readily and unconcernedly, as is the custom in their blythe science, have so often proven that the Reformer had Slavic blood in his veins. For did not this Luther have a round skull, and whoever has a round skull is at least one half Slav, even though, as in this case, German peasants were his ancestors, and the Reformer hailed from a region in which hitherto no trace of Slavic settlements or admixture of Slavic blood has been found.

This Luther therefore undoubtedly is a type, namely, a figure, the features of which have become as fixed to the artists and their public as for instance those of the "Germania," the "Helvetia" and other allegoric females. However, though this Luther is a type, he certainly is not a freely invented wholly unhistoric one like the Apostle Peter or the Charlemagne of mediæval art, but the idealized reproduction of an historical portrait like the "Old Fritz" of Menzel and the "Queen Louise" of Rauch. Everybody knows that in the last analysis this conventional representation is based on the well-nigh innumerable portraits of the Reformer by the great master Lucas Cranach, and that it is found in a truly classic example in the most famous painting by this artist, the altar picture in the city church at Weimar. Who has not repeatedly even in quite modern "highly scientific works" about Cranach and about Luther read this in black and white? In fact this still is the prevailing opinion of to-day.

However, what "everybody" believes to be true usually is not true. If under an expert guidance we submit the artistic legacy of the elder Cranach to an unprejudiced investigation we experience one surprise after the other and meet with disappointment upon disappointment. We note in the first place with considerable misgiving that despite decades of study of the history of art this legacy has not yet been carefully sifted. In the second place, we notice that so far only four portraits of Luther, two paintings in oil and two copper etchings, have been proven to be indubitably genuine works of Cranach. Lastly, we find that the classic representation of the type, the picture in the altar at Weimar, was not created by the elder Cranach, but evidently was made two years after Cranach's and fully nine years after Luther's death by Lucas Cranach the Younger.*

---

*The four genuine portraits are: Luther as monk, front view, copper etching of 1520; Luther as monk, in profile, copper etching of 1521. Luther as Squire George, oil painting, done in December, 1521, poorly preserved, now in the City Library at Leipzig; oil painting, front view, of 1526, in the Kaufmann Gallery at Berlin. To these possibly may be added the small, very poorly preserved round portrait in the Luther Hall at Wittenberg, and an oil painting discovered only this year (1913) by Hans von Cranach, Head Castellan of the Wartburg, about which discussion is not closed as yet. This latter painting represents the aged, gray-haired Luther, though minus the big wart which is visible in the Epitaphium. It is the prototype of many modern portraits. Excellent reproductions may be had directly from Herr von Cranach. Compare also Eduard Flechsig: Cranachstudien, vol. 1, 1897, pp. 257 ff; Cranachwerk of the Saxon Historical Commission, plates 74, 84, 85; Hans Preuss: Lutherbildnisse, pp. 27, 30, 32, 34, 35, and ibid., a tracing very probably executed by Hans Cranach after which portraits of Luther were manufactured in the atelier of the Cranachs. On page 40 is a reproduction of the Epitaphium; on page 42 the Weimar altar painting.

Now, if we examine the few admittedly genuine Cranachs we notice further that the typical Luther head certainly does not go back to these, but rather to some later works from the workshop of the Cranachs about the origin of which the final word has not yet been spoken. The most important of these are the so-called Epitaphium, a woodcut with a lament on Luther's death, and a recently discovered beautifully preserved oil painting. The "type" in the former still makes quite a different impression from that in the altar painting at Weimar, or even in the well-known likenesses by Schwerdgeburth, Gustav Koenig, Ludwig Richter and Spangenberg. The features are much sharper and more energetic, the mouth is firmly closed. On the forehead the hair forms a loose curl (cowlick), a furrow of anger appears between the brows and above the right eye a tremendous wart glowers.

It is impossible for us now to determine whether this really is the true face of Doctor Martin. On the other hand, we can say with assurance that not one of the undoubtedly genuine portraits by the elder Cranach wholly agrees with the descriptions of Luther's face and figure which have been handed down to us by Mosellan, Kessler, Melanchthon and other contemporaries. None shows the peculiar erect bearing, bordering on stiffness—"so that he seemed rather to be bending backward than forward"—none even remotely conveys an idea of the expression in the dark demoniac eyes, "which sparkle and twinkle like a star, so that one cannot well bear their gaze." These falcon's eyes, lion's eyes, basilisk's eyes, which immediately drew the attention of everyone, and this highly characteristic and imposing heroic presence are left to the imagination even in these portraits. Unfortunately imagination never quite makes up for the missing concrete representation. No matter, therefore, how well drawn even these genuine Cranachs may be, they are certainly not successful portraits. Nevertheless, the elder Cranach was by far the ablest of the few artists who personally met Luther. The younger Lucas possessed much less ability, though after all a good deal more than the painter of the well-known picture representing "Luther on the Deathbed," now in the Dresden gallery, the false perspective and bungling execution of which immediately disturbs even a layman, or the anonymous artist in wax who created the famous death mask in the Library of St. Mary in Halle.*

The really great German portrait artists of the sixteenth century, Dürer, Holbein and Amberger, to whom we owe so many portraits of famous contemporaries, unhappily never had an opportunity to see the most renowned of all, Doctor Martin. True, Dürer had the sincere intention "in everlasting memory to portray and make an etching in copper of the God-inspired man who had helped him out of great

---

*This mask is frequently regarded as the most faithful representation of Luther's features. It was, however, taken four days after Luther's death, at a time when decomposition had already set in. Luther succumbed to a stroke of paralysis, and in such cases deterioration is very rapid. Besides, the mask was damaged in the course of time and has evidently been patched considerably about the mouth and nose.

tribulations," but unfortunately he also never came to Saxony. The extent of our loss, owing to the fact that these great artists did not have a chance to portray Luther, may in a measure be judged from a comparison of the portraits of Melanchthon from the atelier of the Cranachs with the well-known copper etching by Dürer and the red pencil drawing by Holbein in Windsor. In the former Magister Philipp always appears so starved, miserable and wretched that one's heart almost aches at the sight. Even in the best picture, that at the Wartburg, he utterly fails to impress us as a great man. Dürer and Holbein, on the contrary, make it immediately evident that the Præceptor Germaniæ was an unusually learned and bright person, so much better were these great artists able to reproduce the spiritual expression in a face.

Hence we must familiarize ourselves with the idea that we possess not many but very few portraits of Luther from the hand of the elder Cranach and that among these few, though they are mostly excellent in technique, there is not a single good likeness. In other words, we must confess that we do not any more exactly know how Luther looked. Nevertheless, we will do well henceforth to picture him to ourselves only as he is depicted in those few unquestionably genuine Cranachs from the second decade of the sixteenth century. If, besides, we desire to have before our eyes also the aging Luther we may add to these the recently discovered oil painting and the Epitaphium of 1546. But we will for all time strike from our memory the affable and corpulent gentleman of fifty with immaculately groomed hair who was gradually made up by idealization from the type furnished by artists who were more well-meaning than expert. We will also consign to oblivion the new, so-called historic Luther whom Hans Fechner produced in 1905 by combining several portraits by Cranach. (Heliogravure published by Stalling in Oldenburg.)

After all, what difference does it make if we no more know and probably never will know exactly how Luther looked, if only we know precisely what he did, was, thought and wished to achieve? This indeed is vastly more important. However, it is not by any chance an easy matter to give a rapid and correct report of what he did, was, thought and wished to achieve. The literature about Luther has grown to such proportions that with its two thousand volumes, large and small, it forms a complete moderately sized library. Withal it is so many-tongued, so multiform and varied that one is struck with fear after a mere cursory glance through the endless list of titles, or upon attempting merely to remember the names of the authors of the more than two hundred biographies of Luther in Latin, German, French, English, Danish, Swedish, Italian, Spanish, Russian, Polish and Lithuanian. Stranger sensations still take hold of one when dipping into a few dozen of these biographies in addition to half a dozen novels on Luther and dramas about him. The most immediate impression derived from this process is that there are as many Luthers as books about him; so widely divergent are the views of the writers about the essence and worth of Luther's person and work. To the one he appears as a prophet of God, to the other as a changeling of Satan; for one he is a model citizen, excellent father, and affectionate husband, for the other a criminal of the deepest moral depravity; for some a productive genius of the foremost order, for others an intellectually inferior, or at least anormal individual; to some he is one of the foremost enlighteners of all times, to others an Obscurantist, a henchman of the princes and a firebrand of the worst type.

Was Luther in reality such a complicated and ill-defined character, or is the tradition about his life so scant, open to so many different interpretations and so vague that historians of necessity arrived at such radically varying conclusions? By no means. Our sources are in this instance as ample, clear and connected as we could wish them to be, and the character of Luther in the genuine documents in no way conveys the impression of being complicated. Hence the fault this time lies with the historians. Some would not, others could not see the real character of Luther. And why? Because they approached the records with concrete, preconceived opinions, and therefore naturally saw only what seemed to suit their view. This failing, however, must not be laid at their door alone. Most of them worked under the influence of a psychological force from which they found it difficult to emancipate themselves. They allowed their judgments to be guided by the ideas and ideals of their religious belief and their age and involuntarily interpreted the sources accordingly. If this fact be taken into account the grotesque differences of conception become psychologically quite intelligible, then this chaos presents a measure of order, sequence and development, and the reader learns to value even the most peculiar products of this literature, if not as scientific achievements, at least as historical documents, as records for the history of the religious, philosophical, political and social ideas since the days of the Reformation.

In the early years of the movement the Evangelical faction generally looked upon Luther as a prophet of God. Indeed sober men like Albrecht Dürer spoke of him outright as an inspired personality. Less well-balanced natures sought and found in the Bible and the utterances of mediæval prophets predictions pointing to him and his work. Enthusiastic artists went so far as to represent him with the dove of the Holy Ghost or with a halo about his head. In the two earliest evangelical biographies of Luther, the Luther Sermons by Cyriacus Spangenberg and John Mathesius, this view still prevails, though it did not cloud the authors' perception of the faults and weaknesses of the Reformer, nor prejudice their judgment with regard to them.

But already Mathesius occasionally emphasizes as the most noteworthy service of his hero the fact "that he again scoured the doctrine clean." Herein a new view of Luther's person and work makes its appearance, one which by this time had become prevalent in wide circles and was destined to maintain itself in the

Lutheran Church down to the last decades of the
seventeenth century. It is the dogmatic conception of
Lutheran Orthodoxy. This view clung to the belief
that the Reformer was the prophet of Germany. The
chief proof of his prophetic mission for these orthodox
groups was the agreement of his doctrines with the
teachings of God's Word. Involuntarily the picture
of the Reformer was modeled on the outlines of the
traditional Catholic conception of a church father.
The Lutheran people, however, at the same time
revered this father of the church as a veritable saint.
They told wonderful tales about his prophecies, his
miracles and his pictures, and diligently cut splinters
from the wooden columns in the house of Luther at
Wittenberg; for as in Catholic lands the relics of Saint
Apollonia, so in Lutheran territory these slivers were
accounted wonderfully efficacious as remedies for
toothache. Pietism broke away from the habits and
point of view of Orthodoxy in these matters also. It
discovered the difference between Luther and Lutheranism and occasionally played off the former effectively against contemporary manifestations of the
latter. Besides, it distinguished a young, middle-
aged and old Luther, and very freely criticized the last
two by calling the early Luther to witness against
them. With the Luther of the middle period, of the
Marburg Colloquy, almost no Pietist would have any
dealings. To the old Luther most of them, with
Albrecht Bengel, the mild patriarch of the Swabian
Hour Men (*Stundenleute*), gave the grade *Good*.
They all were truly enthusiastic only about the young

Luther. Him they extolled not alone as a father of the faith, a man of spiritual power in prayer, a second Samson, a victor over parsons and Philistines, but as the true originator of the pietistic community ideal of "the little churches within the Church." Indeed the greatest and most highly gifted among these pietistic venerators of Luther, Ludwig Zinzendorf, saw salvation for theology only in a return to the theological method of Doctor Luther, and himself made several efforts to bring about such a reform.

The Rationalists stood so far removed from Luther in their religious views that they were wholly unable to understand his religious personality. The struggles of his soul were to them a disease, his doctrines of sin and justification were at best looked upon as a "perversion," or as "the dangerous dogmatic extravagance of a great and courageous, but at times one-sided spirit." Even sincere Protestants with Semler placed "the learned and righteous Erasmus" above him. Men who were wholly apathetic to religion, as, for instance, Frederick the Great, judged him to be "a raving monk and barbarous writer," or taking their cue from Voltaire spoke of him as a man who had missed his calling. These radicals, however, found one phase in the character of the "regenerator of the church," which appealed to them: his hatred of the priests and his ardor in the cause of the "freedom of conscience."

Milder advocates of the faith of reason, though chiefly admiring the Reformer as an enemy of parsons and a restorer of liberty of thought, besides delighted in praising the great man as an "affectionate husband, honest father, magnanimous friend, excellent citizen and as a scholar useful to the public. As late as the Jubilee of 1817 the addresses and poems in honor of the occasion were uniformly pitched in this key. A proof of this is the beautiful "Nightwatchman's Hymn for the Year 1817":

List, ye men, and be advised,
No more in shackles the spirit lies.
Remember Luther, the faithful one,
Who hath this freedom for you won.
Guard well the light, the light of truth,
Guard well the fire, profane it not.

More characteristically perhaps than in these laudatory utterances the spirit of the times is revealed in the critical remarks we encounter occasionally. The German Rationalists highly praised what had been so discomforting to the Pietists, Luther's love of song, the pleasure he found in a game of chess or a drink of good wine, his mild judgment on dancing and the theatre. What disturbed them most, however, was the disrespectful manner in which the Reformer frequently referred to the princes and bigwigs. Their censure of his public burning of the bull of excommunication also was most lively. It above all others was the one act of the Reformer which ran counter to their conception of gentility and civic virtue.

Now and then, however, even in the heyday of

Rationalism, we meet with instances of a deeper understanding of Luther's peculiarities. Hamann even in those days endeavored to grasp the prophetic element in the Reformer and also attempted to evaluate psychologically the harshnesses and paradoxes of his personality. Young Herder is found trying to cut loose from all the artificial criteria of Enlightenment, Pietism and Orthodoxy in forming a judgment about Luther. He endeavors to appreciate the "patriotic and great man" from out of the depth of his own personal being as an independent phenomenon. Nevertheless, for some time no progress was made beyond these imperfect efforts. Herder himself in his later years returned to the method and historical point of view of Rationalism, and even Schiller, who among the intellectual leaders in the Germany of that day was most interested in history, finds no higher epithet of honor for Luther in his "Secular Hymn on the Year 1800" than that of "a champion of the freedom of reason against error and the Vatican."

The Romanticists finally showed signs of adopting a new conception of personality which was likely to benefit Luther also. They viewed individual life from the point of view of the æsthetic ideal. According to this the worth of a human being lies not in the usefulness of his existence for the world of his own and later times, nor even in his moral perfection, but solely in the originality, fullness and force of his nature; briefly, in his genius. The wholly unromantic genius of Luther, however, kept them from ever really coming into closer touch with him. Schelling saw in the Reformation only decline and retrogression, and even Schleiermacher was so little clear about Luther's religious "peculiarity" that in his lectures on church history he still ventured to assert: "the Hussite movement and the Lutheran reform started from the same basic principles." Instead, therefore, of giving a vivid portrayal of Luther to his hearers he warned them not to overestimate the reformers on the very modern grounds that "in them as in projecting points were concentrated the general forces."

The romantic valuation of personality appears wholly without qualification in the utterances of the aged Goethe about the Reformer, when in 1817 he declares that Luther's character is the only factor in that "confused nonsense," i. e., the account of the Reformation, which is of interest to him. And again when in 1826 he testifies to a lively admiration for the unity and wholeness manifested in Luther's attitude, word and action, this is altogether in keeping with the æsthetic historical point of view of the early Romanticists. However, the great poet was no longer completely under the magic influence of the æsthetic view of the world. "Genius" to him connoted not merely a sense for the harmonious development of one's individual existence, but "creative force, of which deeds are born fit to stand before the judgment of God and nature, and which for this very reason brings results and lives on." Pursuant to this definition Goethe in 1827 rates Luther as "an extraordinary genius" who had not then and probably would not within a measurable space of time cease to make his influence felt.

While thus æsthetic minds, untroubled by the brutal misery of the present, were constructing their Cloud-cucoovilles, the ignominious yoke of foreign domination fell heavily on Northern Germany. This immediately caused a revulsion of feeling both in the North and in the South. National enthusiasm replaced the complacent æsthetic philosophical culture, spiritual revelling was supplanted by suspicion, indeed hatred, of the cult of the beautiful and by the harsh pathos of political passions. As a result we find an inevitable change in the judgment of the nation about its own past. While people almost contemptuously turned from Frederick the Great they began under the leadership of Arndt and Jahn to passionately revere Luther as a national hero, as the archetype of German piety, manly courage, and love of liberty. Indeed, they naïvely placed the Reformer by the side of the old Blücher and requisitioned him even in support of the purely political ideals of the time.

In the ranks of rising Liberalism this new nationalistic conception of Luther was still somewhat tinged with the old rationalistic valuation of the Reformer. Leberecht Uhlich, Baltzer and other Friends of Light praised the Wittenberg hero not as the great German only, but also as the supreme enlightener. However, in these strata of the population the interest in Luther, especially after Herwegh's triumphal progress through Germany, had been materially weakened by the enthusiasm for the newly discovered "Saviour,"

Ulrich von Hutten, whose resounding catch phrases were indeed much better suited to these political poets and journalists than the absolutely non-pathetic utterances of "Father Luther."

After all, though, Liberalism never quite dominated public opinion to the extent of Rationalism. On the contrary, intellectual development ever since the days of Romanticism shows a tendency to ever greater cleavage and disintegration. Most characteristically this is brought out in the verdicts about the person and work of Luther. All the manifold views of earlier stages of evolution experienced a sort of resurrection in the course of the nineteenth century. Only the naïveté and assurance with which older scholars had asserted their attitude was lacking. It was impossible now for any party to wholly escape the influences of historical criticism, and each group was therefore forced to defend its standpoint against differing conceptions.

In the historical point of view of the strict New Lutheran school the Reformer again appeared as church father. For that reason they as far as possible caused him to approach Lutheran Orthodoxy and summarily disavowed the younger Luther as "a personality still quite unclarified and wallowing in subjective extravagances." (Kliefoth.) They accepted Luther as master and model only in the middle and later period of his career. Radical Protestants of the Tübingen school, as whose characteristic representative we may regard Heinrich Lang, on the contrary would have no dealings with this later Luther. They venerated only the young Luther, and him only in so far as he was "a genius and national hero." As a reformer Luther was to them merely a representative of the Catholic view of life and in no way the equal of such men as Zwingli, Karlstadt and the leaders of the Anabaptists and rebellious peasants.

Albrecht Ritschl made another attempt to comprehend Luther as a religious prophet. To make this possible he removed him from Lutheran Orthodoxy as far as he could and extolled particularly the young Luther. In his mind the really great achievement of the prophet Luther was the setting up of "the new ideal of perfection." Upon closer inspection, however, this ideal was found not to be a genuine Lutheran product, but a hybrid of purely Lutheran ideas and certain basic religious and ethical principles of the old Rationalism. Therefore it is hardly surprising that for instance the disciples of Ritschl in their appraisement of Luther should also have returned to the views of the radical Rationalists. Harnack's History of Dogma marked the first step in this direction. In it Luther was once again brought closer to Orthodoxy, criticized severely on particular points, and "the great epoch of his life, the years from 1519 to 1521" estimated merely as an episode in which Luther in reality "had not been himself, but had been lifted up out of the limits of his being."

This rationalistic standpoint, though with considerable modification in detail due to points of view of romantic philosophy and modern religious criticism, is again reached in the recent writings of E. Troeltsch.

Herein, as previously in Semler's attempt at a free
theological method, Erasmus of Rotterdam is placed
above Luther and the Reformer's religious attitude, as
H. Lang had done before in his "Luther," is in its
essential phases merely rated as a recasting of the
"mediæval ideal."

While thus theology is once more approaching the
ideas and methods of Rationalism the broader strata
of the cultured world are again being strongly influenced by the æsthetic point of view of Romanticism,
particularly through the writings of Friedrich Nietz-
sche.* As a rule, however, the "genius" Luther is
even less sympathetic to this new school of Romanticists than it had been to the old. "Luther the plebeian,
the great rustic whose mental horizon is bounded by
the space taken up by his hobnailed shoes," "the barbarian," "the demagogue," "the originator of the
peasant rebellion of the North against the Southern
ecclesiastical organism of government which assured
supremacy to the more intellectual man," the "German monk who, filled with all the vindictive instincts
of a priest, cheated Europe out of its last great
cultural harvest, the Renaissance, and who ruined
the prospect resplendent in all the horrors of exquisite
beauty of seeing Cæsar Borgia (he died March 12,
1507!) as Pope abolish Christianity"—this Luther
appears pitiably small to some of these newer Romanticists, over against such vaunted supermen as that
savage son of a pope in whose person "life itself, the

*Who, by the way, was wholly under the spell of Janssen. See
his Letters, Inselverlag, Leipzig, 1911, p. 222.

triumph of life, the great Aye to all that is grand, beautiful and audacious" reached out for mastery in the church.

Whenever these advocates of New Romanticism prove accessible to religious sentiment (and such instances are not rare), they mostly turn to pantheism, as older romanticists had done, and in that case naturally they looked and still look upon the Reformer as a representative of a backward piety, a "Judaist" who, though he learned a great deal from the German Mystics of the fourteenth century, is nevertheless inferior to these godly men "of the last period of originality in Germanic religion."

Popular writing of the more recent past is astonishingly little affected by all these changes of opinion on the person and achievement of the Reformer. It is still dominated chiefly by the narrow conceptions of vulgar Rationalism. To them Luther stands forth as "the affectionate husband, honest father, true friend, the scholar useful to the community, the model citizen, great patriot and undaunted champion against Rome." The austere and sturdy, rough and powerful, popular and original features have magically disappeared from the portrait of the Reformer, the lion has become a tame pussy, the terror of all the Philistines of his day has become a typical German domestic Philistine who, though he after the true manner of German domestic tyrants often growls mightily and makes a scene, is in reality quite harmless and would not injure a fly. However, this trite historical point of view and hero worship have long ago been called to a

halt and relegated to where they will not be able to put
on airs any further.

A noted jurist once said: "The German people have
thrice loved: Karl the Great, Luther and Bismarck."
With equal justice one might say: "The Germans
have three times hated: Karl the Great, Luther and
Bismarck." No man, however, did they love more
strongly and hate more violently, no man is even now
more candidly loved and hated by them than Luther.
Indeed, hatred and aversion toward the Reformer are
to-day perhaps more widespread, certainly more
active, than love for him, for those very men who now
control the masses will have nothing of him.

Already during the lifetime of Luther this antago-
nism and enmity brought together two powerful
parties which otherwise fought one another bitterly:
revolutionary radicalism and Catholicism. In order
to discredit the Reformer's doctrines both attacked
also his person and in their efforts drew a picture of
him which differed from the idealistic portraits of the
Evangelical faction as day from night. The conception of Luther among the revolutionary radicals in its
general outlines harks back to Karlstadt and Thomas
Münzer. The detailed execution of it and the
retouching is the work of the nineteenth century and
was done by such men as Zimmermann, Kautsky and
Blos, the historians of the radical burgher parties and
of social democracy. In less striking colors and
altered to suit the tastes of the national socialists it was
very recently embodied in Barge's bulky book on
"Karlstadt."

Slightly different in shading and argument we now find this picture also in the historical works of the radical Pietists, Darlyists, Adventists, Pentecostmen and whatever else their names may be. The sole criterion of the historical opinion set forth in these treatises is the aversion Luther felt for Karlstadt, Münzer, Schwenckfeld and their associates, and his attitude during the peasant revolt. The former brings him the honorary title, "the dull, self-indulgent beast of Wittenberg," the latter such pleasant names as bloodthirsty firebrand and venal henchman of the princes, also causing the accusation that he is a reactionary parson and hostile to the interests of the people, etc. But Radicalism never was wont to pay very much attention to historical facts. All the more zealously the Catholic party has ever tried to forge from the history of the past weapons for the conflicts of the present.

Before the Lutherans had found time to write a detailed biography of Luther, the first Catholic account of his life appeared (1549). Its author was an old foe of the Evangelical party, the Breslau canon John Cochlaeus from Wendelstein, who ever since the days of Worms had been tirelessly crossing swords with the Reformer. The portrait he paints in his book is the complete antithesis of the ideal conception of the Protestants. While in the latter Luther stands forth as "a divinely inspired man," Cochlaeus depicts him with even greater emphasis as a child of the devil whom Satan himself begot in adulterous union with Margaret Luther. Hence as a mere

infant the unfortunate offspring manifested such
a strange and savage nature that his own mother
later felt sorry that she had not immediately
murdered the changeling in the cradle. In the
monastery also discerning brothers soon saw what
manner of man he was, and later on indeed no sensible
person could harbor any doubts on this point. At
Luther's death, of course, this mysterious "father"
is also brought into play. He appears just in time
and carries his loyal evangelist off to hell.

This conception of the Reformer as the son of Satan
was very popular in the Catholic world down to the
eighteenth century.

But even in the sixteenth century it was not always
believed necessary to conjure up the devil in order to
help elucidate the problem Luther. Occasionally
Luther was permitted to count as a human being, but
in that case he was, as, for instance, by Thomas Münzer as early as 1520, portrayed as the German Catiline, i. e., as a great criminal. Others, with Pallavi-
cini, called him a savage Cyclops whose fertile and
powerful mind had brought forth only colossal mon-
strosities and whose vaunted courage was but the
courage of a despairing beast. This view of Luther
likewise found many adherents. In Bavaria, for
instance, at the opening of the nineteenth century,
peasants were wont still to parade Doctor Luther
and his Katie side by side with the Bavarian Hiesel
and the notorious Schinderhannes in their Shrove
Tuesday processions.

In the days of enlightenment, however, educated

Catholics, who were convinced of the necessity and value of "Church reform" very closely approximated the view of enlightened Protestants. Even Catholic theologians began now to judge the Reformer as "a precious instrument of the Lord," "a great bringer of light," "an honest character" and "the greatest benefactor of humanity." On the other hand, certain among these theologians emphasized even more strongly than Semler that Erasmus had been greater than Luther. One of their number, Franz Berg, Professor of Church History at Würzburg (he died 1821), risked a highly modern assertion: the doctrine of justification in the hand of Luther was just as much a product of superstition as in that of Paul, the Reformation in the same measure a hindrance to enlightenment as the Counter-Reformation. On the whole, however, a tone of joyous recognition, a feeling of spiritual kinship dominates. Individual Catholic Romanticists, as for example, Eichendorf, and romanticizing converts like Leopold von Stolberg still evince a lively sympathy for "Luther's heroic, thoroughly popular personality."

After the July Revolution there is a complete change of sentiment. Old opinions were once more brought to honor though they now wear modern attire and are much more delicately substantiated. Very learned professors like Adam Möhler again know of very intimate relations between Luther and Satan. But they avoid calling the child by its right name, they are content to delicately hint at the hideous secret. Nevertheless, people have come to feel that it has ceased to be modern to cite Satan for the solution of a psychological problem. Therefore they prefer to explain Luther's "possession" as a sort of insanity. This, for example, is done by Friederich van Kerp in 1810. Others, with Bruno Schön, the Austrian monk and alienist, sympathetically affirm that the so-called greatest offspring of the German nation at least temporarily suffered from persecutory mania, megalomania, hallucinations, illusions, sexual hyperæsthesia and "transitory dementia."

When the Reformer is not directly regarded as insane he is looked upon, for example recently by Hartmann Grisar, S. J., as a monomaniac burdened with hereditary nervousness and with a tendency to autochthonous and "exaggerated" ideas. Others again, like the jurist Jarcke, in their judgment of his theologoumena kindly take account of his unusually persistent digestive disturbances by which unfortunately Luther was troubled. While writers thus treated the heretic as a sick man, they robbed themselves of the possibility of dragging him before the judgment seat of morality. For that reason, whenever a case of doubt arose, they reverted to the view which Thomas Münzer had championed as early as 1520; that is, they regarded the accused as the German Catiline, though their method is much more prudent and cautious than that of the old mendicant. They do not any more bluntly and rudely call Luther a great criminal; rather he is in the objective tone of the seasoned criminologist depicted as a wholly impure, deeply immoral individual. (Döllinger, Janssen, Audin, Maraval,

Grisar.) Others are content with Denifle to brand him officially as a "superman," though this in reality is only a euphemism for criminal monster, "knave," degenerate, type of the deepest moral decline and decay.

Taken as a whole the tone of these polemics which masquerade as history has in the course of centuries become materially refined. Its early representatives as it were painted with dirt so that Lutherans justly spoke of their rooting *in excrementis Lutheri*. To-day they not infrequently show an admirable skill in concealing their inbred loathing of the archheretic behind the cold mask of the impartial judge. Their method, however, is still that of the approved masters and models of the wild days of religious warfare. As far as possible the sources themselves are made to give testimony, but only those sources which favor the writer's point of view. In a sense Luther is made his own judge in that authors carefully cull from his works and speeches all utterances which seem to place his character in a bad light. Even these statements, however, are not always reported in full, or they are torn from their natural context and misinterpreted at every point. Grisar furnishes a recent example of this method.

This ingenious process, which has found in Döllinger and Janssen its expert exponents, is now more than three hundred years old, for its real inventor is the Hessian physician John Pistorius, who died in 1608. He had already issued numerous polemics when he hit upon the idea—a very natural one, to be sure, for a medical man—of dissecting the dead Luther. To this end he read the works of that "hellish person" three times from cover to cover and prepared a prodigious collection of quotations from which incontrovertible proof was to be furnished that the so-called Reformer had been possessed by no less than seven evil spirits, namely, the sensuous spirit, the blasphemous spirit, the sloven spirit, the spirits of error, of insolence and of pride, the spirit of fraud and the turncoat spirit. This truly spirited collection nourished the whole Catholic controversial literature for the next two hundred years, though the successors of the wrathful doctor mostly excelled him in ability to strike the popular note.

The Jesuit, Conrad Vetter, for instance, assumed in his "Helle Prob" (Clear Test), the innocent guise of an arch-Lutheran theologian and then brought together from the inexhaustible stock of Swabian vulgar obloquy such a superb collection of epithets that students of German may still use his work with profit. He was outdone by the Strassburg ecclesiastic, Nicholas Weisslinger. The very title of his book, "Root Hog or Die," which appeared in the first edition in 1723, gives promise of much pleasant entertainment to the reader. This hope is not betrayed, for in his treatise the *sacræ theologiæ polemicæ studiosus* so soundly berates the gospelless heretic, the stinking blasphemer, dirty fellow, scamp, boor of boors, mucker, backbiter, blackguard Luther, and all the Lutheran lousiness, the Lutheran vermin, mudlarks and tinker's rabble that it well-nigh takes the reader's breath away. Such geniuses of rudeness, however, have always been able to count on a grateful audience in Germany. We are not surprised, therefore, to find that Weisslinger and his older and younger fellow controversialists are still much read, used and even imitated. The former Jesuit Berlichingen very recently sat in judgment over Luther altogether in the style of Weisslinger. The learned Father Denifle himself has not found it beneath his dignity to draw upon the rich treasury of these ancient and coarse polemics and occasionally to copy their fresh and pithy style.

An old adage has it that love is blind while the eye of hatred is keen. With equal justice it might be affirmed that hatred makes people blind and that the eye of love sees sharply. But this again would be only half the truth. There is a blind love and a blind hatred. Nothing is better proof of this fact than the history of Luther after his death both in polite and learned literature. Whoever seeks the real Luther in these sources will never find him and will always remain uncertain as to who and what the oft-mentioned man really was, whether he was a prophet of God or a son of the devil, a father of the church or a gospelless heretic, the prototype of a true evangelical teacher and man of prayer or a great criminal, an enlightener and mighty liberator of the spirit or a destroyer of the last cultural harvest of Europe, a "genius of the first rank" or an intellectually inferior degenerate, even a poor maniac, the greatest child of the German people or the Catiline of Germany who was responsible for the moral and intellectual decline of his country in the sixteenth and seventeenth centuries, the type of a savage revolutionary or a bloodthirsty firebrand and venal henchman of the princes, "an affectionate husband, honest father, faithful friend, a scholar useful to the community, a good citizen" or "a frantic beast, filthy hog, a vacillating turncoat, frivolous liar, shameless sensualist, wrathy brawler, hyperbolic Thrason (braggart), insolent Goliath, Markolfian ribald, public seducer of nuns."

Whoever desires to acquaint himself with the true Reformer must cast aside all these wild caricatures, these portraits ofttimes too fulsome in their praise of him, and must seek Luther where alone he can be found: in the genuine tradition. Unhappily these genuine sources, like precious metals, are rarely found pure and unalloyed and so readily accessible that one needs only to grasp them. In most cases they must be hunted up and unearthed from libraries and archives and freed from impurities. Even then the product, like gold, is of value only to him who appreciates and knows how to use it.

The age of Orthodoxy and of the Counter-Reformation believed that it knew who Luther was without knowing the sources about him. For that reason it took little trouble to collect the works of the Reformer and the documents relating to his life. Also it solely used them to prove either that he had been a man of God and a saint or that he was an archheretic and great criminal. In the Lutheran camp this purely dogmatic view of history ceased in the days of Pietism.

Criticism then awakened, and with it a scholarly interest in the life and deeds of Luther. Veit Ludwig von Seckendorff furnished the first history of the Reformation based on a study of the documents. In it, despite the apologetic character of the title, a scholar's love of evidence dominates. Thereupon Valentin Ernst Löscher, J. C. Kapp and S. Cyprian began to assemble the documents on the history of the Reformation from the libraries and archives, and the untiring Johann Georg Walch from 1740 on undertook the publication of a new complete edition of Luther's writings. He also was the first to write a strictly scholarly, indeed, in some respects monstrously erudite, biography of Luther.

In the age of Rationalism this scientific enthusiasm for investigation gradually subsided. The generation of antiquarians became extinct. Very little research on Luther was done and what little there was well illustrates the spirit of the age. Men busied themselves with very inadequate means, to be sure, in collecting the sources in which the Luther whom they understood, the "father, educator, friend and citizen," most unconstrainedly revealed himself: the letters of Luther. As for the rest, they were content following the advice of Semler to make excerpts from his best-known works. They were of the opinion that only in such selections could Luther still "be of any service." Plebeian as this persistent emphasis on usefulness even in scientific work may appear to us to-day, we yet must for this reason not overlook the progress which Rationalism marks in the writing of history. It was

the first time that complete intellectual mastery of his
material was demanded of the historian. A psychological interpretation of events and an accurate
ascertaining of their connection, strong emphasis on
essentials and suppression of all mere antiquarian
side issues was required. Certainly, the psychology of
the Rationalists was still indescribably crude, and their
appreciation of the inner connection of events very
superficial, but the narrowness and clumsiness of the
antiquarians at least had been overcome.

Romanticism and the idealistic philosophy springing from it put an end to this purely atomistic view
of history. But it was a case of driving out Baal with
the aid of Beelzebub. The exponents of the new
method realized that conscious influence is of small
importance in history. They discovered the "un-
conscious factor" and conceived the idea of development, they placed historical accident under ban and
excommunication. As a result they dropped into
a new mythology in that they thought of history
as being the strictly regular thought-process of an
all-pervading intelligence, so that the philosopher,
as the organ of this supreme intelligence, was in
the happy position of being able to predict the history
of the unknown past and of the equally unknown
future with the same assurance as the historical development in ages much better authenticated by documentary evidence. Since these men viewed personality merely as an organ of the dominant intelligence
and regarded reason as its really distinguishing characteristic, they were wholly unable to appreciate,

much less understand, a man like Luther, whose life seemed to be swayed by an intimately personal experience which could not be conceived at all as a process of reasoning.

At this time Leopold von Ranke came to the fore. He recognized that it was not the business of the historian to pass judgment on the past, nor even to instruct his contemporaries for the benefit of posterity. He pointed out to the historians their modest task of "showing how things in reality had been," that is, to determine from the sources the actual facts and then to record the result simply and plainly, undeterred by the forward interference of their own enlightened reason. Thus he not only ended the old subservience of History to Philosophy and Theology, but above all showed a clear path to an objective appreciation even of personalities so much under debate as Luther and Loyola. In his "German History in the Age of the Reformation" this possibility was realized. Only since then have we a truly scientific method for the investigation of the history of the Reformation and of Luther. The old dogmatizing brand has been loath to go into well-merited retirement, but it cannot since then do as much harm as formerly. In the circles of the initiated at least it has lost all influence.

Ranke's German History, published in 1839, is one of the few historical works which have outlived their author. Investigation, however, has self-evidently not remained stationary. On the contrary, it has pursued its path assiduously and by dint of new forms of organization and constant improvement of its methods has experienced a tremendous increase in capacity. Supremely important for the judgment about Luther was the coming into being of the modern wholesale methods of historical research, the so-called historical commissions and institutes, for only with their help has a systematic examination of the libraries and archives been rendered possible. This new method permitted the first successful attempt at a critical edition of Luther's works, the so-called Weimar Edition, which is in progress since 1883 and now contains fifty-two volumes. So immense is the mass of the documentary material for the history of the Reformation which the search in libraries and archives has from year to year brought to light that the scholar must needs have the digestive faculty of an ostrich to be able to take in all this fresh matter and to separate the historically valuable portion without feeling too much oppressed by the indigestible residuum.

More important still, perhaps, is the fact that in the course of the last generation investigators have set for themselves new aims and are drawing into the scope of historical perception phenomena which hitherto had been hardly thought worthy of notice. Ranke and his pupils had in the main been content to portray the religious movement and the political events of the age of the Reformation. In their treatments princes, diplomats and theologians hold the stage. The condition of the people, their actions and feelings one learns to know only incidentally.

This deficiency Johannes Janssen was the first to

clearly recognize. In his History of the German People since the End of the Middle Ages, he consciously chose the masses as his hero and made it his object to determine with minute care the economic, social, political, religious and moral conditions of the day and to show the changes wrought in these by the Reformation. It was a significant step forward, but at first only in the putting of the problem. Janssen's solution of the new task was not successful. The reason for his failure lies in the fact that he did not strictly adhere to his purpose, but allowed himself constantly to be driven off the main track by the apologetic argument: the fifteenth century is essentially an age of the highest bloom for the whole of German cultural life, and it is Luther alone who prevented the harvest.

While older investigators easily succumbed to the danger of isolating the leaders from their surroundings and raising them too high above the masses, they also rarely had an eye for the relations existing between Luther and the theologians of the late Middle Ages. Indeed, since A. Ritschl's sharp criticism of the exaggerated estimates of the services rendered by the so-called precursors of the Reformation it had become customary to look upon Luther's theology as an entirely new creation, and to deny any deeper influence of the Middle Ages upon his development.

It was Denifle who saw that no such formal break existed in the history of intellectual life, and in his "Luther" (1904) he endeavored to set forth how the

Reformer was connected with the so-called "Modern Theologian" of the late Middle Ages. However, in this instance also, progress lay merely in the putting of the problem. The question itself was not solved, because Denifle as little as Janssen, could make up his mind to treat it in a purely historical fashion. On the contrary, in his capacity as a Catholic apologist he always wished at the same time to demonstrate that Luther was a typical example of decadence and his theology the degenerate product of declining scholasticism. Side by side with these most influential Catholic scholars, others were busily engaged in bringing back from the dead the almost forgotten Catholic opponents of Luther: Tetzel, Usingen, Eck, Cochlaeus, Emser, Schatzgeyer, Sylvius, Kilian, Leib, and whatever their names may be.

Meanwhile Protestants preferably paid attention to those antagonists of the Reformer who had undeservedly been neglected by all parties, because they had been unwilling to follow either the Pope, the Wittenberg School, or the Zurich reformers: men like Karlstadt and Schwenckfeld, Sebastian Frank and Erasmus of Rotterdam, Thomas Münzer, Hans Denck and other Anabaptists. In competition with a great number of local historians they furthermore tried to ascertain more closely the progress of reform in the several German territories. This resulted in the discovery of a large number of stars of second, third, fourth and fifth magnitude besides the great star Luther. Also it furnished a much clearer and more forceful and realistic conception of the development of the Evangelical movement as a whole.

Naturally the verdict on certain groups and phenomena of the Reformation was thus materially changed. To Ranke and other older students Erasmus of Rotterdam and those who shared his point of view appeared noteworthy almost solely as critics of the Catholic system. Now the positive side of their efforts was stressed. Indeed some writers professed to see in them the direct ancestors of the religious enlightenment of the seventeenth and eighteenth centuries. Forty years ago the Anabaptists were still regarded as blood-red, fanatical revolutionaries, besides as narrow and small-minded reactionaries, that is, they were held to be merely stragglers of the religious movement in the late Middle Ages. People are now agreed that the majority of these severely persecuted pious men were not revolutionaries at all, but rather passive and recluse ascetics like the later Quakers, not merely stragglers of mediæval Waldensianism, Apocalypticism and Mysticism, but in part also late exponents of the Humanistic movement of reform and above all opponents of the crude literal faith and moral laxity of vulgar Lutheranism. Some scholars in fact are now prone to see in these men, as in Erasmus and his school, the precursors of new and powerful religious currents. They exalt them as the direct progenitors of the Independents and Pietists above Luther and his associates. Since the Anabaptists were being given their due it was obvious that those men ought no longer be made to stand back who, as true step-children of Dame Fortune, had also been treated as such by the investigators, men like Caspar von Schwenckfeld and that greatly misunderstood person, Sebastian Frank of Donauwoerth. After long mis-representation these were now at once rated so highly that the revised opinion on them amounted almost to misunderstanding. Schwenckfeld was venerated as the spiritual father of the Pietistic community ideal and Frank even as the prophet and forerunner of the religious views of Schleiermacher.

In the first place, therefore, the clarification and correction of the general picture of the age which resulted from the new focusing of the problem and from special studies demands a revision of the tradi-tional view of Luther in many particulars. But aside from these considerations the wealth of finds in the last decades which bear directly on Luther, and the many monographs caused by them call for a recon-sideration. Naturally these discoveries are often mere minutiæ the knowledge of which makes us neither wiser nor happier. The fact that Luther was very probably baptized by Father Bartholomew Ren-nebecher on November 11, 1483, in the tower room of the church of St. Peter and St. Paul at Eisleben; that he was not the firstborn son as so far has been gener-ally believed, but that he had an older brother; that in Eisenach he used to bring young Schalbe to school with him, and that as a student at Erfurt he lived in the Hall of St. George on Lehmann's Bridge; that the maternal uncle to whom the parents looked for aid when they sent the boy to school at Eisenach was named Conrad Hutter and was sacristan at the church of St. Nicholas there; that in May, 1512, Luther participated in the chapter of his order in Cologne and even viewed the relics of the Holy Three Kings there; that when still a young professor he once gave a course of lectures on Genesis, and that on the Koburg in 1530 he wore spectacles and a long beard—all these facts are certainly not without interest to the student of Luther, but they in no wise compel us to revise our opinion about him and his work.

More important are the lively discussions about the genuineness of the famous Worms utterance: "Here I stand, I cannot hold otherwise, God help me, Amen," or about the time when the hymn "A Mighty Fortress Is Our God" was written, and lastly about the cause and detailed circumstances of his death. Even these points, however, are not as weighty as they seem to the participants in the discussion. Whether "A Mighty Fortress" was composed in 1521 or 1528 is essentially quite immaterial. The haggling over this question is interesting only in as far as it shows how audacious, imaginative and naïve some Luther scholars are even at the present time. All the writers who now with so much assurance give 1521 as the year in which the hymn was produced, and who sometimes believe that they can precisely indicate the day, the hour and even the exact spot which gave Luther the inspiration for the immortal poem, innocently cite as their sole valid proof "The Prayer of Martin Luther at Worms," a very doubtful document, which does not appear until 1564 and then in the possession of John Aurifaber, a very untrustworthy authority.

As for the supposed closing words of Luther at Worms there are perhaps very few students at present who accept them as authentic in the form in which school text-books have transmitted them from generation to generation. We have good evidence only for the words: "God help me." It is true that the words: "I cannot hold otherwise, here I stand," occur as early as 1521 in a Wittenberg print. With this, however, we know Luther had nothing to do. In the conventional form and sequence this dictum does not appear until the complete Wittenberg edition of 1545. It seems advisable, therefore, not to cite this famous sentence henceforth as an utterance of Luther. That will be difficult for many, but for the appreciation of Luther's attitude in Worms one neither gains nor loses by this omission. The important point is not that the Reformer specifically assured the assembly that there he stood and that he could not hold otherwise, but that actually he did stand firm and could not decide otherwise.

The same is true of the recent discussions about Luther's death. The proof given by Tschermack that the Reformer succumbed on the eighteenth of February, 1546, to a stroke of paralysis, and the discovery of Paulus that the report on Luther's death which is most interesting to the medical man, is by a Catholic, the apothecary John Landau of Eisleben, are both significant inasmuch as they once again prove the Catholic legend about the Reformer's suicide to have been a crude falsehood. Earnest students, however, never did believe this untruth which did not appear in Catholic controversial literature until 1591, while the lower type of controversialists are not moved to discard it even by thorough refutations published by scholars of their own faith.*

I shall leave aside all such details, interesting though they may be, and shall select from the mass of. new discoveries and investigations only those through which the general picture of Luther's life, personality and opinions seems to have been modified, enriched or made clearer. If I see aright such a change took place in the main in four directions. We know more than our fathers about Luther's inner development from a "fanatic papist" into a reformer. Furthermore, his

---

*Luther's death did not occur early in the morning of the eighteenth of February (2:45 A. M.) in his sleeping room but in the living room, not in bed but on a bench upholstered in leather. The report by Landau was published as early as 1548 by Cochlaeus as a piece of news from the letter of a citizen of Mansfeld, and since 1565 was regularly reprinted in the appendix of this author's biography of Luther. Despite this fact Paulus was the first student to notice it. In the Catholic camp the fable at first was spread that Luther had been carried off by the devil. In 1568 another legend, to the effect that the Reformer hanged himself from one of his bedposts, can be traced. See Hondorf: Promptuarium Exemplorum, p. 138 b. It was, however, at first found advisable to spread this tale only by word of mouth. In 1591 the Italian Oratorian Bozio had the courage to champion it in writing. See Bozius: De Signis Ecclesiæ, 2, p. 154. He cited as proof the pretended testimony of a supposed valet of Luther. This deposition the Franciscan Sedulius published verbatim in 1606. See Sedulius: Præscriptiones Adversus Hæreses, Antwerp, p. 208 ff. The author asserts that he got the "document" from an anonymous trustworthy person from Freiburg in the Breisgau. This anonymous citizen of Freiburg is said to have acquired it from a second anonymous, "a pious man," and this second anonymous brings into play still another, the supposed valet. The legend therefore operates boldly with three anonymous guarantors. See Nicholas Paulus: Luther's Lebensende, Freiburg, 1898. In spite of this controversialists like Majunke did not find it necessary to drop the tale.

personality in some respects appears to us in a new light. Also the mediæval background and the mediæval elements in his thinking have become clearer to us. Lastly, we have come to realize that only then can we correctly estimate the net results of this great life, if we endeavor to determine its effect upon cultural development in its whole breadth and depth, not upon religion and theology alone but also upon custom and morality, law and government, economic and social life, art and science, literature and language.

This realization, to be sure, has not yet brought forth the desired fruit. So far only one biographer of Luther, Arnold Berger, has tried to portray the Reformer as "Hero of Civilization." And yet, the clear recognition and concrete setting forth of problems is always more important than their solution. The latter requires only diligence, circumspection and learning, in this case, to be sure, probably the industry of whole generations of future investigators. For in some fields of the cultural development of that period, for instance, on the history of theology, morality and language, we are at present only very superficially informed. The task, however, has been clearly recognized, the preliminary work has at many points been done, therefore we may hope that the twentieth century will finally solve also this great and difficult problem.

CHAPTER II.

The Stages in Luther's Conversion to the Year 1513.

A MAN who compels his fellow citizens to take sides for or against a cause championed by him must rest content henceforth to lead his life under the control and criticism of "public opinion." Whatever he may be doing he can never be sure that a good friend or crafty foe will not secretly denounce him to contemporaries and posterity by publishing broadcast his most intimate private affairs and most innocent casual remarks, even though it be merely from a desire for personal notoriety.

This curiosity on the part of his contemporaries, Luther himself, since the Disputation at Leipzig in July, 1519, so amply experienced that finally he registered furious complaints.* His enemies observed with suspicion even the ring he wore, for might not the devil be hidden in it? They watched closely his every word and gesture and devoutly noted every draught of Malvasie and beer which he was careless enough to drink in the presence of others. His friends very early began to save every note and scrap of paper from his study, they busily transcribed not only his sermons and lectures, but since 1531 even his conver-

---

*In order to illustrate Luther's deep resentment over this disconcerting curiosity of his contemporaries, Professor Böhmer quotes an angry remark by the Reformer. It has not been translated because it is not in accordance with modern literary taste.

sation at the supper table, indeed, they minutely
recorded whenever he was troubled with headache or
pains in the chest or was bothered by mosquitoes.
They wrote down when he was cheerful or serious,
angry or in a joking mood.

All this watching and spying, however, would have
helped the curious very little had Luther been as
close-mouthed as Calvin, as reserved and careful and
so completely master of all his gestures and moods as
Loyola.   But the Reformer was a true Thuringian
and hence by nature not silent, nor a "step-easy," nor
given to grand manners and smooth civilities.   Without anxious concern about his dignity, he spoke
before his friends and those who shared his home on
absolutely everything that moved and occupied his
mind.   He freely talked even on matters which the
cultured European of to-day only discusses privately
with his physician.   Ever since 1515 he stated his
opinions without any consideration or precaution
even about persons in high and exalted positions and
felt no compunction after he had begun to feel at
home in pulpit and cathedra, in sermons and lectures,
if he saw fit, to speak very frankly of his own experiences, struggles, errors and faults.

Luther did not drop this unaffected communica-
tiveness even when writing.   For he never wrote
"books" in the sense in which professors nowadays
are wont to do.   In reality he was always merely
"contributing to questions at issue and to problems of
the day," writing theses, pamphlets, polemics, edificatory tracts and sermons the brevity of which was

very early ridiculed by his opponents. In these "booklets" he was in the habit of freely easing his mind without the least worry over ill report or misunderstanding about everything which at the moment engrossed his attention. From these products we can therefore at any time determine what at a given period he thought, felt, hated, loved, desired and wanted. Even his apparently purely learned writings are for this reason "fragments of a great confession" and the sum total of his works a single continuous self-revelation, a collection of confidences such as we hardly possess from any other important man.

However, valuable though this collection of "confessions" may be, it suffers from certain defects which are sorely felt again and again. In the first place, it does not begin until relatively late in his career, and secondly, it is very uneven as regards the number and value of the documents contained therein. For the time from 1505 to 1513 it consists of only three rather meaningless letters, a receipt and a few accidentally preserved marginal notes. During the ensuing six years it is still quite fragmentary. Immediately after that it suddenly grows so voluminous that a novice almost despairs of knowing what to do with this tremendous amount of material.

In the course of the last generation, however, so many hitherto wholly or partially unknown writings by the Reformer and documents relating to the history of his life from the twice seven lean years before the Disputation at Leipzig have come to light again

that students now may bless these meager years as
the period of their most abundant harvests. In the
shop of an antiquary at Cologne in 1877 a student's
notes on Luther's lectures of the year 1516 on the
Epistle to the Galatians reappeared. A decade later
Buchwald discovered in the school library of the
Zwickau city council seven old books which the
Reformer had evidently studied as a monk and had
in accordance with his habit industriously annotated.
In the same place were found in 1885 a few unknown
early sermons, among them the oldest relic of this
kind, the sketch for a pentecostal address from the
year 1514. Shortly before Luther's preparations for
the first lectures on the Psalter (1513-15) came to
light again in Dresden, and simultaneously his own
careful notes for these lectures were for the first time
published completely.

New surprises were furnished by the last years of
the past century. Hermann Vopel in 1899 discovered
in the Vatican Library a copy of Luther's lectures on
Romans (1515-16) and also lecture notes of a student on the Epistle to the Hebrews taken in 1518.
Hardly had the excitement in the learned world subsided somewhat, when it heard, to its greatest astonishment, that Luther's own manuscript of these renowned lectures on Romans was reposing safely
though unnoticed in the show cases of the Berlin
library. This surprise, at first rather more painful
than pleasing to the learned librarians, justifies our
hope that the era of unexpected finds is not yet over,
that somewhere in Germany or in Rome, the remain-

ing "lost manuscripts" from the youthful period of the Reformer are also awaiting discovery. These are: his class notes on the Nichomachian Ethics and Dialectics of Aristotle, on the Epistle to Titus, the unfinished commentary on the Physics of Aristotle and the sorely missed correspondence with Staupitz between 1505 and 1517. Pleasant as it may be to indulge in such dreams it would be ungrateful to forget meanwhile how rich we have already become and how much new material those finds offer which have now ceased to be altogether new.

What we possess enables us to observe the young monk and professor Luther at close range for weeks, months and years while he is at work in the quiet of his cell. This is the first and perhaps most gratifying advance we owe to this new material. For it is most edifying, merely to watch this worker, he is always so engrossed in his task, so painstakingly conscientious and accurate even in seemingly non-essential matters. He writes out in full beforehand not only every sermon but also every lecture, and, as though this were not enough of virtue he later on prepares a very neat and faithful copy of some of the lectures. At times, therefore, his notes have the faultless appearance of well-written books. A professional calligraphist could hardly have done better.

Much less charming is the outward aspect of the books of his library which have come down to us. They fairly swarm with markings, notabenes and marginal glosses of all kinds. Sometimes he has filled every available blank space. However, what un-

der other circumstances would be offensive is here an
agreeable sight. For what do these blemishes prove?
That Luther did not merely page through the books
which he took in hand, but really read them, and while
reading criticized, indeed, criticized very severely.
Thus the mere outward appearance of his academic
tools betrays to us the fact that already the young
professor possessed characteristics very valuable to a
man of his calling, namely, thoroughness and diligence, accuracy and independence of judgment.

If then we examine more closely his lecture notes
and preparations we are struck at the outset by the
prodigious progress made by the young professor as
instructor and scholar in the space of a few years. In
his first theological lectures on the Sentences of Peter
Lombard, 1509-10, he still moves in the beaten path,
as far as we can judge from the available notices.
Also in his lectures on the Psalms he still altogether
follows mediæval pedagogical custom both in arrangement and method. Nevertheless, he is beginning to make considerable use of the Humanists
Faber and Reuchlin; he already feels it necessary to
learn Hebrew and occasionally, as far as his scant
scientific apparatus permits, he refers to the Hebrew
original of which a printed edition lay before him.
The lectures on Romans also still in their external
appearance look typically mediæval.

However, though he faithfully continues to employ the mediæval exegetical apparatus and always
in accordance with mediæval practice expounds the
text two, and even three times, he has in this case

almost entirely overcome the exegetical methods of the Middle Ages. He is now much more impressed by the Humanists than by Lyra and Paul of Burgos. Therefore, as soon as the edition of the New Testament by Erasmus is available he follows the Greek original as a matter of principle and with the aid of his poor dictionaries endeavors in the manner of Erasmus, also to explain the text linguistically.

He is, however, not minded to follow Erasmus and the Humanists through thick and thin. He perceives clearly that they are wanting in just that phase which to him is the main one, that though they translate Paul correctly they do not properly understand him. Hence he guards his independence even over against Erasmus and thus by drawing upon the depths of his own experience for the first time he solves the great problem with which so many scholars of the primitive and the mediæval church, and since Marsilio Ficino also the Humanists, had again and again wrestled in vain.

Luther shows what Paul really felt, thought and taught. Thereby he rediscovers for humanity the great Apostle who so long had been unsuccessfully courted. Viewed purely as a scientific achievement, therefore, this course of lectures is an event which in the history of exegesis has scarcely been equalled. In these lectures the wishes of the Humanists are met as well as the aims of the older expounders who looked more toward an appreciation of the content. But the limitations of both groups have been recognized and as a result overcome and overtaken scientifically.

While advancing in scholarship the young monk in these first years of his instructorial activity also made great strides as a teacher. In the lectures on Peter Lombard, Luther seems even on the teaching platform to have employed altogether the cumbersome chancery style of Scholasticism. In lecturing on the Psalms he occasionally attempts to facilitate the understanding of the text for his hearers by means of similes, comparisons, examples and applications to the present. Not until the lectures on Romans, however, does this tendency so dominate his entire exposition that from his notes one can determine not only the educational level, but to a certain degree also the interests of the better class among the students at Wittenberg.

In ever-recurring digressions Luther expounds the words of the Apostle through striking examples from contemporary life, apt similes, fables and anecdotes. Besides, not infrequently we find him also adducing German proverbs in order to render the textual meaning clearer. Above all, he takes care by means of "able translations" of difficult Greek and Latin expressions that also the less gifted can follow him. In order that no one may spend his time in the lectures altogether without profit to himself Luther regularly summarizes the essentials in a brief dictation. Small wonder, therefore, that so relatively large a number of transcripts of his course by students have been preserved, and that students even at this early date "gladly," indeed enthusiastically, entered his classes. For once they enjoyed the rare good luck of learning something really new in a course of lectures. At the same time this new material was presented to them in such a comprehensible and clear, and in so captivating and interesting a manner that even a dull person needed only to stretch forth his hand in order to make it his lasting possession.

It is more noteworthy still for us to-day to observe how early the temperament and critical vein of his later fighting years becomes evident in the Reformer. In the earliest manuscript notes from his hand which we possess, in a marginal gloss of the years 1508-09 to the works of St. Augustine, he manifests his enthusiasm for this author quite in the passionate manner of his later life, while at the same time he shows his aversion for the prince of mediæval philosophy, Aristotle. Simultaneously he begins to look upon tradition with critical eyes. For example, he closely compares the content and style of the writings in the Basel edition of Augustine and with happy penetration stamps two of them as spurious.

Soon after in his studies on the Psalms he began to risk strictures on conditions in the church of his time. His sympathy for such matters is, however, not yet very active. His interests remain chiefly centered in scholarly investigation and on practical questions of edification. Only in his lectures on Romans does his participation in the happenings of the world outside of the monastery walls become visible. He refers with increasing frequency to events of the day.

With growing energy he points out evils in the
Church and in secular society, ever more briskly,
openly and audaciously he expresses his displeasure,
sorrow and indignation. Though he does not censure indulgences as such, he yet finds fault with their
excessive number and with the greedy and cruel
methods of the givers of indulgences. He does not
object to fasting in itself but condemns compulsory
fasts, nor does he oppose the cult of the saints as
such but he rejects the superstitious out-growths of
saint worship. He openly asserts that canon law
needs a thorough cleansing, that public worship
requires a decided purging of superfluous ceremonies
and tenets and that the number of festal days ought
to be materially reduced. He states that for money
dispensation from all obligations is granted at Rome
and that the new Rome is worse than the old. He
loudly complains about the hardness and violence,
effeminacy and unspiritual attitude of the ecclesiastical princes, the crudeness and inadequate education
of the parish priests, the arrogance of the monks, the
imprudence of the indulgence preachers, the superstitious regard paid to foundations for masses, the
laziness of the craftsmen, the selfishness, dogmatism
and cruelty of the secular princes, the perverse stupidity, superficiality and irreligion of the jurists.
Indeed, he is well-nigh as opposed to this latter group
as he is in later years. Greater, however, is his aversion for the "hog theologians," *i. e.,* the Scholastics
and Scholastic philosophers. He has so completely
done with both of these that he openly advises his stu-

dents to absolve the required courses in philosophy as quickly as possible and then promptly to begin the attack upon philosophy, that is, upon Scholasticism.

Luther is by no means always content with such covert and general judgments. He is not afraid to mention by name, or at least clearly to specify individual sinners in high position so that every attentive auditor knew at once who was meant. Thus, for instance, he speaks of Pope Julius II., Duke George of Saxony, the Bishop of Strassburg and even his own ruler, the Elector Frederick the Wise whom otherwise he held in sincere regard. His criticisms always spring from disappointed love, never from a mere habit of fault-finding. Full of honest loyalty to his Elector he also clings to the Church with his whole soul. He still loves and honors it as his mother, still deems it self-evident that priests ought to be reverenced, in spite of the many bad elements among the clergy, and ardently pleads that people ought for love of the Church punctually to observe also those external ceremonies and ordinances which it had imposed on the faithful. Monasticism remains so high in his regard that he endeavors to prove to his audience that now when the orders were so despised it is more than ever a duty to become a monk.

Nevertheless, in the last chapters of these lectures one always has the feeling that he himself is already at the point of discarding the cowl. For no matter how monkish his utterances occasionally still sound, he has ceased to solely turn his gaze inward and upward as a true monk, he has begun to look about himself freely and with clear eyes. His strictures are no more after the manner of a monk directed alone upon himself, he criticizes the whole world. He is no more desirous in the true monastic spirit to reform merely himself, he has a complete programme of regeneration both for the Church and for Christian society as a whole.

This broadening of his intellectual horizon, this change of sentiment, indeed of his whole point of view in life, is so striking as to elicit the involuntary question: What has made the young monk so clearsighted, fresh, courageous, in fact audacious in the course of a few years? Was this change due merely to a growing familiarity with the dual calling of professor and preacher which had been forced upon him and the greater inner confidence on cathedra and pulpit resulting therefrom? Were this true, it would be impossible to understand why this natural development expressed itself in a growing opposition to precisely those authorities which as professor and preacher he was officially held to respect. The causes of this change must therefore lie deeper. Somehow a transformation in his convictions must have occurred in his first years as instructor, a change which gradually evinced itself in his speech and actions, so that more and more he appeared a different person even to those who knew him less intimately.

If we address our request for enlightenment to the latest biographer of Luther, Hartmann Grisar, S. J. we are given what seems a very simple "psychological" explanation of the above-mentioned facts. He tells us that at the beginning Luther professed the views of the strict, indeed the strictest group among the Augustinian Eremites. For this reason Grisar further contends Luther was sent to Rome as their advocate when Staupitz got into a quarrel with seven monasteries who were zealous for the maintenance of the rules of the order. And how does Luther in reality make use of this trip to Rome? In the first place he learns Hebrew from the Jew Jacob, secondly, he hands in a supplication to the Curia asking leave to remain away from the monastery for ten years so that he might don secular dress and study in Italy. The Curia, however, refused him this permission. Brother Martin willy-nilly had to return to Germany, and there he then tried indirectly to gain his desired object. As a first step to this end "he deserted to his friend Staupitz," that is, he now suddenly opposed the seven Observantist monasteries whose cause he had up to this time championed with such vehemence. Thereupon with increasing openness and regardlessness he attacked the Observantists in pulpit and platform and after 1515 as district vicar endeavored with all means in his power to gain control for "the liberal party within the order which was devoted to him," in the ten or eleven monasteries under his jurisdiction. In the Black Cloister at Wittenberg where he held full sway no true monastic discipline obtained as early as the beginning of the year 1517 according to his own words, and he himself had long ago become a monk "of liberal views and practice." Therefore these critical statements in the lectures on Romans merely reflect the progressive desertion of the young professor from the old faith for which he had had no real inner sympathy ever since 1510, in fact really not since the celebration of his first mass on the second of May, 1507, as his aversion to the reading of masses shows.

This is a rather surprising psychological explanation. We therefore justly inquire: How does the learned father know all this? His chief witness is a chronicler from lower Saxony, Jan Oldekop of Hildesheim, who in 1515-16 had heard Luther, but did not find time to put his thoughts and reminiscences to paper until the last years of his life beginning 1561. This man who hates Doctor Martin so bitterly that he flatly holds him responsible for all the mischief and disorder of the time, even for the custom of wearing trunk breeches and the rise in the price of bread, butter, cheese and eggs is the only one of the innumerable opponents and enemies of Luther who relates the neat little yarn about the Jew Jacob and about the petition to the Holy See. Unfortunately, he is not an unobjectionable authority. We can prove, that especially in Rome, Oldekop permitted himself to be duped outrageously. More serious still is the fact that he occasionally slights the truth with great unconcern. Displaying the greatest honesty and without batting an eye, in the style of an honest old tar he relates events as personal experiences which he never can have experienced, because they never took place. Consequently, he must be given credence only as far as other witnesses confirm his testimony. Where this is not the case, where, in fact, he conflicts with trustworthy authorities of his own party like John Cochlaeus, we must always count with the possibility that he is indulging a little in fibbery or is lying outright.

This witness is therefore worthless. With his other proofs the learned father also cannot make a great showing. His method of dealing with the monk Luther reminds one of the manner of an ambitious young lawyer who is preparing to be state's attorney and of his treatment of the accused who are brought before him. He does not listen carefully to what his defendant is saying, very important depositions he fails to hear at all, while step by step he cross-examines into his victim just those things he wishes to hear from him. If we try to avoid this little blunder and to determine what the Reformer and the other credible witnesses actually say, what picture do we get of Luther's development?

In the first place it is true that a conflict occurred in the German Congregation of the Augustinians to which Luther belonged. The cause of the trouble was an attempt by Staupitz, the Vicar General, to unite with the Congregation twenty-five non-reformed Augustinian houses. The purpose of Staupitz, of course, was to thus gradually reform these monasteries also. Since the General of the Augustinians in the Spring of 1510 consented to the plan, everything seemed to be in the best of order when, just at the crucial moment, seven of the thirty-one members of the Congregation protested against the proposed

union. Among the protestants were the two large
and influential convents at Erfurt and Nürnberg.
Whether this opposition was very wise may be hon-
estly doubted. However this may be, the seven feared
for the continuance of the observances and therefore
sent two brothers to Rome before the end of 1510
there to register their protest before the constituted
authorities, in accordance with the explicit permission in the statutes of the order. One of the envoys
was the Erfurt monk Martin Luther, though manifestly he was not chosen as spokesman. He was altogether too young for that task; besides, and this was
the most important prerequisite, he did not know how
to pull the wires at Rome. As was to be expected,
the embassy met with a rebuff. The procurator of the
order, acting wholly within his rights, refused even to
allow an appeal to the Curia.

Nevertheless, the stay of four weeks in the Eternal
City did not remain without fruit and blessing for the
monk Luther. In the first place he made a general
confession, though he had twice done so before in
Erfurt. Thereupon he undertook the difficult pilgrimage to the seven principal churches which con-
sumed a whole day, but was rewarded with abundant
indulgences. Finally, he in accordance with the directions prayerfully ascended the Scala Santa of the
Lateran on his knees, and like a "mad saint" visited
all churches and catacombs in which a miracle-work-
ing picture or relic was to be seen, or any indulgence,
great or small, to be obtained. All this he did in common with other pilgrims to Rome. Otherwise he un-

dertook or experienced nothing peculiar. He saw and heard, as all pilgrims did, a number of things about the unholy Rome of his day, but these impressions in his case also were not strong enough to eradicate the reminiscence of the sacred Rome of the apostles and martyrs and to shake his faith in the grandeur of the Catholic Church.

Meanwhile the General of the Order had taken steps to settle the conflict within the German Congregation. Staupitz entered into his plans without opposition. About the middle of June, 1511, in a conference with the priors of the seven protesting monasteries at Jena he declared his willingness to recede from the main point of his project, the union into one chapter of the thirty-one old Observantist monasteries with the twenty-five newly added convents. But the success which had been hoped for did not materialize. Only a few of the protesting monks, among them Luther, were satisfied and joined his side. What now was the next move of Staupitz? At the meeting of the chapter at Cologne, in May, 1512, he simply dropped his whole plan of union, while in return it seems the Nürnberg convent assumed the very considerable expenses of the conflict.

Thereby the difference was ended and forgotten. It is clear from the foregoing that the whole controversy was not one about principles of monastic discipline, but about purely practical, almost political questions over which divided opinions, in spite of complete agreement on monastic principles, were quite possible. But did not Luther probably later on make out of a squabble over matters of organization one about principial issues? By no means. True, the negotiations of the summer of 1511 had for him personally a very important consequence. Because at Erfurt he had championed the cause of peace and probably for this reason, as a black sheep, was treated badly by his brothers in the convent he was, possibly in the late summer of 1511, recalled to Wittenberg by Staupitz, and in October, 1512, through the influence of his patron, given the professorship for Old and New Testament Theology vacated by Staupitz. This undoubtedly for Luther and for mankind constituted the most important result of the whole controversy. That Wittenberg became the forum, and Electoral Saxony the outpost, of the Reformation, and whatever else resulted therefrom for Saxony as well as for the Reformation, is indirectly connected with this event which to none of those implicated seemed to be of sufficient importance to even once mention it in passing. Indeed, the Reformer Luther did not exist at this time, only Luther the Professor. As such Luther for the present did only what all professors of theology have always done, he gave lectures and occasionally besides preached sermons distinctly professorial in tone.

In the course of these lectures, which were heard also by many young Augustinians he twice, in passing, criticizes the attitude of the opposing monasteries toward Staupitz in the recent fight on unification. Also on occasion he attacks certain excrescences of monastic life which showed themselves not only among the Augustinians but in all orders. Finally, exactly as the Italian and Spanish bishops at the Lateran Council of the same time, he once discusses the scruples which had arisen among Catholics about the excessive privileges of the mendicant orders, doubts which were fully justified. In all these utterances, however, we have to deal with mere doubts and criticisms of actual conditions, never with opposition in principle to the organization of which he himself was a member. His fellow Augustinians fully recognized this fact. They saw in this occasional criticism no more than "a holy zeal for the house of the Lord," and therefore, in May, 1515, elected him district vicar at the chapter convened at Gotha, right after one of these criticizing speeches.

Did he as vicar subsequently endeavor to place in control in the monasteries subject to him "the liberal party in the order which was devoted to him?" The answer to this is simply that there was no such party. What we know about his activity as vicar, and it is not so very little, merely proves that he was attempting on the basis of the statutes to maintain or re-establish order in the convents. But why did he not make a beginning in Wittenberg itself, where by his own admission at the opening of 1517 a true monastic order of life had ceased to exist? Does he really admit this? No. What modern inquirers call disorder was the normal order of things in all the monasteries of the province with the exception of Erfurt, namely, the monks did not chant high mass, did not sing the monastic hours, but merely recited them *recto tono*. As far as possible they concentrated the hours, etc., that they might have the necessary time for other matters which seemed of more importance to them, namely, pastoral care, preaching and study—these being "the rites and regulations" mentioned in the now almost famous confession.

Thus nothing is left of "the monk of liberal views and practice" except a complaint made by the Reformer in October, 1516: "Seldom do I get the requisite time to pray the hours and to celebrate the mass." Upon these words people immediately but wrongly, "with calculated tactics"—to use a favorite phrase of modern "Luther psychologists"—based the accusation: therefore he even neglected to perform his hours and read a daily mass in obedience to the rules. Furthermore, there remains the fact that the Reformer after the opening of the public conflict, that is, after the thirty-first of October, 1517, frequently was unable for two, even three weeks to read the prayers of the breviary, and that he therefore occasionally on Saturday locked himself in for three days without partaking of food or drink in order that he might make up at one sitting what he had missed.

The psychological exposition of Father Grisar therefore unfortunately does not lead us to the goal. Hence let us turn to another interpreter of the soul of Luther who is perchance better acquainted with its depths and shallows than the learned Jesuit, since, to use an adage, "he was next to it," namely, Doctor Luther himself. It is well known that he ever wore his heart upon his sleeve. We therefore do not expect him to carefully conceal what agitated his soul during his sojourn in the Babylonian Captivity of the "Papacy."

Quite to the contrary! He often and gladly told why once upon a time he had entered the monastery and what brought him out again. Indeed, once at the end of his life, in the historical introduction to the first volume of his complete works on the fifth of March, 1545, he made an attempt at a formal autobiography. This effort can hardly be termed a success from the point of view of form. Like so many old people—even aged professors—he continually goes off at a tangent while narrating his story; one incident always suggests to him another which he has passed over.

Luther begins with the publication of the Theses on the thirty-first of October, 1517, as present-day writers are still doing and thereupon *deinceps secundum ordinem* reports on the events up to the debate at Leipzig in July, 1519. Having arrived at this point without accident he suddenly remembers that he has not said a word about the famous golden rose and the even more significant affair with Miltitz. Directly he sets about making up thoroughly for this neglect, and then continues in a languid narrative strain: "In the same year, 1519, I had for the second time undertaken the commentary on the Psalms, confident that I now possessed greater practice after having meanwhile in lectures dealt with the Epistles of Paul to the Romans, Galatians and Hebrews." Barely had he written the word "Romans" when suddenly and

powerfully there stood before his soul all that he
owed to this epistle. Forthwith he turns back a few
years in the course of events and writes a whole page
about his initial and decisive encounter with the Epistle to the Romans. After ten sentences he then again
resumes the narrative with the words: "Better prepared by such thoughts I began for the second time
to expound the Psalms," whereupon he quickly concludes the whole with a single statement about the
Diet of Worms.

Anyone who has associated much with old people
will not be surprised at this somewhat disorderly account by the aged Reformer. Much less will such a
person be amazed about the fact that the old man says
the most important and interesting things in a digres-
sion. That occurs frequently, especially with old professors. The most significant and interesting parts of
his story are naturally the ten sentences about his
first meeting with the Apostle Paul. Luther says in
his narrative that he had felt a strange longing to
know the Apostle, but one thing had always made
him shrink back again, "the righteousness of God,"
in the seventeenth verse of the very first chapter of
the Epistle to the Romans. Luther says that he had
been in the habit of explaining this concept in the manner of the philosophers, that is, to understand it as having reference to the punishing and rewarding righteousness of God, and that he had concluded therefrom that God in the gospel also revealed himself only
as a merciless and angry judge. For this God of ven-
geance and judgment who already by the law of the

Old Covenant had entangled mankind in all manner of misery he had felt a downright hatred. After days and nights of meditation he claims that the idea once struck him to compare these words with the following sentence: "The just shall live by faith." And suddenly the meaning of the words of the Apostle had become clear to him. Not the punishing and rewarding righteousness of God was meant, but the righteousness which absolves through grace. Directly he had felt as though the gates of paradise had opened wide before him. The Reformer relates how a short while later he read the treatise by Augustine "About the Spirit and the Letter," and how he there found, if not exactly the same, at least a very similar exposition of the words which to him now had become the door to paradise.

The very same story is told by Luther repeatedly in earlier years. Indeed, he adds a few interesting supplementary details in these other mentions of the fact. In a sermon he once says: "When I was made a Doctor (18-19 of October, 1512) I did not yet know the light." (Weimar edition, vol. 45, p. 86.) Substantially in agreement with this statement he says on another occasion during conversation at supper: "In this tower—that is, in the Black Cloister at Wittenberg—the Holy Spirit gave me this understanding."

Can we without further inquiry accept this testimony on faith? From a marginal note which the young monk in the year 1509-10, at Erfurt, made in his copy of Peter Lombard, we perceive that even then he was at one time engaged upon Romans 1:17, and had indeed referred to a commentary in which the words "the righteousness of God" are, if not correctly, certainly not wrongly and "philosophically" interpreted, as Luther himself according to his own words still understands them in 1512. It is true, he did not consult the commentary for the sake of these words but with an eye to the following phrase: "from faith to faith." We must, therefore, grant that at this time he overlooked this first passage, as is likely to happen when one seeks for a definite expression in a bulky volume in the nature of a dictionary.

Another observation is more suspicious at least upon first impression. In the introduction just quoted he seems to claim that all expounders with the exception of Augustine had explained the righteousness of God in this passage of the first chapter of Romans "philosophically." In fact, in his lectures on Genesis of the year 1511-12 this charge is literally made. (Weimar edition, vol. 43, p. 537.) These lectures, however, he did not personally write down and publish. The part in question was not made public until long after his death and is based upon the not always legible notes of one of his students. Besides, the publishers showed no scruples in making all sorts of additions upon their own responsibility even in the sections published during his lifetime. (See Weimar edition, vol. 42, pp. 213 and 357.) Nevertheless, Luther must have made a similar statement at some time. How otherwise could Melanchthon in his famous "Life of Luther" of the first of June, 1546, directly assert the identical thing? Let us therefore calmly assume that this assertion goes back to an utterance made by Luther himself. What would be the result? That he made a mistake in this introduction. For what he says in it about the exegesis of the Epistle to the Romans has been proven to be false.

However, is the designation "mistake" perhaps not too mild? If we read the later reports and verdicts of the Reformer about his life in the monastery we might easily be led to the belief that not for one hour did he feel happy and content in the cowl. On the other hand, he relates that when celebrating his first mass on the second of May, 1507, he praised the life in the monastery to his father as fine, peaceful and godly, and also that during his stay in the convent he had experienced hours of mystic exaltation like a proud saint, during which he imagined himself among choirs of angels. Is not this an intolerable contradiction? Not in the least. Indeed, it is but another proof for the old psychological truth that with men of hypochondriac temperament the remembrance of struggles, anxiety, distress and disappointments through which they have passed impresses itself much more vividly upon the soul than the remembrance of happy hours, which after all are not lacking even in the most miserable and sorrowful existence.

Even so, however, the details of the stories, especially such as he personally told some of his companions as a sort of relish or dessert at the supper-table in the Black Cloister, are not always wholly correct. Occasionally he is mistaken in the matter of dates, at times he errs also in points of fact. On the other hand, we must guard against drawing too far-reaching conclusions from minor contradictions. If, for example, he at one time says: I was born in 1483, and at another time gives the date 1484; if once he refers to Eisleben as the place of his birth, and then again says that it was Mansfeld, this only proves that he, as so many people of his day, did not know the facts exactly. Even the person who could most readily have given information on this subject, his good mother, had, as we are in a position to prove, entirely forgotten the year though not the place of birth of her son Martin. Nevertheless, these little contradictions, uncertainties and errors make it our duty in every case closely to examine his reminiscences and communications, and never to let them pass without scrutiny or investigation.

Is this sufficient? Some scholars say no. Who errs once is not worthy of credence, even if he speak the truth. All these stories about his life in the convent and under the Papacy, they aver, are legends and originated in the third decade of the sixteenth century. Moreover, they claim that they are "lies" (Legende: Luegende), intentional falsehoods calculated to glorify his own person, a romance gotten up later in order to defame the religious orders of the Catholic Church. Undoubtedly this is but another instance of a very simple "psychological" explanation of the facts. Is such an interpretation on the other hand necessary, likely, or even possible? It would be had Luther elsewhere also been in the habit of lying without any sense or object, like an hysterical woman. For it is absolutely impossible to see what "advantage" or purpose these utility lies which are so often told in complete agreement with one another and are in the common sense of the word altogether uninteresting should have served. Again, this view would be possible if the Reformer had really not begun to tell of the struggles of his soul, his doubts and pangs of conscience until 1530, as Denifle claims. This, however, is not the case. As early as 1515, years before his breach with the old Church, the monk Luther tells his pupils about conflicts, doubts and troubles of conscience now happily overcome. Early in 1516 he declares that once he knew nothing of the "righteousness of God," but that now, though not without internal conflicts, he had come to understand clearly the meaning of this term in Scriptures. Almost at the same time he further confesses that he actually felt "seasick" whenever he heard anyone use the word "righteousness" in the strict sense of the law.

It follows from this that the aged Luther's supposed "romance of the convent" is in its essential features quite firmly fixed in the mind of the Reformer as early as 1515 and 1516, though at that time he does not yet mention self-castigation, freezing, wakeful nights and fasts. But of these things his cell at Erfurt and his oldest portrait speak all the more eloquently. His room in the monastery had no arrangement for heating, so he really did suffer from cold as he later asserts. His oldest likeness dates from the year 1520. On it his features are still those described by Mosellan in July of the previous year. He looks morbidly tired, with sunken eyes and hollow cheeks and seems mere skin and bones. Hence it is also true that he starved himself and otherwise lived like an assiduous ascetic "in waking, praying and other labors." For it is quite unlikely that a healthy and robust man of thirty-six—this was his age then—should look so cadaverous if he be in the least careful about his physical well-being. As soon as Luther took the trouble to pay attention to his health his outward appearance began visibly to improve. Evidence of this is his next picture from the spring of 1521. In it the hollow cheeks and eyes have become filled out, the bony neck is round and firm, indeed, the first signs of a double chin are to be seen, so that one is almost led to believe that meanwhile the ascetic hermit had become a comfortably situated prelate.

While thus we have no reason whatsoever to impugn the veracity of the Reformer in this respect, are not on the other hand the blunders, errors and exaggerations in his statement so incriminating that we would do well wholly to dispense with information given by him in his later years? If this were the case we would be forced radically to discard as mere idle prattle well-nigh all memoirs and autobiographies and absolutely all biographical reminiscences of older people. For Luther had the same experience as all famous writers of memoirs who were not in a position to use contemporary documents and notes.

Goethe in his "Dichtung und Wahrheit" not only very frequently combines facts in an arbitrary way, but is besides guilty of the gravest errors in chronol-

ogy, especially when he deals with the date of origin
of his works. There is no doubt, however, that on
these questions particularly the great poet wishes to
present truth and not poetry. It is well known that
Bismarck in his "Gedanken und Erinnerungen"
often sets down mistaken reminiscences and wrong
thoughts. Yet no one would for a minute think of
branding him a liar because of this or refuse to accept
his memoirs as an historical source. The same is true
of all such works in modern times, no matter who the
author may be. None of them is free from blunders
and errors, yet without a doubt they are sources which
no historian dare leave unread. Consequently, no
psychologist will be surprised about these errors and
contradictions in chronology and fact in the reminiscences of the aging Luther. At most he will wonder
that the old man did not err more often. For Luther
did not have access to diaries and journals like Goethe,
he had no well-ordered collection of materials and no
expert collaborator like Bismarck. Above all, his
stories are always told incidentally and mostly by
word of mouth only, without long previous prepara-
tion and careful testing of his remembrance—altogether on the promptings of the moment.

Is it possible in this way to explain all mistakes,
all exaggerated and unjust verdicts which the Reformer in later years renders about the "Papacy,"
that is, the Catholic Church in all its phases? He
makes the well-known declaration that as a child he
knew nothing about the mercy of God and of his
grace, and that he became acquainted with Christ

only in the capacity of an angry judge of the world
enthroned upon a rainbow. He says that even in the
monastery he still hated Christ, so that he was frightened whenever he saw a painting or likeness of him,
or heard his name mentioned in passing. Indeed,
here especially Luther claims to have suffered the
keenest doubts about God's mercy. This was due,
he asserts, not merely to the frailty of human nature
but to the Pope's theology. Is this true?

Upon reading the beautiful prayers and hymns
which Denifle cites from the breviary and missal used
by the Augustinian hermits one is tempted at the first
blush to join him in his negative answer. For in these
prayers and hymns we everywhere meet not the angry
judge but the merciful and gracious God of whom
Luther at the time claims to have been ignorant. Since
then it can be proven that he knew these books thoroughly, in fact, had committed a goodly portion of
their contents to memory, the conclusion seems unavoidable that all his later stories about his doubting
the mercy of God are pure invention. Luther never
sincerely doubted and struggled. It was impossible
for him ever to fall into such inner conflicts and troubles, for almost hourly and daily he heard that very
grace praised in hymns and talked about in the most
impressive manner.

True, if in the monastery he had never done anything but sing and pray, hear and read mass, then this
conclusion would not only be permissible but impera-
tive, then we would always need only to open the
missal and breviary of the Augustinians in order to

determine what at the time were Luther's beliefs, hopes and fears. However, we know very distinctly that he did and had to do many other things besides. Even as a novice he read and became acquainted with the Bible and a few mystic and theological authors in addition to the missal and breviary. Above all, it was his duty to memorize the rules and constitutions of the order, and to accustom himself to the tremendous task set for the monk, and ever new from day to day for the novice: the problem of subduing his old self and of becoming a superman after the monastic ideal, that is, a man who, free and rid of all selfishness, loves and desires God alone. This task demanded his whole force of will and action. It not only compelled him to submit his whole outer and inner life completely to the control and training of the master of novices, to chastize himself and to take upon himself all sorts of external exercises of humility and obedience, but also constrained him to continually observe himself, to register faithfully every sinful thought and with all his might to "torment and torture," to discipline and train his soul, so that gradually it might be capable of the high art of loving nothing and desiring nothing but God alone.

After taking the vows in September, 1506, a new task immediately confronted him which deeply stirred his soul: the duty of preparing for his consecration to the priesthood. Hardly had he with this end in view thoroughly and with a "bleeding" heart studied the prescribed book by Gabriel Biel on the canon of the mass and received holy orders (February, 1507) when his superiors again imposed upon him an altogether new duty. Once more he was forced to become a pupil and as "cursor" to study the masters of "modern theology," Okkam, d'Ailly, Gerson, Biel under the teachers of the order, Paltz and Nathin. This he accordingly did with such zeal and success that after autumn, 1508, he was employed as instructor. From that time on naturally his days were more than ever given to study, for in order that he might teach well Luther also was at first compelled to study harder than ever before.

All these facts sufficiently show that in these decisive years his soul was occupied much more with numerous other matters than with singing and praying in the choir. From his very first day in the monastery he was naturally more vitally concerned in the great life question of his new state: how will I gain complete freedom from the natural instincts of self-love and arrive at a perfect love of God? Also his attention was deeply centered upon all those problems which he met again and again in the course of his studies. For they were most intimately connected with this practical question and ever again forced him to the closest and most earnest meditation. Meanwhile he on the other hand increasingly felt the daily hours and readings of the breviary to be "ass's work," indeed mere sound, drawl, murmur and bleating at the walls, which made one feel dull in the head.

If therefore we wish to find out what it was that engaged his inner self during the first years of his sojourn in the monastery, we must not have recourse

to the prayers and hymns which year in year out he
read and recited together with all his fellow monks exactly in accordance with the rule, but we must remember also the high and strict ideal after which he
then endeavored to mould his outer and inner life.
We must besides study the great theologians and
edificatory writers whom he so completely followed
at the time that he read even the Bible through their
eyes, men like Okkam and d'Ailly, Gerson and Biel,
Bernard of Clairvaux and Bonaventura, John Mauburnus and Gerard of Zuetphen.   Only thus will we
be able to determine whether he really struggled and
fought as mightily in the monastery as after 1515 he
declares that he did.

The young monk had heard lectures at the university only with the Okkamists or philosophers of the
"modern" school, and thus when he entered into the
monastery he had the firm conviction: man can do
all that he wills.   He can, for instance, fulfill the Ten
Commandments to the last letter, if only he wants to;
he can love God with his whole heart, with his whole
soul and with all his powers, if only he wants to; he
can even force his reason to believe that black is white,
in fact, he can create in himself every imaginable concept, sensation and feeling, moral and immoral passion, and do this at any time, unhampered and completely, if only he uses his will.   For, because the will
is the all-determining psychic force it is itself determined by nothing, never weakened or strengthened,
increased or decreased at any time by any good or
evil deed.   On the contrary, it remains ever un-

changed, the same in quantity and quality; like the needle of a compass it always returns to its characteristic stabile balance, no matter how often it is diverted in the direction of "good" or in the direction of "evil."

This well-nigh mythological conception of the essence and force of the will was strengthened in the young monk during the first part of his stay in the monastery. In the first place, here also he heard only Okkamists and very soon studied the great masters of the school, Okkam, d'Ailly, Gerson and Biel themselves. Furthermore, all that these philosophers declared theoretically possible, the perfect fulfillment of all commandments, even of the command to love God, in the monastery immediately confronted him as a practical requirement. Lastly, he found this point of view confirmed time and again also in the ascetic writers with whom he had already become familiar as a novice. For no matter how much these latter authors spoke of "grace," not one of them doubted that man through ascetic practices, prayer and meditation could himself prepare his soul for becoming one with God. And none of them omitted most earnestly to encourage his readers to the highest exertion of the will. Indeed, the greatest of them all, Bernard of Clairvaux, ventures to affirm that it were possible through a careful control and regulation of the process of perception gradually to convert the impulse of natural egotism into the noble passion of the true love of God. In his book on the love of God he minutely describes the methods to be used for that purpose.

The deepest impression along these lines was undoubtedly made upon the young monk in the confessional where again and again his attention was drawn to these conceptions. For wholly in keeping with Master Gabriel Biel who, though he was not a strict Okkamist, was nevertheless in the monastery, and everywhere among the "moderns," accounted a model theologian, the Augustinians of Erfurt taught: Man achieves absolution from the eternal punishment for sin or from the guilt of sin only if he sincerely hates and loathes evil. Whoever, therefore, thinks that he needs only to confess and in so doing evinces a measure of fear of hell and purgatory in order to receive absolution from the father confessor is seriously mistaken. The so-called "contrition of the gallows," or the sorrow over the evil external consequences of sin alone never brings about a change in the attitude of God, and even confession and priestly absolution make no difference in this. For, though these latter are useful and necessary, one must not forget that the priest in the confessional remits only the penances imposed by the Church and a part of the temporal penalties of sin, never the eternal punishment of wrong-doing. But is it not expecting the impossible of man to demand that out of his own power he must be completely repentant? By no means. All he needs to do is to subject his inner life to the psychological process of ennobling suggested by Bernard of Clairvaux, and thereby gradually transform the natural self-love which manifests itself in fear of punishment and the contrition of the gallows into perfect love of God. This love by its very nature always includes sincere hatred of all evil, and thus the prerequisite of perfect repentance is attained by the sinner's own efforts. In this way the young monk by all that he did and heard was most energetically encouraged to torment, torture and train his soul in a manner in which otherwise only the body is trained, to the end that he might wrest from it the perfect love of God. If he desired to be saved from purgatory and hell, to be free from all pangs of conscience, if he wished to be a true monk, the initial stipulation was always the same: love God above everything. And ever again the alluring inducement was added to this condition: you can, if only you want to.

But then, was man really able to do everything he wanted to do, in fact, could he even in this case will earnestly and with all his power what he himself wished and desired? Since his university days Luther knew no other attitude, and now under his Okkamist teachers he read and heard the same tenet repeated over and over: God in his innermost being is *Will*, exactly like man, but absolute, eternal and almighty Will. If therefore mere human will can be determined by nothing and yet completely dominate the life of the soul, God is in the highest sense of the word the all-determining Will, determined and limited solely by itself, that is, in the last analysis he is eternal and almighty arbitrariness. This is clearly shown in his actions as Creator. Out of pure arbitrariness he called this particular world, and no other, into being, and altogether like a despot he now disposes and gov-

erns in it, bound only by the "constitution" he himself
gave it, to be in force as long as he wished and subject to the condition of good behavior. It is secondly
manifest in his actions as a Lawgiver. Arbitrarily he
declared one deed to be good and worthy of reward,
another as bad and meriting punishment, for nothing
is in itself either good or bad. Hence he could at any
time to-day declare good what only yesterday was accounted evil, and to-morrow punish as a vice what to-
day was rewarded as a. virtue.

Most flagrantly God reveals himself as personified
arbitrariness in the third place in his actions as Saviour. No rational consideration, but simple arbitrariness led him to bring about salvation through a god-
man, and not through a god-stone, or a god-animal—
to predestine a portion of humanity for salvation and
the others for damnation, while nevertheless he makes
eternal bliss depend upon the fulfillment of certain
conditions. Indeed, it was arbitrariness and nothing
else which made him feel that salvation was at all
necessary, and above all that he made it depend upon
the sacramental practices of the Church. For if anything is certain, it is surely this that man by dint of
his own reason and strength can do everything that
God asks of him. Even the greatest and most severe
task, the pure and disinterested love of God, is not too
difficult for man. In spite of this, every human being
is in need of salvation, though not for inner reasons
but rather for a very external one.

It has pleased God in his absolutism to look only
upon those actions as worthy of reward which he in a

sense has stamped with the "spiritual ornament' of "grace" and thereby transformed from mere good deeds (*merita de congruo*) into merits (*merita de condigno*). Also it further pleased him to closely link this stamping process to the sacraments of the Church. Not in the sense that the Church has the power to directly bring about this stamping or application of "grace" through its sacraments; that is always done by God himself. But he has so arranged it that the stamping always occurs simultaneously with the sacramental acts of the Church. In this way man, though he can do everything that God asks of him out of his own power, nevertheless is always in need of the Church and of "grace"—not in order to become a changed man internally, but merely to gain the recognition of the despot "God." This is not very difficult to attain if man does what he can. God unfailingly gives his works the character of merits and thereby makes them legal tender in heaven. Not that man could force God to do this,—but the Lord of the Universe has contractually bound himself on this point, and since he is unchangeable and truthful man may count on it that God will always scrupulously observe this pact.

This was the God whom the young Luther had before his eyes, whom he wanted to love and was told to love, indeed, as he believed, had to love if he wished to gain forgiveness for his sins, salvation and eternal happiness. If we consider these facts we will step by step be able to realize with him what he felt and what since 1515 he tells of the struggles of his soul. Only then will we be able wholly to comprehend that he feared, indeed, hated God, and was so terribly worried over the problem of predestination. For at all times he had before his mind's eye the God of Okkam, the God of absolute omnipotence and arbitrariness who damned and saved as it pleased him. Further, we will then understand that he tortured himself incessantly "to do sufficient good works to win a merciful God," and that at times, like a mad and haughty saint, he believed to have "done his part." For he knew no other view than this that man was able and obliged to earn "grace" by his own power. Furthermore, we then see that the promises of grace in Scriptures and in the liturgy could make no impression upon him, no matter how tempting and consolatory they might sound. The word "grace" necessarily always called to his mind first of all the spiritual "ornament" by which God was said to give to good works the character of merit, and he was firmly convinced that this "spiritual ornament" also must first be deserved.

Such considerations enable us to understand why Luther never could or would cease worrying over his sin, for upon conscientious self-examination he never found in himself as much humility and love of God as Biel and Bernard and other monkish saints demanded. Lastly, we understand in view of these facts why the priestly absolution dispensed in the sacrament of penance was to him an altogether insufficient consolation. He had learned from Biel that it is not absolution which brings about forgiveness of sins, but alone true contrition springing from the perfect love of God. It is, therefore, not an exaggeration to assert that it is the "modern" theology, Biel's doctrine on penance and the monastic teaching about the royal road of humility and love which first plunged Luther into the terrible doubts and troubles of conscience, about which later on he speaks so frequently, and always so vividly and impressively.

Granting that this is true, how came it that just Luther was so strongly and peculiarly affected by this modern theology, that he particularly was so powerfully shaken by Biel's teaching on penance and the old monastic doctrine of humility, and that especially he was so sorely troubled by the fear of sin? Other monks who studied exactly the same things and undertook the very same exercises were not so affected. Does this observation not make the supposition very probable that his nerves were not quite in order, especially since not even so experienced a mentor of souls as John von Staupitz understood his "temptations" and evidently regarded Luther's fear of sin as abnormal? Certainly his condition was not "normal," and it is very probable that his nervous system suffered severely under the strain of hard study, fasting, waking and living in an unheated cell. But does this justify us to forthwith conclude that his fear of sin was nothing more than a symptom of psychic derangement caused by the unaccustomed physical and emotional exertions of monastery life? That would be overshooting the mark altogether. The psychic abnormality which was at bottom of all this worry was not acquired by Luther after his entrance into the monastery. It can be shown that he suffered from it already as a student and never again got rid of it as long as he lived though otherwise he was a person of robust health of body and soul.

What was the character of this abnormality? It consisted simply in a particularly delicate and sensitive conscience, and an unusually keen and live sense of truth. In this tender conscience and this inexorably rigid truthfulness in the judgment of himself we must see the real cause of these internal tribulations. On the other hand, the old monastic teaching of humility, Biel's doctrine of penance, the hard and cruel picture of God and the fantastic conception of man found in "modern" theology must be looked upon merely as the occasion and external impetus which set in motion this strongest and most sensitive chord of his inner self and for a long time kept it in a state of quivering excitement and susceptibility.

Had Luther not been so unusually sensitive, Biel, Okkam and the old monkish teachers would certainly have been as little able to touch him as his more coarse-grained comrades in the monastery. He would then, however, have turned out to be only a good average person like these, and every trace of his sojourn on earth would like his ashes have long since disappeared. This very conscience with its sensitive organism which now caused him so much unrest, on the other hand, like the restless mechanism of a watch was also the live-force which drove him on. As time wore on it pushed him ever farther from the beaten path of the old faith, and with increasing energy urged him to give to the religious problem that altogether personal formulation by which unbeknown to himself, he already stepped outside of the limits of the Catholic system. The problem as he put it was: How will I, the single individual, become absolutely certain of forgiveness of sin and thereby of the grace of God?

What Luther tells us of the conflicts of his soul is thus indirectly confirmed by the books which he studied in the monastery. It is merely necessary for us to give serious heed to the demand made by Denifle and Grisar, and to peruse these books with the eyes of a psychologist, that is, always attempt while reading to feel what impression they must necessarily make upon a thoughtful, serious young monk with a tendency to "scruples" who in his anguish of heart thrice made the great confession, and for a time daily went to be shriven. But naturally this method does not yet prove that the statements of the Reformer about the time and turning point of his severe inner crisis, the experience in the tower of the Black Cloister, are all correct. At any rate, it is advisable for us here also to adopt the method of getting down to the documents themselves, that is, that for once we make a close study of the manuscripts of the period in which he himself places this event, the late autumn of 1512 (Weimar edition, vol. 45, p. 86) to March, 1515. Period of his becoming acquainted with Augustine's treatise on the Letter and the Spirit.

A study of this kind must above all deal with the preparations and notes for his first course of lectures on the Psalms delivered between July or August,

1513, and March, 1515. What do these teach us? In the first place, they indicate that Luther must have been quite closely conversant with the Epistle to the Romans as early as the summer of 1513, for he cites it on every occasion, even in his marginal notes to the commentary by Faber which he used for the Psalms. Secondly, they prove that even at this time he understood the Epistle, and thirdly, that the decisive turn in his inner development must have been passed some time before, since all those views which pre-eminently stamp him a heretic are already found in these documents though often still in a clouded and conflicting form.

Thus, for instance, we meet the conviction: the greatest evil is guilt, the greatest good the cancellation of this guilt, in other words, the possession of a "secure conscience." Furthermore, we find the recognition that no man can force this security of conscience from himself or earn it by his own efforts. It is obtained solely through the aid of God who instills into the soul the trust in his mercy. Further we note the firm conviction: in and with this trust or faith God gives to man also the power to do good. Lastly these old notebooks show beyond a doubt that the passage Romans 1:17 must have had a very special importance for the young instructor, so often is he busy with the concept of the righteousness of God, so emphatically does he ever anew develop the religious ideas previously derived from a correct understanding of it. In short, these notes furnish us the documentary proof for the fact that Romans 1:17 really had for Luther become the gate of paradise, and that the enlightening of which he speaks in later years in reality took place in the period which he himself indicates, that is, in the end of the year 1512 or the opening of 1513, in the first months, therefore, after his promotion to a professorship in the theological faculty at Wittenberg.

But we must guard against misinterpreting this result. The young professor who in his cramped study is bothering his head about the concept of the righteousness of God, and the Reformer Luther who in the same small room writes against the Papacy are two entirely different persons. The former still remained a true monk and Scholastic for years to come. He grows into his new religious point of view only very gradually, and the old ideals and authorities lose their power over his soul by slow degrees only. It is not until some time in 1515 that he completely succeeds in shaking off the last remnant of the network of the Okkamistic doctrine on salvation which he had torn long before. Thereafter, in the course of the year 1516 he overcomes the monkish views on humility and learns that humble submission to the will of God is not sufficient, but that there must be added thereto the glad trust in his mercy. Not until the turning of the year 1516-17, however, does he dare to discard altogether his pastoral doubts about the doctrine of the certainty of salvation, and his monkish aversion to the thought that a pious person may confidently count on the mercy of God without seeming to infringe on humility. Only after all this does he frankly and freely assert: It is impossible to trust in

God without at the same time being absolutely certain of salvation and eternal bliss.

Because this forward movement was so slow and so gradual Luther himself never fully realized how diametrically opposite to the basic views of Catholic piety his attitude had become and was destined increasingly to become. "In error and ignorance," "as a horse whose eyes had been blinded, God led him onward and upward," until finally he had been so far matured and steadied internally that he was able, though again not "knowingly and with foresight," but without the least presentiment whither his course would lead him to challenge publicly the "misguided seducers of the people" whom he had previously so sharply attacked in his lectures on Romans.

CHAPTER III.

Luther's Helpers and Guides During the Conversion.

DID this development, as it has just been sketched, take place without external influences, or did the young monk find helpers and guides upon the lonely path which he was treading almost like a somnambulist, securely, but without clearly realizing his fate? Did Luther have mentors and guides who pointed out to him the right way, accompanied him, or even preceded him?

This question has also been much discussed of late but very differently answered. According to Denifle we ought to look upon William of Okkam as his foremost teacher and master; Albert Maria Weiss, O. P., holds that John Wiclif must be given this place; Braun and John Ficker believe that the mediæval Mystics and John von Staupitz were responsible for his views; Loofs names St. Augustine and Bernard of Clairvaux; Büttner, Stange and Mandel mention John Tauler and the anonymous author of the "German Theology"; H. Barge claims that Karlstadt, though not acting as his forerunner exactly, at least preceded him in the battle, while Kampschulte, Janssen, Pastor and other Catholic investigators assert that even after the beginning of the public conflict the Humanists Crotus Rubeanus and Ulrich von Hutten decisively influenced his actions and convictions, in-

86

deed, really trained him up and induced him to assume
the rôle of leader of the nation against Rome.

Attempts to solve this interesting educational problem are therefore not lacking. Naturally not all of
these solutions are real solutions. Barge's statement,
for example, about the influence of Karlstadt on the
Reformer is disproven by a mere glance into the lectures on Romans of the years 1515-16. Here we find
the whole ensemble of opinions which Karlstadt on the
twenty-sixth of April, 1517, proposed in his 152
theses. But not always is it possible so quickly to sift
truth and error. For that reason we will have to tarry
a moment over some of these attempted explanations.

Early in the summer of 1515 the Reformer summarily refers to the Okkamists as "hog theologians."
One might conclude from this that he had even then
severed connections for all time with Okkam and his
fellows. But such a conclusion would be overhasty.
Luther never quite got through with the hog theologians. In a measure he remained an Okkamist during his whole life, in fact, in some of his doctrines he
must, as Denifle declares, actually be regarded as a
disciple of Okkam, who carried on and developed his
work. Luther's teachings about the eucharist and
about the omnipresence of the body of Christ, and all
that he puts forth in concepts, proofs and analogies in
the conflict over these doctrines goes back directly to
this source and to d'Ailly and Biel. Indeed, it seems
almost as though Luther had had the feeling that he
could bring this controversy to a successful issue only
if he fought as an Okkamist, so abruptly and without

reservation does he at the time in his polemics use for his purpose the Okkamist view on revelation as a sum of non-rational teachings, so unconditionally does he after the manner of this authority demand in the name of faith, the sacrifice of intellect, the captivity of reason and a blind submission to the non-rational "tenets" of Christian doctrine.

But not only on this point, and not exclusively in those dogmas which were later on so frequently regarded as arch-Lutheran does the Reformer appear as a true pupil of Okkam. He followed the Invincible Doctor elsewhere also more often than is commonly suspected both in his ideas and methods of thought. Classic examples are his much-discussed doctrines on the inviolability of the confessional and on the permissibility of the white lie. Other instances substantiating his dependence are his teachings on the law of nature and natural right, on the position of the secular government over against natural and written law, on the right of the civil power to reform the Church, and furthermore his deprecatory judgment on jurisprudence and the jurists, his gruff verdict on the "blind and mad heathen Aristotle," and all the philosophers, who like the Stagyrite give themselves up to metaphysics, his views on the relation of reason to revelation, and his highly characteristic utterances on the hopeless inadequacy of reason in an inquiry into the ultimate causes of all existence which lie altogether beyond the realm of experience.

It is therefore downright impossible to comprehend Luther's theology, in fact his whole point of view in

life, without continually bearing in mind that he
passed through the school of the "moderns," the
"Modernists" of those days. However, dare we for
this reason like Denifle summarily dispose of him as
an "ossified Okkamist"? That would mean doing
plain violence to the truth. For if we center our attention upon the religious basis of his message, his
concept of evil and sin, of forgiveness and of grace, of
law and gospel, of piety as a religious and as a moral
attitude, we recognize without difficulty that these
fundamental ideas were arrived at in a struggle with
the theology of Okkam.

Luther's Christianity, therefore, is everything but
ossified or softened Okkamism. Quite to the contrary,
it is in all its essential features the most complete contrast to the teachings of this theologian that can be
imagined. This does not preclude the fact that Okkam, even if he did not directly aid Luther, at least
materially eased his task of overcoming mediæval religion. For Okkam was not only the Antichrist but
also the anti-Catholic among the great thinkers of
the Middle Ages, not merely the confessed antipode
of mediæval Christianity but also the sharpest critic
of the *mediæval features* in this Christianity.

The classical Middle Ages were as yet incapable
of comprehending the spiritual in a purely spiritual
sense. Just as they always conceived God in some
manner as a substance so they also viewed sin, if not
directly as a substance, at least as a lack of substance,
and looked upon grace as the heavenly material which
compensates for this lack; while justification to them

was the process by which this deficiency is equalized and man in a trice converted from a sinner into a righteous person.

Duns Skotus was the first to attack these "massive" concepts, and he was soon followed with greater authoritativeness by Okkam. While the latter conceived God strictly as will, he also saw in sin only a functioning of the will and in grace actually only a "spiritual ornament" or a sort of stamp by which God recognizes as acceptable the performances of man. Accordingly, he understood forgiveness of sin no more to mean the infusion of the substance of righteousness into man, but held that it signified merely the non-imputation of sin to man. Augustine's "justification" he allows to stand as an independent process following the non-imputation of sin, but for practical purposes this dogma seemed to him perfectly meaningless and superfluous. He was altogether at a loss what to do with it. Meanwhile he evidently desired to destroy to the very root the old Christian idea of salvation by grace. In reality, however, he killed only the belief in the old imperfect massive formulation of this doctrine.

Thus Luther had only to throw overboard entirely the now wholly sterile and empty concepts of grace and justification which the great Englishman had retained and to give a new content to the very hollow idea of "non-imputation of sin" in accordance with his own religious point of view, and he had done with the Catholic system in this particular. This was self-evidently not as easily or quickly done as it would seem to us to-day. On the contrary, it cost Luther hard struggles and weary labor. Nevertheless, there remains no doubt that Okkam made this task easier for him and furnished him in the concept of "non-imputation of sin" with a formula which he could readily employ for the presentation of his own views.

The critical work of Okkam and his school was equally important for Luther in another matter. As in the doctrine of salvation, so these wise "advocates of the cause of man versus Augustine" tried also in the dogma and the sacrament of penance to show that man could by his own power do all God required of him, and that hence for internal reasons he really in penance needed "grace" just as little as the Church. Therefore Biel, for example, regards non-sacramental penance as much more important than the sacrament of penance. What are the elements of this non-sacramental penance according to Biel? They consist in a "change of attitude" in man which necessarily in turn brings about a change in the attitude of God, that is, it causes God to cancel the threatened sentence and to again regard the sinner as fit for eternal salvation.

On the face of it this theory reminds one so strikingly of Luther's later point of view that one would feign believe that he had learned directly from Biel on this point. Upon closer inspection, however, this impression vanishes. In the case of Luther the "change of attitude" on the part of God comes first, while Biel always conceived it as the result of the "change of attitude" in man. Luther believes that

God alone can bring this change in man about, while Biel contends that man can and must effect it himself. With Luther, therefore, the whole emphasis lies upon the act of God, with Biel it rests upon the act of man. This alone shows that Biel's doctrine of penance at first necessarily precipitated Luther into ever new doubts and fears. Only after he had gained the mastery over the in his opinion deadly fundamental idea of Biel was he able to draw honey even from this poisonous flower. Not until then did Biel's criticism of the Church's doctrine of penance become important and valuable to him as a means by which he might break and throw aside the hollow shells of the old dogma which had been left over in this process of criticism.

However, Okkam was not only the most acute critic of the Catholic dogma of salvation whom the Middle Ages had seen, he was likewise one of the sharpest critics and antagonists of the hierarchical system. He already asserted tersely and without equivocation: Popes and councils can err; he declared it an open question whether the monarchical form of government were beneficial to the Church; he denied that the Pope and the clergy had any right whatsoever to mix in secular affairs, and would at most permit the former to count as a cult official who in secular matters was quite as much subject to the Emperor as all other men.

We do not know how far the Reformer before 1517 became acquainted with these radical opinions. In any case it was not immaterial for his development that he grew up amidst the views of a theological school whose founders and most influential spokesmen were pronounced enemies of the Papal system. He certainly never was a "Papist" in the strict sense of the word, not even when he still held very high notions of the sanctity of the Roman Church. At most he may be called an Episcopalist. Therefore, when Prierias and Eck forced him to take a stand over against the curialistic point of view he was able to do so in a relatively short time and without experiencing serious inner conflicts.

Did the Okkamists thus give him only negative aid through their critical work? Did they not also immediately, by means of positive suggestion and hints, assist him out of the labyrinth of doubt and terrors of conscience into which they themselves among others had plunged him? If we read what the "Invincible Doctor" himself says about the Bible in his renowned Dialogue and elsewhere, it would indeed seem that though he did not directly show the young monk the way out of his inner disturbances he nevertheless emphatically pointed out to him the source where alone he would find right advice. Among other things, for instance, Okkam says: Holy Writ alone is infallible, therefore a Christian is in duty bound to believe only what is found in the Bible or what can with logical consistency be deduced from its words. Could this suggestion be of much help to Luther? Only if Okkam at the same time opened up to him an understanding of Scriptures. For the mere study of the Bible Luther practised diligently enough in accordance with the precepts of his order and from his own volition. Was Okkam fitted to teach Luther the understanding of Holy Writ? In reply it is sufficient to note the fact that in Okkam's eyes the Bible was merely a haphazard collection of non-rational divine oracles; that he always saw in the teaching of the Church the correct interpretation of these, and that he believed his own doctrine of salvation in turn to be an accurate rendering of the dogmas of the Church. He was thus in reality not a biblicist, and consequently could never have made one out of Luther. Indeed, had Luther followed him, the Bible would ever have remained to him a book with seven seals, and he would never even have thought of seriously and with an unbiased mind determining the true content of the sacred book.

Not until after the Reformer comprehended the Bible and was quite certain of his new convictions did the teaching of the moderns relative to the Bible assume a certain significance also for him. But again this was due not to the positive content of this teaching but merely on account of its negative conclusions, that is, because of its polemics against the infallibility of the Pope and the councils. It is therefore hardly possible to rate too highly the influence of Okkamist *criticism* upon the development of Luther. It offered him a whole arsenal of weapons for the fight against the Catholic dogma, and against the Catholic constitutional and legal system. Furthermore, step by step it rendered his internal conflict with the old faith less difficult, and in fact furnished him in the clearly worked out formula of the "non-imputation of guilt by the grace of God" a scaffolding of concepts admirably suited to the presentation of his new convictions. But for these convictions themselves the Okkamists must in no way be held responsible, these he did not receive from them. On the contrary, he attained and was forced to attain them by dint of steady battling against this theological school.

Perhaps the young monk was most aided in his troubles by Biel and not by Okkam himself, in that this "leading publicist of Okkamist orthodoxy" who, of course, is no longer an altogether sound representative of the system, emphatically pointed *Augustine* out to Luther again and again as the greatest of all theologians.

Luther began to study Augustine no later than 1508. The very first impression of the Church Father upon him was so profound that the monk continued to read him "until he had read and made his own almost the entire writings of the great teacher." What was it that so captivated Luther? If we may place faith in the marginal notes by his own hand in his desk copy it was at first especially the mystic philosophical speculation of Augustine about God, the world, the soul, the valuelessness of all earthly things and the eternal happiness in God.

These thoughts of course were hardly new to Luther. He had met them before in Bernard of Clairvaux and other mystics and was soon after confronted by them in a still more pronounced form in Dionysius Areopagita. But now seemingly for the first time was he so powerfully gripped by them that he endeavored quite in the manner of the young Augustine and the Neoplatonists to raise himself up to the level of God through mystic speculation, "to climb up into the Majesty," to "behold the pure Majesty," to become immediately conscious of and one with God through visions and ecstasies. And actually there were hours when he believed himself to be "amidst the choirs of angels." But sober reaction never failed to set in. The terrors of conscience returned, and a real confidence in the method of the Mystics would never appear. It was impossible for him thus rapidly to completely transform his nature by speculation, or to forget entirely what he had learned in the school of Okkam about the absolute incapacity of human reason to fathom God's nature, will and work. Therefore he never could—as his marginal glosses show—really assimilate completely the fundamental dogma of the Mystics about the divine ideas. Instead of moving freely and unhampered in the rare ether of speculation, he always dropped back again into the old "method of authority," which Augustine himself had never scorned, and which directed him to seek God in the historical revelation.

The unrest and motion which hereby entered into his thinking is still faithfully mirrored in the lectures on the Psalms given in 1513-15. Here we find, first, the fundamental ideas of his new religious point of view, however secondly, side by side with them, also occasional genuinely Okkamistic reflections, and thirdly, a number of passages that sound almost Neoplatonic and Mystic. A closer study reveals the fact that the basic dogmas of Neoplatonic metaphysics had remained strange to Luther. He neither believes that the general concepts of human reason accurately correspond to the "ideas," nor the invisible and eternal original forces which supposedly condition and determine the nature and essence of individual phenomena, nor does he see in the world of being a system of graduated forces and existences which all spring from the original being, God, and are continually connected with him as with their living focus. Likewise he knows of no methodical and gradual upward trend of the process of thinking from the lower to the highest forms of being, nor does he with the Neoplatonists regard that which is carnal, perceptible and visible as merely an illusion or as non-existing, much though he occasionally stresses the absolute value of the transcendental, spiritual and invisible, and emphasizes the worthlessness of that which is visible. If we ask what, so to speak, immunized Luther against these doctrines the answer can only be: Okkam's criticism of the pure speculative intelligence, which had accustomed Luther to regard general concepts merely as symbols or signs for a wholly unknown and unknowable thing in itself, and to see in the divine ideas only the concepts of God about an individual phenomenon. That is, Okkam after all in this point retained the victory over Augustine.

However, was Luther's association with Neoplatonic Mysticism for this reason without value for his development? By no means. Though he did not find in it the solution of his doubts and internal troubles it acted as an antidote to the hypnotic influence which the Okkamist doctrine of salvation had up to this time exerted upon his thinking. He recognized that it was possible to judge quite differently about God, man, sin and grace than the "Invincible Doctor" and was thereby not a little encouraged to throw overboard the old theories of his school.

Is this the only service which Augustine and Mysticism rendered Luther at this juncture? The answer to this question is found in the fact that at the time (1508-14) he learned to know not only Augustine's Mystic philosophy, but also his teachings about sin and grace, and further, in the circumstance that the Mystics who most deeply affected him were two of a pronounced Christian type: Bernard of Clairvaux and John von Staupitz.

Though Luther did not himself become clearly conscious of it, Augustine, after 1509, became ever more the standard of his views on salvation. In 1513, therefore, at the beginning of his lectures on the Psalms he stood much closer to Augustine than to Okkam on this point. But not until some time in 1515 after he had read Augustine's treatise on the Letter and the Spirit did he succeed in overcoming the last vestige of Okkam's doctrine on salvation which remained in his thinking, and thus finally vanquish utterly the "Invincible Doctor."

Augustine, however, was by no means the only ally of Luther in the long and desperate struggle with Okkam and his school. As early as 1505-07 two other advisers, Bernard of Clairvaux and John von Staupitz, stood by him. The former (he died in 1153) though by conviction an adherent of Mystic speculation and especially in his theological writings a zealous advocate of the common Catholic views on good works, the law, the meritorious value of ascetic practices by the monks, nevertheless manifested certain Evangelical elements in his religious attitude. Occasionally he looked upon forgiveness of sin as the supreme blessing. At times he praised justification through faith alone and in so doing clearly conceived justification as the foundation of a new relationship between God and man on the strength of which God no longer charged sin to the account of man, though the sinner might not yet have overcome his sin. On occasion, Bernard, also therefore like Luther, regarded penance in the celebrated opening thesis in the Ninety-five as a moral process of purification which continued through the whole life of the converted person. Once, in fact, he insisted quite in the manner of the later Luther: It is not sufficient merely to believe in a general way that God pardons sin, you must also believe that he forgives you personally. Above all Bernard continually pointed to the cross of Christ as the incontrovertible proof of the compassionate love of God for sinful mankind and over and over emphatically designated humility which is conscious of no merit and constant sorrow over sin as the fitting attitude and sentiment of man in his intercourse with God.

In view of these facts it is easy to understand why

Bernard very early made an impression upon Luther. The words: you must also believe that God has forgiven you personally, were forcibly called to the attention of the perturbed young monk by the master of novices of the Augustinians at Erfurt in 1505-06 and directly lodged in his soul to remain there unforgotten throughout his life as the first bit of consolation which had comforted him in his misery. With equal force he was influenced by Bernard's continual reference to the cross of Christ, for the more he followed this direction, the more the bleeding head and wounded side dislodged from his religious consciousness the terrible picture of the Judge of the world seated upon a rainbow, the more certain he grew of the incomprehensible fact of the compassionate love of God for the sinner, the more firm also, on the other hand, waxed in him the knowledge that sin is the direst of evils and that it were blasphemy to persist in speaking of merits and good works in the face of the crucified Saviour.

These new convictions, however, came to be his permanent property only during the intimate personal association with a genuine disciple of Bernard, John von Staupitz, Vicar of the order. Staupitz himself, in his last letter to Luther, explicitly confessed that "alone Brother Martin had led him from the husks of the swine to the pasture of life." Nevertheless, there was a time when conversely the Vicar was the guide of Brother Martin. He led Luther along exactly the same paths as Bernard, however. Ever again he pointed the young monk to the wounds of Christ as the great proof of the love of God; he encouraged him to cling with his whole soul to this overpowering revelation of the true sentiment of God and urged him to stop the useless speculations about predestination. On the other hand he admonished him to accustom himself to the thought that he was in truth and reality a sinner, and above all convinced Luther that he must cease torturing and tormenting himself in accordance with the prescription of Biel in the endeavor to gradually transform his natural self-love into the pure love of God by a systematic training of his ideas and feelings. He did this by calling to the attention of the young monk the words "which remained fixed in his soul as the arrow of a mighty one": the love of God and of righteousness is not the end but the beginning of true penance. In this wise the desperate young man in his associations with Staupitz learned to know God from an entirely different angle from that which had been presented to him in the school of Okkam. Simultaneously he was freed from the futile self-torture which he had so far assiduously practised in order that he might wrest from himself true love of God and true penitence.

Despite all, however, Staupitz was unable to entirely free Luther from his tribulations. Brother Martin's fear of sin appeared quite unintelligible, indeed absurd, also to his patron, for the Vicar himself did not regard sin in such a serious light, and the mysterious striving of the young monk for personal assurance of forgiveness he failed utterly to comprehend, because his own convictions on this point were the orthodox Catholic ones. In full agreement with St. Bernard he deemed it impious even to pray for such assurance. But, though he did not understand Brother Martin, Staupitz, nevertheless, without coddling, always made Luther feel his high personal regard for him, and his willingness to assist him. The lonesome young man who still associated with the word father the idea of unbending severity and strictness which life in the paternal home had taught him thus for the first time came to know a father's love, and that was perhaps of even greater moment for his psychic condition than all the comforting directions and knowledge which he owed to the pious Vicar.

Staupitz and Bernard stood by the Reformer in the hardest years of his development. Later on a number of other Mystics crossed his path, among them Bonaventura and Gerson, and besides the two Dutchmen, John Mauburnus and Gerard Zerbolt von Zuetphen who so profoundly impressed also his great antipode Inigo Loyola. A short time only before Luther entered the lists, at the end of 1515 or the beginning of 1516, he further made the close acquaintance of two of the great German Mystics of the fourteenth century, John Tauler and the so-called Frankfurt Anonymous, the author of the "German Theology." He forthwith recommended the former to his students as an excellent German religious writer. The latter he himself edited, in an incomplete form in 1516 and completely in 1518, confessing that outside of the Bible and St. Augustine he had found no other book which had taught him more about the nature of God, Christ, man and all things.

This enthusiastic verdict is responsible for a whole literature. Even to-day a considerable group of scholars on the basis of it assert: "Not until he met the Frankfurt Mystic did Luther develop from a despairing struggler in a dark sea into a Reformer." (H. Büttner) Mandel says: "As a reforming theologian Luther is a pupil of Tauler and the Frankfurt Anonymous," hence his conversion occurred in the period when he came to know these two old seekers after God. "German Mysticism is the cradle of the Reformation" and similar statements abound. The proof for this weighty assertion these students have always magnanimously left to the common hod carriers of the historical profession. Are the historians in the happy position of being able to provide the necessary confirmatory evidence for these rather large contentions? Unfortunately not. Luther had at the end of 1515 long ago ceased to be "a despairing struggler in a dark sea." His new religious point of view was at that time already fixed. This is shown by the seven first chapters of his lectures on Romans at every point. He had by this time also begun his reformatory criticism of conditions in the Church. Only one thing he still lacked, the clear recognition that the faithful Christian not alone dared be sure of his salvation, but that he *must* be certain of it.

What then was it that so strongly attracted him to Tauler and the Frankfurt Anonymous? Was it the pantheistic speculation which he found there? No, that was not new to him any more. These speculations were neither a peculiar feature of German Mysticism, let alone the last forceful manifestation of the ancient Germanic religion over against the "domiciled Hebraizing worship of foreign gods." This trait the German Mystics held in common with all other Mystics of Germanic, Romanic, Slavic, Semitic, Persian, Hindoo, Greek and Chinese origin. What attracted Luther were naturally those phases which are peculiar to these two seekers after God, the things that were new to him. What was the character of these captivating novelties? He answers this question himself as plainly as possible in the passage of the lectures on Romans where he first mentions and lauds Tauler, furthermore, in the resolution of the fifteenth of the Ninety-five Theses where in part he almost verbally uses the eleventh chapter of the German Theology, and indirectly besides in the marginals to his personal copy of the sermons of Tauler. No other sermon in this volume is so heavily underscored and so profusely glossed as the one which he had in mind during the lectures on Romans and which in its whole content shows close relationship to the eleventh chapter of the German Theology.

What do Tauler and the Frankfurt Anonymous discuss in these passages which were so important for Luther? They treat exhaustively of internal tribulation, the sense of oppression, the distress, fear and unrest, the despair and complete inner collapse which normally precede the rebirth or the regeneration in God. For, as the soul of Christ first descended into hell and only after that ascended to heaven, so man also must first experience the torments of one who

feels himself completely forsaken before he can taste
of the peace, happiness, delight and pleasure of the
eternal God. In this hell nothing pains man more than
his own sin and wickedness, and nothing can console
him on that score. One thing only will avail, to let the
wound fester out, to bear patiently the visitation of
God. Man gets into this state of torment without
knowing why and without having given cause for it
by his own deeds or omissions. His desperate condition is God's visitation upon him. From this in itself
follows that all is not well with man until he feels
disconsolate and desperate, or until he feels happy
and joyful in God. For even in these sore tribulations he is not forsaken by God as he imagines. He
is that only if he himself abandons God, busies himself with created things and flits hither and thither
in doubt without knowing to whom he belongs. But
why does God lead especially his chosen people such
wondrous ways? Because he wants to drive out of
man pride and arrogance, the wish to be somebody,
and wants to show him that he must give himself up
to God in unrestricted humility whether it be for salvation or damnation.

This was the new doctrine which Luther found in
Tauler and the Frankfurtian. Why did it mean so
much to him? In the first place, because it gave him
the firm conviction that every man whom God saves
must pass through the hell of pangs of conscience;
secondly, because in it he again found the knowledge
confirmed that man has no other alternative than to
give himself up unconditionally to God for life and

death and to wholly relinquish all idea of personal choice; thirdly, because he clearly saw from this doctrine that the path he had himself trodden was not a false one, nor a roundabout way, but that it was the direct road to salvation, and that he himself had already been "safe" in God while he was experiencing his hours of greatest inner tribulation. From this necessarily followed also the conviction with reference to the future that he need not and dare not allow new temptations to rob him of the blessed feeling of "security in God."

It is, therefore, not accidental that only after his acquaintance with Tauler and the Frankfurtian Luther ventured freely and openly to confess that the believer must feel certain of his salvation, for only after this had the doubts which so far had held him back from this assurance been set at naught. Now he was unable further to feel that it was a precept of humility to doubt God's everlasting gracious providence, now he no more needed to fear that ignorance and frivolity would abuse this knowledge, for now he could always sober a frivolous person by asking whether he had already passed through the hell of despair. This all enables us to comprehend why in the next years he places Tauler and the Frankfurt Anonymous as the best theologians right after Paul and Augustine. Though they were not the first to teach him what God, Christ, man and all things were, he yet owed to them the clear insight into the apparent tangle of his own development and thereby liberation from the last scruples and doubts about the blessed knowledge that he could and must feel absolutely certain of his God. He did not by any means find this knowledge in a ready and complete form in these two old men of God. He had to arrive at and win it independently, but they indirectly helped him to succeed by making the unfolding of his own religious life clear to him.

Luther's growth, therefore, also confirms the old truth that the human spirit like a plant absorbs from its environment only the nourishment which agrees with its nature: "modern" theology and philosophy the old monastic teaching on humility and of the perfect love of God, the Neoplatonic speculations of Augustine and the Pseudo-Dionysius, the doctrines of Augustine about sin and grace, the edificatory reflections of Bernard of Clairvaux, Tauler and the Frankfurt Anonymous, the personal counsel and encouragement of John von Staupitz—all these had to serve his growth without, however, at any time enslaving him, or forcing him from the path upon which undeterred he advanced toward a goal unknown to himself.

At first, to be sure, it did seem as though Luther were entirely under the domination of modern philosophy and theology, as though his whole feeling and thinking were governed by the old ideal of the monastery and by the desire to transform natural self-love by a radical cure after the prescription of Biel into pure love of God. Gradually, however, with the aid of Neoplatonic speculation, Augustine's doctrine of grace, the religious convictions of Bernard and of Staupitz, he mastered the Okkamistic notions about

God, man and salvation, and at the same time Biel's teaching of the amenability of natural self-love to the process of ennobilization. Simultaneously, however, with the aid of the critical work of Okkam and his school on the dogma, he escaped the pernicious grasp of fantastic mystical speculations and the massive concepts of the Augustinian doctrine of salvation. Furthermore, he made Okkam furnish him the formulas and concepts for his new views on sin, grace, justification and penance. Barely had he completed this long and silent struggle in which his opponents and allies continually changed, when once more Mysticism, as represented by Tauler and the Frankfurtian, was made to assist him in severing the last ties which still connected his new attitude toward religion with the old faith. And contrary to their own convictions as well to the tenets of ancient and mediæval theology, they had to aid him in arriving at the conclusion that the faithful Christian can and must be certain of his salvation.

The ideal which Luther thus acquired in the main still corresponds to the ideal with which he in 1505 had entered into this inner conflict. It still was an answer to the old question: How will I attain complete devotion to God? But his opinions about the way to this goal, and his ideas on the relationship between God and man had in the mean time undergone a revolution which in its kind was as momentous and full of consequences as that wrought by the discoveries of Copernicus in the views about the sun, moon and stars. While in 1505 his own ego still had seemed to him an independent center of inexhaustible energy which ever moved freely in its own orbit without at any time requiring an external impetus, it now was to him only a small dependent star which without proper motion circles about the immense sun, God, and must receive from this sovereign luminary all energy and all light in order that it might illumine itself and others. Thus, while formerly he had expected everything from his own personal will and effort, he now hoped for all from the power and mercy of God.

It is evident that in this revolution of his thoughts, next to Paul and Augustine the greatest influence was exercised by Mysticism. But is it permissible for this reason to regard his religious point of view merely as a development from Mystic piety? No. The Mystic is content with the consciousness of his dependence on God, with the duty of patiently bearing the visitations of God, and with the enjoyment of God. Whatever activity Mysticism contains is completely used up by the task of bringing about this condition in which the will is as it were switched off. With Luther it is not merely a question of passive suffering, but a question of experiencing God in a manner which requires of all forces of the soul a passionate tension. It is with the Reformer not a mere matter of an apathetic attitude, but of an active and joyous feeling of trust and faith which in its nature is not rest, but "a live, busy, active, mighty thing," a continual driving impulse to do what is good. Therefore any attempts to derive his views from any specific earlier doctrine or form of piety have always failed. For no matter how much his whole course of development seems to be conditioned by late mediæval theology and philosophy, by Augustine and Mysticism, the final product is in no way the logical result of these several educational factors, but is something new and original, something that had never existed before, for the explanation of which one must always again point to a wholly uncommensurable quantity: the personal peculiarity of the Reformer.

Luther's whole course of development is just as original as the result, if measured by the career of other heroes of Christian piety. He does not attain calmness and clarity as August Hermann Franke in the space of a few hours, or like Loyola after a few hard weeks—it takes him about eight years. Also he never has a peculiar experience during this period like other pious individuals, he hears no voices like George Fox, has no "photisma" (visions of light) and visions like Loyola, he does not experience a moral collapse like Augustine or John Wesley, he does nothing more than other monks do, he prays, meditates and studies. Even his "conversion," therefore, has not in the least an air of romance about it, for it consists in nothing more than the sudden comprehension of a concept of Pauline theology which hundreds before him had already correctly understood.

Like his conversion the clarification of his new knowledge also proceeds altogether in the quiet of his cell, without convulsing external or moral catastrophes, without any change in his mode of life or form of activity. Luther goes right on praying, meditating and studying, only he perhaps studies even harder than before. For it was impossible for him to get a firm grasp on the new knowledge unless he gained freedom from the old Okkamistic doctrine of salvation which was stamped upon his whole inner life, and unless in addition he gradually acquired an altogether new theology.

How much industry, what a tremendous amount of intellectual energy was necessary for the attainment of this end can in a measure be gauged only if following his footsteps one personally studies all the folios and quartos which he read in these years and allows the truly confounding variety of views they contain to act upon oneself, and if one at the same time endeavors to understand all the highly complicated concepts and subtle arguments with which the Okkamists, for example, operate. Only one of the great representatives of Christianity before Luther was similarly forced to perform and did perform so tremendous a task, the Christian whose development can most readily be compared with his own, the Apostle Paul.

However, Luther was not alone a religious thinker and character, he was also a Reformer. The question arises, is he as original and independent in this capacity as in that of religious thinker? Is the Luther who casts the bull of excommunication into the flames, who as spokesman of the nation places himself at the head of the national movement away from Rome, and who with incomparable audacity and openness pronounces on all the great and small issues of the time like a prophet, is that Luther only the more mature brother of the monk, who like a true fighting theologian fights only with theologians, or did this young champion develop into a reformer only under the educative influence of freer and stronger spirits, into the sphere of whose power he came since about the end of 1519?

This question also has engrossed the attention of scholars and has called forth very different answers. Some see no problem here at all; to others the Reformer Luther is but the docile pupil of Ulrich von Hutten* and of his friend Crotus Rubeanus, the chief author of the Letters of the Obscure Men. Even today it is still claimed that not until after his association with these revolutionary patriots did the young monk who knew nothing of the world discover his German heart, that their example alone encouraged him to appeal to the whole nation? They say, the spirit of Hutten and his challenging boldness speaks in the lines of the great reformatory writings of 1520. Indeed, they claim that the most powerful of all of these, the Address to the Nobility, is nothing more than an extract from Hutten's great satire Vadiscus, or "Trias Romana," and that it is at the same time the documentary proof for Luther's connection with the "Hutten-Sickingen Revolutionary Party." Evidences for this contention are seemingly not lacking, but the question is: Are the methods of proof flawless, and are the facts which are cited always correctly interpreted?

---

*Ulrich von Hutten was notorious for his loose morals. The detractors of Luther group him here with von Hutten and apply to the latter an epithet which is perfectly correct, but which in the translation we have omitted.

A cursory glance into the lectures on Romans and into the sermons of the monk Luther from the period of 1513-17 suffices to show that the monk "who knew nothing of the world" even then knew the world quite well, and that Luther the Reformer was already in the field, though for the present he was content to use the lecture platform and the pulpit as his rostrum. In these sermons he undismayed attacks the excrescences of saint-worship and the indulgences. In the lectures, as we have seen above, he very frankly states his opinion on all sorts of evils in Church and society, indeed, he is no longer satisfied with mere criticism, he sets up quite a list of definite demands for reform. Simultaneously he begins to take a stand over against the problem of nationality. He keenly deplores the fact that so often the peoples in their disputes and jealousies forget that they are Christians. Meanwhile he notes with a certain satisfaction that the Greeks had been even greater gluttons than were the Germans of his day. He further shows the warmest admiration and sympathy for his ruler Frederick the Wise. Three years later, in June, 1518, he assails the supercilious and overbearing attitude of the foreigners toward the German theologians, and with reference to the "German Theology" he expresses the hope that his countrymen might some day still be recognized generally as the foremost theologians.

For the present, however, he was destined to experience personally how far the Italians dared to go in their presumption over against a German. The Italian Dominican, Sylvester da Prierio, attacked him as a leper and a dog in an unspeakably superficial and arrogant treatise. From the moment when this "typically Italian product" came to his hands (August, 1518) he feels the contrast between Italian and German just as strongly and gives it just as undisguised expression as Ulrich von Hutten. In October, 1518, he publicly chastizes the Roman Church's insatiable thirst for gold. In December he voices the suspicion that Antichrist is ruling at the Curia. In February, 1519, he even calls Rome a Babylon and declares angrily: "We Germans alone have helped the popes to the limit of our power. As a punishment we have had to endure them as masters in anathematization and flaying and now also in the exploitation of archdioceses and bishoprics." At the same time he gives in the prologue to his commentary on Galatians a veritable prelude for his Address to the Nobility: "These ungodly windbags, Prierias, Cajetan and their fellows, abuse us as German blockheads, beasts and barbarians, and deride the unbelievable patience with which we permit ourselves to be deceived and plundered. Praise be therefore to the German princes who recently at Augsburg (1518) refused the Roman Curia the tenth, the twentieth and the fiftieth, though they were aware that the most accursed Roman council had sanctioned these taxes. They recognized that pope and council had erred, . . . that the legates of the Curia are only looking for money and nothing but money. The example of these lay-theologians, therefore, is most worthy of emulation . . . it is evidence of a greater piety if princes, and whoever else it may be, opposed the Curia than if they took the field against the Turks." Surely, one who dared to write publicly in this strain a whole year before Hutten sounded the trumpet of battle does not first need to borrow national anger and pathos from Hutten, or be inspired with courage by a writer of the caliber of Crotus Rubeanus who at bottom of his soul was cowardly and without conviction.

However, if accordingly the patriot Luther had been long in the field when Hutten declared war upon Rome, and though the challenging boldness and regardlessness of this German beast was offensive to the Italians and a joy to the Germans when the people still knew nothing of Hutten, this does not exclude the possibility that the patriotic monk in later years learned from Hutten and Crotus Rubeanus. The latter, in fact, since October, 1519, wrote long letters to Luther. The Reformer, however, nowhere refers to their contents. Manifestly they made no deep impression on him. Hutten did not approach Luther until February, 1520. At this early date he already offered him, through the mediation of Melanchthon, the protection of Franz von Sickingen. In April he renewed this proposal, and finally in July he for the first time addressed himself to Luther in person, and forthwith proposed to him a regular alliance. Even this enthusiastic missive, however, did not result in a more lively intercourse between the two men. We know only four letters of Hutten to the Reformer and only four letters of Luther to Hutten. The latter, therefore, was quite right when, in the spring of 1523,

he asserted that Luther had never been his confeder-
ate. But he neglected to mention that he himself had
very earnestly though always wholly in vain sought for
Luther's alliance. The ostensible confederacy of the
Reformer with the "Hutten-Sickingen Reform
Party" is, therefore, nothing more than a legend, or—
to use a favorite term of Luther's—a lie-gend, a tradition which is not rendered more trustworthy by the
fact that it was current in the camp of Luther's adversaries as early as 1521. This venerable age it
shares with many other legends about Luther.

Even so the contact with Hutten did not remain
without abiding results either for Luther or for Hutten. On the contrary, both men doubtless learned
from each other. As soon as Luther enters Hutten's
horizon the Frankish knight suddenly strikes a different note in his writings. The Humanist becomes
a national publicist, the celebrated Latinist learns to
write German and to compose poetry in the language
of his country, the frivolous poet suddenly places the
full extent of his wild passion and extraordinary talent into the service of the national movement away
from Rome and the pagan scoffer condescends to read
the Bible and talks like a pious Lutheran.

The Reformer is indebted to Hutten above all for
the publication of Lorenzo di Valla's treatise on the
forged Donation of Constantine. The reading of
this work made an immense impression on him. Since
then he felt quite convinced that the Pope was the
Antichrist. He was much less able to profit from
Hutten's other writings against Rome, dated Febru-

ary and March, 1520. He certainly read them before he undertook to write his Address to the Christian Nobility. A comparison shows, however, that he had at his command much better and more accurate data about the "Roman greed, love of display and arrogance" than Hutten was able to offer him. Therefore he did not at all need to excerpt the Vadiscus as Hutten could tell him nothing new, the enthusiastic applause of the Frankish knight was as little a matter of indifference to him as the proposal of protection and alliance made by Franz von Sickingen and Silvester von Schauënberg, the favorable opinion of Erasmus and other Humanists, the encouraging messages of the Bohemian Utraquists, the growing sympathy of the German clergy and monks, the mighty stir among the student youth and the news of the increasing excitement of the masses.

From all these storm signals he saw with increasing clearness that he was not standing alone but that his cause had become the concern of the whole nation. Ever more strongly he was overcome in view of these events with the mighty sensation that the people as a whole were preparing to rally around him. In view of these facts, since he had vainly addressed himself to Pope and council, the impulse grew stronger within him to appeal to his people, the people who as it seemed were only waiting for him to issue the call to arms. In such a frame of mind he after June, 1520, wrote his powerful manifesto of war against Rome, the Address to the Christian Nobility. In it he by no means addresses solely the knights, he speaks to his "dear Germans" generally. Also he does not by any chance expect the reform of the Christian estate from the knights, but in the first place from "the noble blood, Charles" and the secular princes, from those lay-theologians, therefore, whose actions he had earlier, in September, 1519, praised so highly. For to him "nobility" signifies not only the knights, barons and counts, but the whole noble class. Only in the one well-known passage of his treatise where he expressly sanctions the claims of the younger sons of noblemen to the benefices of the great religious foundations of the Empire is it permissible to see a reference to the wishes of the lesser non-princely nobles and a sort of thanks for the magnanimous promises of Sickingen and Schauënberg. Truly, he did not need to make use of the "hundred faithful knights" whose help the latter had held out to him, and he was able to decline the protection of Sickingen. Nevertheless, the mere fact that so many members of a class which just then was once more beginning to show energetic signs of life, and which was still quite a power, were willing to answer for his security, filled him with joyous faith in the victory of his cause. Furthermore, it freed him from the uncomfortable duty of so closely considering the timid disposition of his ruler, the Elector Frederick the Wise, as he had up to this time been forced to do.

For these reasons, therefore, it is gross exaggeration to ascribe the transformation of Luther from a reforming theologian into a national and religious reformer purely to the influence of Hutten. The observation which serves as the basis of this contention is undoubtedly correct. The Luther of 1520 is indeed a different person from the Luther of the Ninety-five Theses. His aims are grander, his view much broader and clearer, his self-confidence vastly mightier. But this progress is not the work of Hutten, it is the result of all those struggles which the Reformer had had to endure since 1517 and likewise the reaction to the ever more powerfully growing movement which had already begun before he appeared in the open. Luther himself, without realizing it, was in its service since 1517, and Hutten also after the last months of 1519 had given himself up to it with passionate enthusiasm. Naturally the Reformer did not become clearly aware of the ungaugeable influence of public opinion upon his development. He felt the current carry him ever farther on, but he did not know from whence the flood of waters came. With all the greater zeal he gave credit to his opponents especially since 1519 for being his teachers. Indeed, under their "paternal and kindly guidance" he had been led onward step by step, had ever more clearly come to know himself, until finally he was absolutely certain of his call and ceased to doubt against whom he would have to battle: against the Antichrist and his apostles.

CHAPTER IV.

The Beginning of the Open Conflict With the Old Church.

THE Protestant world celebrates the thirty-first of October, 1517, as the birthday of the Reformation. This is quite justifiable, but easily leads to the erroneous idea that Luther's opposition to the authorities and conditions in the Church of his time did not commence until then, and that it was John Tetzel and the Mayence Indulgence which caused him to issue the battle cry. In reality he had entered the lists long before. Ever since 1515 both in the pulpit and in his lectures he continually criticized with steadily increasing frankness the abuses and evils in all fields of the religious activity of the Church. However, nothing was heard of this outside of Wittenberg. Besides, Luther personally was for the present more interested in another question than in the betterment of the Church, his attention was centered upon the reform of the theological curriculum.

In Wittenberg Luther had already in the middle of the year 1517 succeeded in breaking the sole rule of Scholasticism and in making the study of the Bible the central point of theological instruction. Now he wished to smooth the way for this reform also outside of Wittenberg. Thus for the first time he came to issue a public declaration of war, the Ninety-seven

120

Theses, against Scholasticism of the fourth of September, 1517. He had them printed and sent copies to his friends in Erfurt and Nürnberg, he even dispatched them to the learned and clever Dr. Eck. Then in extraordinary suspense he awaited the opinion of the academic world. But the expected echo failed to materialize. These Ninety-seven Theses, which Luther himself valued so highly, are to-day known only to the specialist. Of the Ninety-five Theses, however, which he tacked to the door of the castle church at noon on the thirty-first of October, every child knows, though he did not submit them to his friends until after they had spread through almost the whole of Germany. Thus strangely in this case also the words proved true: a good work must be wrought in error and ignorance.

Well-known though the Ninety-five Theses are, we, nevertheless, have only in the last few years learned positively what it is of which this renowned document treats. Although even children at school spoke so glibly about indulgences as though they had seen them sprout, green and flower, the indulgence was nevertheless in fact a great unknown quantity in the search for which the scholar ever again with a sigh asked himself the question: From where does it hail? This lack of knowledge was in the last analysis due to a wrong method of approach. People had become accustomed to look at indulgences from below, from the angle of the purchaser. They felt justified in seeing in the motives which manifestly or supposedly governed people in their purchase of indulgences the causes for the origin of the whole enigmatical institution. This method, however, will never result in a clear view of the matter. For that reason Adolf Gottlob in 1906 for a change tried the opposite manner of approach. As a matter of principle he for once studied the indulgences from above, from the point of view of the grantor. He inquired: What moved the popes and bishops to issue indulgences? And lo and behold, the riddle solved itself and the confused picture became clear. The family tree, origin and development of the great unknown suddenly came clearly to light and the doubts about its original significance were ended. The indulgence stood forth as a genuine offspring of the period of the great struggle between Christianity and Mohammedanism and at the same time as a most characteristic product of the so-called Germanic Christianity.

At this point it will suffice to prove this for the complete or plenary indulgence of the Papacy only. In religious wars between Christians and Mohammedans the questions arose very early: How about the salvation of the warriors who fall in these battles? For the faithful Moslem Mohammed had solved this problem. The worshiper of Allah entered the holy war with the firm conviction that in case of death the gates of paradise would forthwith be opened to him. Not so in the case of the Christian fighter for the faith. He asked himself: Will paradise open to me also if I have not duly performed penance for my sins? Such doubts might easily induce him to rather remain at home. Very early, therefore, the popes who especially had at heart the struggle against Islam attempted to dispel misgivings of this nature. With this end in view Pope Leo IV, when in 853 he summoned the Franks to the holy war, very confidently held out to the·soldiers of faith a heavenly reward should they fall in battle. Indeed one of his next successors, Pope John VIII, as early as 877 granted to such warriors absolution for their transgressions.

These promises of salvation were as yet no indulgence. They had reference not to living penitents but to dead soldiers of the faith. However, they prove that the idea which became the mother earth and the nourishing soil of indulgences existed as early as the ninth century, namely, the idea that participation in a war against the unbeliever or other enemies of religion is an achievement of religious value, in fact, that death in a religious war is a sort of martyrdom. Who suffers this fate is immediately laid to rest among the flowers of paradise by St. Gabriel and St. Michael, as the Song of Roland later has it.

Once this high estimate of fighting in the cause of religion had gained ground it was but a short step to look upon participation in such warfare as an equivalent for the penitential acts, the incomplete fulfillment of which might prompt many a warrior to keep his charger in the stable. It was an easy matter to promise remission of these penitential punishments in return for military expeditions against the foes of the faith, that is, to use the remission of penances as a means of recruiting. Thereby the Crusading Indulgence, that is, the complete remission of the penitential punishment as reward for taking part in a religious war was complete. When this kind of indulgence originated is not certain. Very probably, however, it is a German pope, Leo IX, who first ventured to use this type of remission as a means of getting soldiers when in 1052 he made ready for a campaign against the Normans. It is certain that such indulgences were granted by Alexander II in 1063 to the warriors who went to Spain to fight the Moors, also by Gregory VII in 1080 to the faithful who were willing to fight for the anti-king Rudolf of Swabia against the Emperor Henry the Fourth. In 1087 Victor II issued them for participation in the struggle against the Arabs in Africa and Urban II in 1095 for the crusade to Jerusalem. Since then the Crusading Indulgence is a firmly established instrument of Papal world politics. If now we remember the inconveniences, the ecclesiastical and civil disadvantages involved in the penances of the Church, we can understand why the penitents eagerly sought this indulgence.

However, another motive acted even more strongly. The ecclesiastical penance was regarded as a substitute punishment for the purificatory penalties in purgatory. Whoever acquired indulgence, therefore, gained not only liberation from the acts of penance but at the same time also from the corresponding punishments in purgatory. Thus from the very outset a transcendental effect was ascribed to the institution, an influence upon purgatory, and this is what made it seem so desirable to everyone.

Indulgences, however, did not for very long remain a recruiting measure. Already Pope Urban II absolved old and decrepit persons from the duty of personal service in war on the condition that they furnish and equip a substitute at their own expense. Thereupon Pope Eugene III, as early as 1145 or 1146, promised to persons who supported the crusading order of the Templars with a donation of money the remission of a seventh part of their penance. Finally, Innocent III in 1199 formally recognized the giving of alms as sufficient for the sharing in the graces of the Crusading Indulgences. Thus, early in the twelfth century we find in place of a personal performance a material one, a money payment. Thereby a momentous change was wrought in the whole character of the indulgence. From a means of recruiting soldiers it grew into a method of making money, into an expedient of taxing the faithful which was ever more frequently and rigidly employed in the interest of the papal finances.

Meanwhile, in the course of the thirteenth century the crusading ideal more and more lost its power over the minds of the people. If, therefore, the popes desired to retain the important source of income provided by indulgences, they would have to invent new and efficient stimuli for the purchase of these favors. It is the merit of Pope Boniface VIII to have clearly recognized this. By creating the Jubilee Indulgence in 1300 he assured the institution a long further development highly beneficial to the papal finances. Originally the Jubilee demanded of the purchaser as his share of the bargain a pilgrimage to Rome. But very soon this later form experienced identically the development of the earlier Crusading Indulgence. The personal was supplanted by the material service, the making of a payment in money. And just as once upon a time Innocent III had finally made the Crusading Indulgence possible in return for alms in every parish, so now Pope Boniface IX saw to it that the Jubilee could also be purchased everywhere by offering it for sale after 1393 through agents in all the territories of the Church. Thus the indulgence became a movable ware, the sale of these favors a "sacred business."

In order to facilitate this sacred business still more the purchase of the sacred commodity was now receipted for by means of ecclesiastical documents, the so-called indulgence letters. At the same time the priests to whom the undertaking was entrusted were equipped with the most extensive confessional powers, so that the believer was now in the convenient position of being able most expeditiously to acquire, in the first place, remission from the pains of hell by confessing to the indulgence priest, and secondly, to gain freedom from the penalties of purgatory and the penances imposed by the Church by buying an indulgence letter. As a result of these innovations by Boniface IX confession and purchasing of indulgences had therefore become a connected act. For this reason among others the wise popes could refer to this new form of granting indulgence in brief, also as "remission of guilt and punishment." For through it the successor of Peter in reality made it possible for the faithful first by confession to rid themselves of guilt, and then by the indulgence at the same time to gain freedom from all the temporal penalties of sin.

However, this did not complete the development of the sacred commodity. Long ago the question had arisen whether the Pope were in the position to free also the dead from purgatory in case a surviving descendant, relative or friend bought indulgences for them. Since the canon lawyers mostly answered this question in the negative it remained open until the middle of the fifteenth century. Pope Calixtus III in 1457 seems to have been the first who dared assert the right and not until Sixtus IV were indulgences for the dead completely established. This pope on the twenty-seventh of November, 1477, issued a dogmatic declaration about the force of indulgences which set at rest all doubts about their usefulness for the poor souls in purgatory, and which at the same time though only indirectly claimed for the pope jurisdiction also over purgatory.

In the Middle Ages, however, many things were actually practised which rigid theologians and canon lawyers did not approve and would not recognize as "Catholic truth." This is partly true also of indulgences. They were centuries old before the theologians found it expedient to seriously consider them. But the first one who did take them up, Alexander of Hales, then performed the task so thoroughly that little was left for later ages to add. Above all, he

succeeded in discovering the transcendental capital
on the basis of which the Church as its usufructuary
could dispense indulgences: the treasury of good
works, of the merits of Christ and the saints. This
discovery was generally hailed with approval and was
generally accepted. As early as 1343 it was given
dogmatic sanction by Clement VI when he expressly
recognized it in his supplement to the canon law. Together with the doctrine of the treasure the same pope
approved the view that indulgence was the remission
of all or part of the temporal penalties for sin, though
he expressly refrained from including the punishments of purgatory. Thus he still left the teaching
on indulgence undetermined in some essential points.
And this condition also prevailed in the future, for the
declaration of Sixtus IV recognizing indulgences for
the dead was not incorporated in the canon law. As
far as the ecclesiastical courts were concerned it did
not exist. As a dogma it was received only by the
strict papalists, but these were not very numerous at
the end of the fifteenth and the beginning of the sixteenth centuries. The theologians who regarded the
council as the highest tribunal in matters of faith
were decidedly in the majority in France, Spain and
England, and also in Germany.

There was therefore not a complete dogma about
indulgences when, forty years after Sixtus IV, Luther submitted to the learned world his declaration
about the force of indulgences. In particular, an
official doctrine regarding the effect of indulgences on
purgatory was still lacking. Consequently, the Re-

former was not guilty of heresy, but at most of having made "an assertion which was insulting to pious ears" when he refused to accept the institution as valid beyond the remission of the ecclesiastical penances. Hence also Cardinal Cajetan found it impossible to proceed against him for heresy on account of the Ninety-five Theses, though he certainly did not lack willingness to do so.

In spite of this unsettled status of its legal aspect the popes promulgated one plenary indulgence and Jubilee after the other, not only for the living but also for the dead. Indeed they saw no harm in especially commending to their indulgence agents the sale of the latter variety. It was the most lucrative of the two. It is therefore not difficult to understand why efficient agents like the well-known John Tetzel spent their best energies on this branch of the business. "Do you not hear your deceased parents wail and cry out: Have mercy on us! We are suffering grievous punishment and pain from which you can save us with a trifling alms." Thus did the eloquent and bold but also quite dignified and corpulent monk preach. And to strengthen his plea he added, either in prose or verse, the old saying which as early as 1482 had been condemned by the theological faculty of Paris:

> "*As soon as the money does clink in the chest,*
> *The soul it will flit into heavenly rest.*"

If in the period from 1515-20, in spite of Luther's preaching, the papal indulgence still netted such a large profit in the territory of the German Empire doubtless a big portion, if not the biggest part, was derived from the sale of indulgence letters for the poor souls in purgatory.

This was the indulgence as Luther found it. Even to-day there are plenty of apologists who feel that they can justify the "sacred business" by comparing it to the modern popular missions and evangelizations. But the comparison limps. Peoples' missions are true *missions,* while the traffic in indulgences was a real *"business."* The popular missionary aims at the saving of souls, the indulgence seller was purely and simply after the money. Pastoral motives never played a roll in the granting of these documents, especially not in the indulgences which were given out by the popes in an almost unbroken sequence since the Jubilee of 1300. In these the sole and only object was the filling of the papal coffers.

For that reason among others from the time of Alexander VI a banking house, the renowned Fugger of Augsburg, played the most important rôle in negotiating the "sacred business." This firm gradually gained control over well-nigh all the business of the Curia with Germany, Poland and the Scandinavian states. It was consequently in the interest of this house to stimulate the intercourse between these countries and Rome as much as possible, thereby at the same time increasing the flow of moneys to the Eternal City. For this very natural reason its Roman representatives were especially active among other things in bringing about the issuance of new indulgences, because ever since 1507 by virtue of a private agreement of which, however, the purchaser never had any knowledge one-third of the total income from all indulgences whether or not they were officially designated as intended for the restoration of churches, the building of dikes or for pious purposes otherwise, flowed into the papal treasury. Indeed, in the beginning of 1514 this firm formally appears as an indulgence agency. At that time it obtained from the Curia the right to offer papal indulgences for sale everywhere in Germany to those interested, with the secret proviso that fifty per cent. of the net gain be turned over to the Curia. The Fuggers were immediately successful in disposing of quite a number of such indulgences in Germany. Outwardly they were not alike, however. In one at least the Papacy was named as the recipient of the proceeds, while privately one-half was promised to a person to whom the Curia felt under obligations. This one, the Mayence Indulgence of the thirty-first of March, 1515, is the indulgence which called Luther into the lists.

On the thirtieth of August, 1513, the Margrave Albrecht of Brandenburg had been postulated as Archbishop of Magdeburg and shortly after as administrator of the episcopate of Halberstadt. The holding of two bishoprics by one person was illegal. Besides, the twice chosen candidate was only twenty-three years old. He was therefore in need of a double papal dispensation. Pope Leo X, however, made no objections. On the sixteenth of December, 1513, he confirmed the young Hohenzollern prince as administrator of Magdeburg and Halberstadt. As legal fee for this confirmation Albrecht paid 1079 ducats. One ducat has a value of about $2.25 in gold, or is worth at present money rates between $6.25 and $7.50.)

Hardly had the Fuggers closed this deal when the prospect of a third bishopric opened up to the fortunate prince. On the ninth of March, 1514, "evidently through divine inspiration," as the Berlin court forthwith claimed, he was also elected Archbishop of Mayence. Now, the Curia had occasionally granted to one of its cardinals three or more episcopal sees, but it was an altogether unprecedented situation that a German prince who had not even reached the canonical age should demand for himself three large bishoprics. Albrecht himself at first did not press the matter. With all the more vigor therefore his brother, the Elector Joachim, began to work upon the Curia through Dr. Blankenfeld from Berlin. The increase of power which the luck of Albrecht promised for the house of Brandenburg was so great that even the Elector was interested in seeing the affair terminate favorably. As a result Brandenburg would at one stroke gain the ascendency in Northern Germany over its old rival, Electoral Saxony. At the same time this increase of territory would effectively block further extension of the latter's power in Thuringia.

The Curia long fought the plans and wishes of the two Hohenzollerns tenaciously. But finally it was in this case also persuaded to change its mind by a splendid bargain. Upon advice from an unknown person Albrecht offered the Pope in addition to the legal fees for the confirmation as Archbishop of Mayence, amounting to 12,300 ducats, a composition of 10,000 ducats on the condition that he be confirmed and recognized in all three bishoprics. In principle the Pope immediately entered upon this suggestion. But for a long time still the two parties haggled about the size of the composition. The Curia first demanded 15,000 ducats, thereupon it asked 12,-000 on the plea that twelve was the number of the apostles. One of Albrecht's agents retorted to this that there were, however, only seven deadly sins. Finally the parties agreed to the original sum.

In order, however, to strengthen the somewhat dubious solvency of the young ecclesiastical prince Leo at the same time proffered to him a Jubilee Indulgence for the Archbishopric of Mayence on condition that he deliver fifty per-cent. of the proceeds to the Curia. Albrecht naturally made no objections to this plan. Whereupon he was on the eighteenth of August, 1514, finally confirmed as Archbishop of Mayence, Archbishop of Magdeburg and Bishop of Halberstadt. A few months later on the thirty-first of March, 1515, the Pope announced the promised plenary indulgence to run for eight years in the Archdioceses of Mayence and Magdeburg, as well as in all the Brandenburg territories. The income from it, according to the official announcement, was to be used solely for the building of St. Peter's, but one-half had already, in accordance with the contract of August, 1514, been secretly written over to the young Hohenzollern.

The Curia could well afford to feel satisfied with the deal. It gained directly about $120,000 in cash. Besides, it had once more assured itself of one-half of the proceeds of an indulgence which promised to be very lucrative, inasmuch as the Pope had in the territories in question suspended in its favor all other indulgences, with the exception of some of those placed by the house of Fugger. Such a thing had never been done before. The young Hohenzollern was not so fortunate. He had from the first become heavily indebted to the Fuggers. These obligations, however, might be borne considering the tremendous success which his house had gained over the house of Wettin.

This was the indulgence against which Luther directed his Theses of the thirty-first of October, 1517. He did not even surmise then the sordid means by which the sacred business this time particularly had been concluded. Had he done so his criticism of the abuse of indulgences would very likely have been much more severe. But it must not be forgotten that in the Theses he merely criticized. He did not wish to destroy the institution. He only desired to make it again what in his opinion it had originally been, a mere remission of the canonical penance. His strictures, therefore, still move altogether within the limits of the mediæval system. He was not attacking a "formal dogma" of the Church. Furthermore, and this also is of the utmost importance, Luther chose for his criticism the most modest and unobtrusive form. He merely invited academic discussion on the value of indulgences and thus distinctly addressed himself to the narrow circle of specialists. Nevertheless, the Church forthwith adopted most decisive measures by opening without delay that renowned heresy trial which, after lasting for more than three years, finally ended with the outlawing of the Wittenberg professor by the Church and the Empire.

In November, 1517, the Elector Albrecht of Mayence in all haste denounced the stubborn monk to the Holy See for seducing the common people and promulgating new doctrines. At the same time he turned over to his councillors at Halle the task of bringing suit against the poisonous heretic "through Master John Tetzel." In doing this Albrecht had merely fulfilled his duties as bishop. Personally he had no interest in the matter. Hence the suit which had been left in the hands of the electoral councillors came to naught. On the other hand, Albrecht's denunciation to which had been added as documentary evidence a copy of the Ninety-five Theses, the treatise against Scholastic theology and the Reformer's writing on the penitential Psalms made a deep impression at Rome, not on the Pope but on Tetzel's powerful friends and fellow Dominicans at the Curia. The General of the Dominicans, Cardinal Cajetan, seemingly under the impression of the Theses, on the eighth of December wrote a treatise on indulgences in which he attempted with much learning to defend the opinions attacked by Luther.

However, the Pope was careful not to proceed too vigorously at the outset. At first on the fifth of February, 1518, through the medium of the head of the Augustinian order, Gabriel della Volta, he tried in a conciliatory manner to bring the disturbing monk to his senses. Thereupon Volta not only transmitted a warning to Luther, but at the same time he prevailed upon the chapter general of the Augustinians which met at the end of April, 1518, in Heidelberg to take up the affair. This induced the presumptuous brother in May, 1518, to make a detailed justification of his teachings on indulgences before the Pope by submitting his Resolutions to the Ninety-five Theses. On the main point, however, Volta suffered complete defeat. Luther refused to recant and to obey the behests of the government of the order, which found itself powerless to force him to obedience, inasmuch as not only the Vicar-general Staupitz but also the Elector of Saxony supported the monk in his opposition.

Meanwhile the Dominicans had not remained idle. Possibly as early as the end of January, at their meeting in Frankfurt on the Oder upon the occasion of Tetzel's promotion to the doctorate in theology, they seem to have decided to denounce Luther not only for spreading new doctrines but for heresy. This accusation also, however, was not immediately acted upon by the Curia. It waited to see whether Volta would succeed in forcing Luther to recant. Only after this attempt seemed to be a complete failure did the Fiscal Procurator Perusco upon renewed pressure by the Dominicans in June, 1518, induce the Pope to empower him to open the trial of Luther in the usual form under the indictment of "suspicion of heresy."

At the suggestion of Perusco the Pope entrusted the conduct of the preliminary investigation to the highest judge of the Curia, the Auditor-general, Jerome Ghinucci. Simultaneously the official expert of the Curia on matters of faith, the Magister Sacri Palatii, Prierias was commissioned to furnish a theological opinion cn the Theses of Luther. On the basis of this opinion, should there be need of it, the proceedings against the Augustinian were to be further set in motion. Prierias was a Dominican, a strict adherent of St. Thomas Aquinas and a curialist. He therefore fulfilled his task with youthful fire. Inside of three days he wrote an opinion in which he dispatched the new heretic with extreme rudeness and tactlessness. Personally he was so proud of his performance that he immediately published it. It made the desired impression at least on Ghinucci, the judge delegated for the case. In the beginning of June, 1518, then, Prierias and Ghinucci jointly issued the citation to Luther in the customary form asking him to appear in Rome for the hearing. He was ordered to justify himself at latest within sixty days after the receipt of the citation before Perusco, Ghinucci and Prierias at Rome on the score of suspected heresy and revolt against the papal authority. In support of these charges the papal chancery had enclosed the opinion of Prierias. Thus the trial of Luther for heresy had been opened in due form.

The summons reached Wittenberg on the seventh of August. It seemed therefore that until the beginning of October, Luther would have time to decide on his attitude in the matter. But things proceeded differently from what he and his friends expected. Already on the twenty-third of August the Pope ordered Cardinal Cajetan, who at the time was attending the Diet at Augsburg, to examine the Wittenberg monk without delay and in case he did not recant to immediately arrest him and have him brought to Rome. Should Luther escape apprehension the cardinal was directly and without further ado to excommunicate him and all his adherents and patrons. Only two days later the General of the Augustinians, Volta, commissioned the Provincial of the order in Saxony, Gerhard Hecker, to forthwith apprehend and bind the heretic.

What had happened meanwhile? Cajetan had in the course of the summer in Augsburg succeeded in taking advantage of the dissension between the Emperor and the Elector of Saxony and had induced the former to send a letter to the Pope which, while very unfavorable to Luther, was very flattering for the Pope. At the same time he had busily collected information on Luther's teachings and opinions and made a detailed report on them to the Curia. From these the powers at Rome derived the impression that the presumptuous Augustinian, as the Dominicans kept on insisting, was in reality a notorious heretic, and further that it would be possible with the aid of the imperial power to bag him immediately. Therefore Rome adopted the method prescribed by the canon law for the treatment of notorious heretics. The Papacy had thus in keeping with the wishes of the Dominicans decided to conclude the trial as quickly as possible.

But the plan, which had been so well prepared from the juridical and political point of view, failed because of the opposition of the Elector of Saxony. Though Luther appeared before Cajetan in Augsburg he did not do so before his Elector had insured him against arrest. At the same time the cardinal convinced himself in his conference with the "German beast" that the necessary dogmatic basis for a condemnation of the heretic was lacking. Instead, therefore, of directly proceeding against Luther and his adherents with ban and interdict he for the present wholly laid aside his instructions and the bull of excommunication which Miltiz in the interval had brought from Rome all complete in order that he might first clear away these hindrances.

The Curia willingly entered upon his proposals. On the ninth of November the Pope issued a decretal on indulgences in which Luther's teachings were condemned as heretical, though their author was not mentioned by name. At the same time Karl von Miltiz was sent to the court of Saxony to persuade the old Elector by amicable means to deliver up the heretic. The cheerful chamberlain soon forgot his very precisely worded instructions. On his own responsibility he exchanged the office of bailiff with which he had been charged for the more congenial one of mediator. Why did the Curia tranquilly tolerate this arbitrary act? Undoubtedly even the Pope allowed himself to be deceived by the clever talker. He also seriously believed that Luther was ready to recant. Therefore, he still, on the twenty-ninth of March, 1519, addressed a very friendly letter to the declared heretic inviting him to come to Rome. Indeed, he even promised him to refund his traveling expenses.

The deciding motive, however, was another. Emperor Maximilian had died in January, 1519. His grandson, the later Charles V, and Francis I of France, were candidates for the succession in the Empire. But the prospects of Francis, the ally of the Pope, were so slim that already at the end of January Leo X, who wished to hinder the succession of Charles at all hazards, began to consider the candidacy of the Elector of Saxony. Miltiz's arbitrary policy of mediation was therefore at the moment very welcome to the Curia. Indeed, it is quite possible that in order to win over the Elector the Pope held out the promise of elevating Luther to the cardinalate. The consequence was that the trial rested for fully fourteen months.

However, by the summer of 1519 all the hopes of the Papacy had been shattered. On the twenty-eighth of June Charles of Spain was elected Emperor and in July at the Disputation at Leipzig Luther formally declared war on the Papacy. After this even Rome could have no further delusions about the planless and vacillating humbug-policy of Miltiz. It decided to reopen the heresy trial. Before doing so one more attempt was made through Miltiz to intimidate the Elector of Saxony by summarily threatening him with the interdict if he did not drop Luther. This threat, however, did not have the desired effect. The otherwise very timid old gentleman in a very voluminous memoir very courteously but very firmly set forth that the Curia had no power to excommunicate his professor or place his lands under the inderdict as long as the attempt at mediation to be made by the Archbishop of Treves and ordered by Miltiz had not taken place.

This document had the effect of a declaration of war at Rome. On the ninth of January, 1520, an Italian official of the Curia replied to it in the papal consistory with a thundering oration which proved that Rome also knew very well how to use the abusive style of the day. In this answer the old Elector, who was so ready to be pliant and yielding and who suffered so much for the sake of peace, was depicted in the blackest colors as a raging, cruel tyrant, as the executioner of the clergy, the Apostolic See, indeed, the whole Christian religion, and finally even set down as the twin head of the horrible hydra, Luther. The oratorical masterpiece culminated in the proposal to immediately reopen the proceedings against Luther in due form.

The Pope acted upon the suggestion without delay. On the first of February he formed a committee of several mendicant monks and two cardinals to prepare a bull of excommunication. The overhasty work of this body proved unacceptable and its place was taken by a new commission, on the eleventh of February, consisting of the cardinals Cajetan and Accolti, and the most eminent theologians of Rome. About the middle of March this board proposed to the Pope the condemnation of a part only of Luther's Theses as directly heretical, while it advised that the rest merely be branded as "offensive to pious ears." Further, it suggested that this decision be published for the present in the form of a decretal without the mention of Luther's name, and finally that the accused be once more in a papal breve asked to recant.

At first the Pope entered upon this proposition. On the fifteenth of March the general of the Augustinians, Volta, at his command requested Staupitz to induce Luther to retract. But upon the instigation of Eck who had come to Rome at the Pope's summons the proposal of the committee was after all declined by the head of the Church. In April he commanded the cardinals Accolti and Cajetan, Dr. Eck and Dr. John Hispanus to forthwith prepare a bull of excommunication. Eck thereupon on the second of May submitted to the Pope in his hunting lodge Magliana where Leo loved to pursue the princely sport of boar baiting the completed draft. Wholly in keeping with the genius of the locality the document opened with the noble words: "Rise up, O Lord, a wild boar has invaded your vineyard." In the sessions on the twenty-first, twenty-third, twenty-fifth of May and on the first of June the bull was submitted to the college of cardinals. On the latter date they also accepted it without alteration. The objection of Cardinal Carvajal against condemning the appeal to a general council as Luther's worst heresy was disregarded by the body which simply proceeded with the order of business for the day. Thereupon the draft was forwarded to the chancery and was finally issued by it officially in the customary form on the fifteenth of June.

The bull is a very voluminous document. The text for it was furnished by the jurist Accolti, the theological evidence by Eck and the Dominicans of Louvain. It orders the burning of all books written by Luther and anathematizes forty-one of his Theses. Luther himself, however, is for the present merely threatened with the great ban. He was to remain free to retract within sixty days after the publication of the document in Rome and in the dioceses of Brandenburg, Meissen and Merseburg. Is not this last clause strange, a proof of truly apostolic patience and clemency? Not at all. In accordance with the canon law every heretic had to be given such an "evangelic warning" before he could be personally condemned.

There is nothing striking or unusual whatsoever in this renowned trial for heresy, not even the peculiar intermingling of ecclesiastical and purely secular political interests which in its course becomes so manifest in the attitude of the Curia. This combination is a common characteristic of the papal ecclesiastical régime of those days. At most the share which the Dominicans bore in the whole trial is noteworthy. In the first place, they are responsible for the fact that it came about at all. They furnished the theological reporter as a result of whose expert opinion the citation was issued to Luther in June, 1518. By untiring machinations they further carried the point of opening the trial for notorious heresy on the twenty-third of August of the same year. They also are to blame for the fact that the charges were later taken up again after the interlude of the political campaign instigated by the Medici—who in matters of theology was quite innocent—in connection with the scramble for the imperial crown. They also predominated in the commission which prepared the verdict and lastly furnished the greater part of the incriminatory evidence used in the bull. It is therefore just to say that Tetzel's order omitted nothing to avenge him. Perhaps the most interesting fact in connection with the action of the order is this that next to the General of the order, Cajetan, the lion's share in the proceedings was borne by a countryman of Tetzel, the Meissonian nobleman, Nicholas von Schoenberg. Of him it is said that once upon a time he was won over to the order by the preaching of Savonarola. But by this time he had long since gone over into the camp of this great Dominican's mortal enemies, the Medici. As the confidant of Cardinal Giulio Medici (Clement VII) he played the most important rôle at the Curia in these fateful days.

Since the bull was not published in Germany by Eck until the end of September the period of grace vouchsafed therein to Luther did not expire until the twenty-eighth of November. What use the Reformer made of it is well known. On the tenth of December he publicly and solemnly renounced the Antichrist by consigning the bull to the flames with the words: "Because thou hast condemned the truth of God may God condemn thee to this fire." Thereupon the Antichrist at last spoke his final word. On the third of January the bull *Decet Romanum Pontificem* placed Luther under the major ban. This second and actual bull of excommunication, however, contained "so many errors detrimental to the cause of the Church" that Aleander, the papal legate, from the Diet of Worms sent it back directly to Rome to be rewritten. The improved form of the "sacred curse" was not returned to Worms until the sixth of May. By that time, however, it was no longer needed at the Diet. The "Holy Empire" had already arrived at a decision on the basis of the sentence of June, 1520, and two days before the great heretic had disappeared without leaving a trace. He abode in full security "in the hills, the region of the birds and the air," and from his home in the clouds ridiculed the plots of the Antichrist which to him seemed merely "an imposing cloud of smoke" like unto the vapors he so frequently saw rising skyward in thick swaths from the charcoal kilns in the green wilds about his Patmos.

CHAPTER V.

The First Practical Attempts at Reform.

IS it true that the aforementioned plots against Luther and the imperial statute which permitted them, the Edict of Worms of the twenty-fifth (28) of May, 1521, were really so harmless, in reality nothing more than a large "imposing cloud of smoke which acts as though it meant to storm the sun, but is quickly scattered by a light breeze so that no one knows whither it has gone"? If we look only upon Luther and the external progress of the Evangelical movement it is indeed hardly possible to judge otherwise. The Reformer himself suffered no harm from the edict, and the movement went forward unchecked, even though in certain localities, as, for instance, in the Netherlands, it met with energetic opposition.

According to the traditional point of view, however, it is thought that after all the edict had one disagreeable indeed ominous result. At the very moment when the time seemed ripe for the change from words to deeds, from mere criticism to the practical work of reform, it robbed the Evangelical party of the life-giving presence and aid of its born leader. Thus it came about that radical spirits got the upper hand in Wittenberg who by their fanaticism severely compromised the cause, and further that at the turning of the year, 1521, a dangerous crisis developed in the

146

capital and forum of the movement which the young party was not able to overcome without loss of strength and prestige.

Is this customary view of the so-called Wittenberg Unrest of 1521-22 still in agreement with the present status of our knowledge? Heinrich Barge emphatically denies it. He claims that not the sudden disappearance but the unexpected return of Luther to Wittenberg was fraught with danger for the Evangelical cause. Luther's sudden vanishing from the scene rather benefited than harmed it, he says. According to him it cleared the path for a new religious tendency which through its moral power and practical energy distinguished itself favorably from that championed by Luther. This new tendency was the lay-Christian Puritanism of Karlstadt who was successful in reforming divine service, the care of the poor and the morals police in Wittenberg in accordance with the ideas of this group. Barge believes, furthermore, that it was not Karlstadt's fault that the students committed a few innocent excesses in November and December, 1521, and that out of this movement grew the iconoclasm of 1522. This leader he holds, would, in spite of the transgressions of individual followers, undoubtedly have maintained his supremacy had not the Catholic Duke George of Saxony succeeded in intimidating his cousin, the aged Elector, by the threat that the Catholic imperial administration would at the next opportunity take steps against the Wittenbergers. Barge thinks that the Elector thereupon in fear dropped the reforms at his capital, but at the

same time recalled Luther from the Wartburg that
he might calm the spirit of unrest in Wittenberg.
Thus in Barge's opinion Luther in March, 1522, unwittingly came to Wittenberg as the executor of the
Catholic imperial administration, made an end of the
promising efforts of the lay-Christian Puritanism and
formally reintroduced the Catholic ritual.

This interpretation of the facts is absolutely new
but for that very reason was much applauded. Does
it do justice to the attitude and motives of Luther,
and does it rest on a correct judgment of Luther's
and Karlstadt's importance and endowments? Before answering this question it is necessary first to
fix the principles which then and later determined the
practical conduct of the Reformer. They are very
simple and in part generally known. The first one
was: No forcible subversion of the existing ecclesiastical order of things with the help of the rude fists of
"Mr. Everyman," that is the mob, in revolutionary excitement. Such an overturning of things by force is
in the first place unnecessary, for the gospel will clear
a path for itself. Every honest person who hears it
must and will sooner or later side with it, even though
the Papists try every means to hinder its progress.
This opinion the Reformer himself later on characterized as a pious dream. Secondly, however, he believed that rebellion was never justified, no matter
how just the cause might be. It is always a work of
the devil, it always merely aggravates the evil which
it means to curb.

In the third place, Luther held that persons who

take recourse to revolution assume an office which does not rightfully belong to them but alone to the Christian nobility (governing class) or the Christian governments. As Christians the nobles are in duty bound to care for the common good, but as lords they also have the sole right to forciby put an end to existing abuses if there be no other remedy. These evils, he claims, are all of them in some way connected with the ordering of material existence and as such are subject to the coercive power of the government. This power, however, as Okkam already taught, has but one limitation: the natural law, or the law of reason, that is, it is neither bound by ecclesiastical law, for that is purely fictitious, nor by the written secular law: the imperial law or law of the land. For all written law has sprung from the natural law or from reason, its heart and fountain, consequently it must also be reformed from out of reason, that is, in accordance with natural law; indeed, if necessary, it must be supplanted by the law of reason. Is it then not possible for people who have no governmental authority to do anything at all for the gospel? They can do very much, in fact, they can do that which is most important, they can speak, preach and write and thus practice the gospel and assist in carrying it on so that the Papists will find their sphere of influence growing ever smaller and more restricted. Further they can by exhortation and counsel induce the government to interfere. In short, they can by word and writing in zealous propaganda serve the cause of the gospel in exactly the same manner as the Reformer himself.

However, if the government neglects to perform its functions, what is then to become of the many evangelical-minded who, for instance, look upon the mass as blasphemy or who like the Evangelical parish priests, for example, are forced by virtue of their office to keep on celebrating the mass? The Reformer answered this question as early as 1520 tersely and without equivocation. They must quietly continue to attend and celebrate mass until also the simple folk have been so far instructed that it becomes everywhere possible to institute a celebration of the eucharist in the German language and in accordance with the sacramental words of Christ. They can in his opinion afford to wait until then because they may for the present spiritually re-interpret the prayers of offering and the ceremonies of the mass and thus do away with all those features in the practice which are offensive to their personal feelings. Besides, it is their duty to be patient, for everyone who through faith in the gospel has been freed from the false belief that salvation depends on any kind of ceremony, must, shall and can tolerate these practices for love of those among his brethren who for the present are not able to do without them, as long as he always frankly and openly, in speech and writing, insists that only for love of his weak brethren he still obeys these tyrannical ordinances.

This patient waiting is directly a duty for the priest whose office it is to perform the public ceremonies of worship. No matter how difficult it may be for him to say the sacrificial prayers and to perform the cere-

monies, he is not privileged on his own responsibility
to change one word in the liturgy or omit a single one
of the prescribed cultual acts. In fact, this intolerable
constraint with which, as one who is spiritually free,
he can after all always come to terms, is for him to be a
spur to preach the gospel as energetically as possible.
Thereby he can enlighten and educate up to Evangelical freedom the weak and simple members of his
flock who still with fettered spirit cling to the old
system. However, is it also the duty of a priest to
take such consideration in case he celebrates the mass
only for himself or for like-minded people? By no
means. On the contrary, it is praiseworthy if an
Evangelical priest refuses further to read private
masses, or if a convent of monks by common action
abolishes the ceremony of the mass in its own church.
For in this case an injury of the weak and simple is
not to be feared directly.

These are the principles which determined Luther's
practical conduct as early as 1520-21. Obviously they
are wholly in keeping with the status of the Evangelical movement of the time and also do not expect anything impossible from those having Evangelical convictions. But it is possible for a man to have very
clear principles and yet be wholly unable to create
new forms and organizations through which they may
become of practical value. It is customary to affirm
that the Reformer absolutely lacked this latter gift.
Is such a position justified? Not at all! While Luther cannot be ranked with the great organizers of
the type of Paul, Calvin or Laski, he yet possessed

sufficient knowledge of men and the world to solve
the problems of organization which confronted him.

It will suffice to point to two renowned documents
which play an important rôle in the work of Barge,
because that author believes he can ascribe them to his
hero Karlstadt.   The one is the so-called Treasury
Ordinance (*Beutelordnung*) for Wittenberg of November, 1521, which regulates the care of the poor in
accordance with altogether new principles.   In all
likelihood it was drawn up by Luther himself,
certainly its passage was due to his urging and co-
operation.   The other document is the well-known
charter of the city of Wittenberg dated January 24,
1522.   It is an established fact that Karlstadt had a
share in its shaping.   But that portion of it which
owed its origin to him, the regulations about church
service and about the destruction of pictures and altars had no permanence.   Everything else contained
in the document, the articles on the care of the poor,
against beggary, prostitution and brothels, is merely
a repetition or further elaboration of older ideas of
Luther.

Nevertheless, though Karlstadt is not the author of
the two renowned ordinances, he may yet, as Barge
claims, be the originator of a new type of piety which
distinguishes itself favorably from the Lutheran type.
The fact is that he did "enrich" Lutheranism by a few
new ideas of his own.   But how curious are these
ideas?   No priest may be given a charge unless he is
married and is the father of one or two children; whoever in communion partakes only of the host and not
also of the cup commits sin; the recipient in the eu-

charist must take the host and chalice with his own hands, for Christ says: Take, eat! To have pictures in the churches is contrary to the first commandment; it is even more harmful to place them on altars, and to paint likenesses is worse than adultery and theft. Fasting and confession is not commanded in Scriptures and must therefore be abolished. The government is in duty bound to prohibit priests under heavy penalty from preaching anything but what is contained in and taught by Holy Writ. Should the government prove neglectful in this matter and not clear the houses of God of pictures and altars the congregation "is empowered to assume control of affairs itself" and to forcibly inaugurate those reforms which it, deems necessary.

These sentences certainly breathe a spirit quite at variance with that of Luther's book on "the Freedom of a Christian." The old system of law has again come to honor therein, "the lowest has been placed uppermost, the least important substituted for the best, the last has been given the place of the first" and all manner of external practices have been "so dressed and puffed up as though the salvation of the world depended more on them than on Christ." The fanatical strain always associated with legalistic piety is also not absent. That such fanatical legalism is not Evangelical is hardly a matter of contention among Evangelical Christians, and it is not likely that Barge himself would support that view. In the heat of the controversy he merely overlooked the harsh, narrow and stupid features in the attitude of his hero.

All this, however, still does not prove that Karlstadt during the Wittenberg Unrest was guilty also of fanatical acts, that we have to deal in this turbulent period with really revolutionary deeds and not only, as Barge thinks, with quite harmless excesses in which outside students played the chief part. Let us therefore for once present the course of this "commotion" wholly on the basis of the genuine documents and then in conclusion ask ourselves whether Luther and the electoral government of Saxony did Karlstadt and his associates an injustice.

A person arriving at Wittenberg in the summer of 1521 might at the first moment well believe that the Reformer was still present in person and performing the work of his office at the customary place. So strongly did his influence manifest itself in the whole life of the town even in external affairs. The shopkeepers and brewers who belonged to the esteemed sodalities of the "Sharp-shooters of St. Sebastian and St. Anne" were just then abolishing the fraternal drinking bouts which Luther had so severely censured. Instigated and aided by him the city council made efforts to create an entirely new system of poor relief, while the professors, students, canons and monks busily kept on debating and considering the problems which he had formulated for them. Three of these were at the time being discussed with especial liveliness: Should priests marry in spite of the vow of celibacy? May the monks also throw aside their monastic oath? What is to become of the mass? The first question the Reformer himself had roundly answered in

the affirmative. Consequently, there was not much
further dispute about it. It was merely a question
now of drawing the practical conclusions from that
which he held to be good and right. The first person
who mustered the necessary courage to do this was
significantly a personal pupil of Luther and a respected member of the university, the provost Bartholomew Bernhardi of Kemberg. On the thirtieth of
May he married his housekeeper. This act practically
settles the question. The other two points were not as
quickly and clearly decided, for with regard to these
no distinct declaration of the Reformer was as yet
available. Only when he had stated his views on the
mass in a letter of the first of August, and made clear
his standpoint on the monastic vows in the themes
of the ninth of September, did the discussion about
these become intense and the wish grow active to proceed in these matters also from mere cogitation to
resolute action.

But did his adherents herein always strictly follow
the principles and direction of the distant master?
On the twenty-ninth of September Melanchthon with
a few of his pupils for the first time privately celebrated communion in both kinds at the parish church.
This was wholly in accordance with Luther's opinions.
Thereupon, in the afternoon of the sixth of October,
the Augustinian Gabriel Zwilling in the chapel of the
order preached a great sermon against the mass in
which he declared that he would henceforth not celebrate any. On the same day his brothers in the monastery decided to cease holding private masses in their

chapel and henceforth not to raise or exhibit the host for adoration. This also was wholly in keeping with Luther's wishes. However, Zwilling immediately went one step further. He asserted that whoever in the future hears mass commits idolatry and that it is a sin to take only the bread in holy communion. Had Luther ever said this? No. This stand was altogether contrary to his principles and opinions.

In the very same month Zwilling in his sermons also took up the matter of the monastic vows. Herein again he was not content to state with Luther that the vows were contrary to the gospel and that the monks were therefore at liberty to cast aside the cowl. He went so far as to say: the monks must give up their status and if they are unwilling to do so, why, use force, insult them in public, starve them and destroy their cloisters until they give in. Clearly, Zwilling is beginning to sound a fanatical note. The result was quickly apparent. After the fourth of November successively fifteen Augustinians left the monastery. This in itself could only please Luther for he saw in it only a voluntary step of his old brethren. He was not aware that Zwilling was demanding the forcible unfrocking of all those living under the vow. This attitude he would have fought most energetically had he been advised of it. For Luther was absolutely averse to the use of force in such matters.

How was the bold proceeding of the Augustinians received by the authoritative circles at Wittenberg, in the university and in the cathedral chapter? At first they were not at all in full agreement with it. A committee of six members of the faculties which the professors and the chapter appointed right after Zwilling's first sermon (October 8) on the twelfth of October requested the Augustinians "to cease their innovations for the present." But on the twentieth of that month they approached the Elector with the petition that as a Christian prince he abolish the abuse of the mass within his territories as soon and as speedily as possible so that disorder and unrest in any form might be avoided. This was a rather naïve demand, naïve especially when addressed to so careful a man as Frederick the Wise. Frederick therefore answered them very quickly (October 25) with the command not to be too hasty in anything and not to do aught which might cause dissension, turbulence and complaint. Further, he requested the chapter and the university to first officially state their view in the matter.

However, the movement was now in progress and could not any more be made to turn back by a simple order. On the first of November a second communion in both kinds took place in the parish church and on this occasion not only members of the university but citizens also participated. This shows that the new ideas had by this time penetrated also the burgher class. In these same days the city council proposed to the cathedral chapter that Melanchthon be made pastor of the city, and that the twenty-one sodalities connected with the parish church be disbanded. The chapter refused both propositions and recognized only the new poor law which, as has been stated, placed the care of the paupers in the hands of the council. Nevertheless, these events show that this latter body was now also beginning energetically to take a hand in the Evangelic cause. In the course of November quite a number of other ecclesiastics discontinued their private masses. In short, the old cultual forms were beginning to dissolve themselves.

There was among the students and burghers, however, no dearth of people for whom this gradual development was too slow altogether. As a result a number of bad riots occurred in the otherwise quiet town on the third and fourth of December. On the morning of the third of this month the altar clergy of the parish Church were driven from their post with stones, as they were about to chant the offices of Mary, so that the first mass had to be omitted. The scene was repeated when the first regular mass of the day was to be celebrated. A few students and citizens simply took the missal away from the priest and drove him from the altar. The bailiffs of the council and the beadles of the university immediately interfered and arrested all the black sheep whom they could apprehend. However, the students were not so readily brought to their senses again. On the following day they affixed a revolutionary placard to the door of the Franciscan Church. Fourteen of them appeared before the monastery and there intimidated the poor monks so that they dared to read only one mass in the choir and lived in fear of seeing their monastery stormed during the night. However, the council was on its guard. They stationed watches and thus induced the wild fellows to abandon their project.

On the same day a handsomely dressed horseman
with a dark beard stopped off at the house of Professor Amsdorf. None of the inmates at first recognized him. It was Luther. Five whole days he
secretly remained in town and on the ninth of December he again disappeared as mysteriously as he had
come. The treatise which he wrote immediately after
his arrival at the Wartburg shows with what kind of
impressions and misgivings he rode away. It bore the
title: A True Warning to All Christians to Guard
Against Sedition and Revolt. Already in the middle
of December he sent the manuscript to Spalatin with
the request that it be published as quickly as possible.
However, Spalatin did not possess the courage to
place upon the market a book written by the outlaw.
Thus the splendid treatise literally appeared *post
festum,* not until March, 1522, after the spirit it was
designed to check had already perpetrated its mis-
chievous deeds.

Ever since the riot on the third of December the
burghers of Wittenberg were in a state of latent fer-
ment. All who were closely allied with those who had
been arrested and who shared their hostility toward
the idolatry of the mass were highly dissatisfied with
the attitude of the council. Finally, the malcontents
formally organized, drew up a series of articles and on
about the ninth of December suddenly stormed the
sessions of the council. There they defiantly demanded the immediate release of their imprisoned
associates and the acceptance of their articles. These
are quite creditable to the good-will of their authors.
They demand free preaching of God's Word, aboli-

tion of all compulsory masses, the cessation of all votive and nuptial masses, all masses for the soul and all other cultual ceremonies for the benefit of the dead. Further, they requested the admission of all citizens to the Evangelical communions, the closing of all taverns in which excessive drinking was in vogue, abolition of the brothels and strict punishment of all forms of adultery.

To the people who year after year had heard the preaching of Luther this all was not new. However, the manner in which the framers of these articles presented their demands could not but rouse certain misgivings. The council in the first moment was so helpless that it actually liberated the prisoners, but thereafter it wisely turned to the Elector for help. He immediately dispatched two of his officials, and these on the seventeenth of the month in a large congregational meeting at the castle, thoroughly laid down the law to the Wittenbergers in the matter at hand. They forbade any further insult to the priesthood under dire penalty and disfavor, had the rioters of the third of December as far as they could lay hold of them arrested again, directed the punishment of the ringleaders among the framers of the articles and commanded the congregation to desist from any further innovation until the Elector himself should propose new regulations to them. This, however, did not re-establish peace in the city. The malcontents now grumbled more than ever, indeed, they sent letters of complaint directly to the Elector. Worst of all, now, one of the best-known teachers at the university placed himself at the head of the citizen movement.

The professors (of the university) had in these very days, from the tenth to the twelfth of December, finally answered the questions regarding the mass which had been submitted to them by the Elector. As was to be expected they had been utterly unable to "come to an agreement of doctrine." Eight, among them Melanchthon and Karlstadt, recommended that all soul and votive masses be abolished and that the mass be reformed after the manner and form of the apostles. Seven decided that all was to remain as of old, and one even handed in a separate opinion. It is therefore easy to conceive why on the nineteenth of December the aged Elector from Lochau sent the resolution: If you few Doctors have not been able to agree in this affair, how much less will that be the case if the thing be brought before the mass of the people. Therefore the old system must remain in force until others also take up the matter. This was very clearly spoken.

But the professors did not accede to this very positive order. Despite all, Karlstadt on the twenty-second publicly announced in the castle church that on the first of January he would celebrate an Evangelical communion service minus all the customary "froth." When news of this reached Lochau the old Elector forthwith (December 23-24) repeated the deliberate command once more to the recalcitrant professor personally instructing him not to make any changes in the mass. Karlstadt had undoubtedly expected this. In order to forestall his ruler he therefore held his Evangelical eucharist a week earlier.

His example was on the same day followed by the altarist Ambrose Wilken in the neighboring village Dobien, on the first of January, by Nicasius Claij in Schmiedeberg, by Franz Guenther in Lochau, Zwilling in Eilenburg and somewhat later by the parish priests at Jessen and Herzberg. This shows sufficiently that Karlstadt's step was not improvised, but was a well-prepared and pre-arranged move by himself and his closest confederates.

The time for this action had, however, been most inauspiciously chosen. In the period from Christmas to the New Year the ancient ecclesiastical fools' feasts were celebrated during which all manner of mummery and nonsense was practised and tolerated in the churches. We must therefore not judge too tragically the excesses which occurred in Wittenberg on Christmas eve. But it certainly was rather questionable that the same wild fellows who had raged and caroused through the night, thereupon, their heads heavy with beer, attend the communion service of Karlstadt, and that otherwise also in the course of the reform the crude instincts of Mr. Everyman occasionally revealed themselves in a very ugly manner. At Eilenburg, for instance, Zwilling's adherents became so enthusiastic as a result of the ceremony that they immediately afterward plundered the parsonage and got into a terrible brawl with the adherents of the old faith.

Even worse things, however, were in store. On the twenty-seventh of December three strangers arrived in the city who were much talked of in the future: the famous Zwickau prophets. They had come to Wittenberg with an eye especially to the professors for whom they made considerable trouble. They did not much concern themselves about the people. Their chief, Nickel Storch, soon left again.

Much deeper was the impression made upon the citizens by the events which soon after transpired in the Black Cloister. There the chapter of the German Augustinian Congregation had been in session since the sixth of January. In the meeting the Evangelical faction was in the majority. Therefore the assembly actually decided to disestablish the Congregation. Whoever wished to sever connection with it was to do so, while those who for the present had no such desire were quietly to remain in their monastery. No compulsion was desired and earnest endeavors were made to proceed with moderation. But the assembly did not lack men who failed to comprehend such a course of action. Zwilling, for example, who had hastened to the meeting from Eilenburg, though he had long ago ceased to wear the cowl, now announced: It is wrong henceforth to go to confession, to fast or to do any so-called good work. He asserted that every festival, with the exception of Sunday, must be dropped, that likewise the pictures and altars in the churches must be done away with. Only what is commanded by the law of God must be allowed to remain.

These utterances made such an impression on the Wittenberg brethren that after the close of the meeting of the chapter they determined upon a new step which created an immense stir. On the eleventh of

January they burned every picture and statue in their
chapel and on the next day they leveled the altars with
the floor.   Thus Zwilling had again raised a new question which was forthwith discussed most assiduously:
Are pictures and altars henceforth to be tolerated?
Melanchthon and other respected professors would
not hear of Zwilling's radicalism, whereupon they
were immediately called to task from the public pulpit
by this person.   Karlstadt, on the other hand, entered
with fiery zeal upon the fanatical ideas of the ex-monk
and in spite of some opposition brought it about that
a regulation to that effect was on the twenty-fourth
of January incorporated into the new "Statutes of
the City of Wittenberg."

What are the facts about this famous ordinance,
the passing of which may well be called the apex of
the Wittenberg movement?   In the first place, who
is the author?   The council, the clergy, Karlstadt,
Melanchthon and other professors.   Did the council
and the professors possess any authority to pass such
an instrument?   By no means.   They acted wholly
in self-arrogated authority and in open violation of
repeated unmistakable commands of the Elector.
That the latter could not afford to tolerate such
disobedience seems not to have been quite clear either
to the professors or to the council.   With the best of
intentions they cheerfully went on reforming, without
considering that they had neither the right nor the
power, nor were capable of putting into effect their
new regulations against even the will of the Elector,
should that become necessary.

What were these reforms?. The customary masses were now abolished also in the parish church, and the church building was henceforth closed during the week.   Only on Sundays and on the holidays were divine services and communion after the method of Karlstadt to be celebrated in the future.   Priests who so far had had no other duty than the reading of masses were put out of office.   The older ones among them were given an annual pension of six gulden, the younger were told to learn a trade.   From the income of endowed masses, prebends, the twenty-one sodalities and the chapels connected with the parish church a "common chest" was formed.   Out of this fund, to which were added also the alms collected in the church, not only the salaries of the clergymen, but in addition the expenses of the municipal poor relief were to be paid.   Begging is strictly forbidden also to monks, pupils and students.   Since the monks were leaving the monasteries—there were really only five or six left in the Black Cloister—the council directed them to vacate their convents by the thirtieth of March and decided to make an inventory of their goods and income so that disorder might be avoided.   The houses of ill-fame were closed, the municipal brothel was converted into a hospital.   The inmates were asked either to marry or leave the city.   The pictures were removed from the churches by the council and all but three altars taken down.

The authors of the previous set of articles might well feel satisfied with this ordinance since all their demands were granted in the same.   Even Luther, however, would on the whole have been able to make friends with this statute, for it contained a great deal that he had himself since 1520 preached unceasingly. Only those portions which are directly traceable to Karlstadt, the regulations about pictures and altars and the new order of service he would not have been in a position to accept. The direct introduction of the new apostolic mass by force of law at this early date, the fact that the council following Karlstadt flatly decreed that in the eucharist the communicants must henceforth take the bread and the cup with their own hands, this all ran counter to the principles which so far he had strictly followed in such matters.

The worst defect of the "ordinance," however, was that it had come into being in direct contravention of the commands of the Elector. This mistake from the very outset jeopardized the success of the whole well-intentioned work of reform which contained so much that was excellent. For the present, however, prospects seemed bright. The prostitutes and beggars disappeared from the city. The students who had so far lived by begging or had studied in the hope of being well cared for through prebends, left the university in large numbers. Monks and priests permitted their hair to grow over their tonsures, they married and courageously endeavored to make their living as shoemakers, carpenters, bakers and salt carters. Several members of the electoral court also voluntarily gave up their benefices, and the eighteen new municipal wardens of the poor were able to enter upon their duties without hindrance.

One point only brought on trouble and dissension. The council had assumed the burdensome task of removing the pictures and altars from the parish church. But it hesitated to fulfill its obligation. Karlstadt felt that he could not tolerate this remissness any longer, for him the matter of images was now the foremost question of faith. Not only did he write about it in a most fanatical manner, he also in his sermons thundered passionately against this abomination in the house of the Lord and added the threatening words: If the government is negligent the congregation has the authority to assume powers of self-government and from out of commiseration and love to undertake necessary changes itself. It is therefore not surprising that the congregation now in reality usurped governmental authority on the question of the images. On about the sixth of February an enraged mob broke into the parish church, took possession of the pictures, crosses and crucifixes and broke, chopped up and burned them. The council interfered on the spot, imprisoned the evil-doers and hastily dispatched a courier to the Elector. However, the mischief was done and the news of it soon penetrated all the German lands.

Involuntarily we ask ourselves: Why did the Elector calmly tolerate all that had happened in Wittenberg against his wishes and command since the twenty-fifth of December? Partly because in January he had moved his court to Allstedt in Thuringia. Not until the fifth or sixth of February did he learn about the occurrences in the city from a complaint of the canons who adhered to the old faith and from reports of the burgomaster of Wittenberg and his own private secretary Einsiedel who had once before, on his own responsibility, unsuccessfully tried to silence Karlstadt. Frederick instantly ordered Einsiedel to interfere. When the latter received this order the iconoclastic outbreak had meanwhile also taken place. The measures of the agent of the Elector were correspondingly more energetic. On the thirteenth of February he cited the professors Karlstadt, Jonas, Melanchthon, Amsdorf and Eisermann into his presence at Eilenburg and pressed them so closely that all of them, including Karlstadt, immediately "toppled over" as the saying goes. Karlstadt admitted that he had caused the iconoclasm by his addresses. He declared himself ready to avoid making such sermons in the future and to suffer punishment willingly should he fail to keep his promise. Zwilling, who alarmed over the effect of his own words, had already left Wittenberg at the time of the iconoclastic outbreak, made the same promise.

The chief point, however, was that the professors accepted a new "order of mass" in which they relinquished all their reforms with the exception of consecration in the German language and communion in both kinds. What was the significance of this? The Wittenbergers, Karlstadt himself leading, themselves gave up their "apostolic mass" in its essential features after it had existed barely three weeks.

Worse things, however, were in store for them. On the eighteenth or nineteenth of February an electoral order arrived at Wittenberg from Lochau to the effect that the whole Catholic mass was to be re-established, that is, even the German consecration and communion in both kinds were again to be set aside. The Wittenbergers could do nothing against this. They were completely done for. There was only one man who might possibly still be able to save them from the entanglement into which they had fallen by their own fault, one man who might perchance be able to conjure the spirit of revolt which had taken possession of the simple man and the student alike and to re-establish the good relations with the electoral court. This man was Luther. We do not know who first pointed this out to them, we do know, however, that seemingly as early as the twentieth of February the council without saying a word about it to the Elector sent a mounted messenger to the Wartburg urgently inviting the Reformer to return to Wittenberg without delay.

Luther had had no news from Wittenberg for weeks. The greater now was his indignation. At first he believed that it would be sufficient if he reprimanded the authors of the mischief by letter. But the longer he wrote, the more clearly he saw that he would have to go personally to see to things. He, therefore, in all haste informed the Elector, very probably on the same day, that he would arrive directly. The old gentleman was frightened. He at once commanded his bailiff Oswald at Eisenach to make the most earnest representations to the Doctor that he must "for the present by no means betake himself to Wittenberg."

But Luther was not to be held back any longer.

Early on the first of March he departed. His state of mind is well illustrated by the famous letter which on the fifth he sent to the Elector from Borna. He says that he knows he is again venturing into the field of battle and that in so doing he is acting in defiance of the wishes of his master. He is also aware that the Elector will be absolutely unable to protect him should the imperial government feel inclined to execute the sentence of outlawry against him. But Luther wanted no protection or help from man. In glorious words he summarily requests the Elector not to give him any further aid, but to do his duty toward the Emperor and the Empire, even if he were commanded to "apprehend and kill him."

Some time on the sixth of March the Reformer arrived in Wittenberg. On the next day already the Elector requested from him through Professor Schurpff a written declaration that he had returned to Wittenberg "without Our leave." This statement was to serve as a measure of defense should the enemies of the Elector raise their voice. Luther immediately complied. Indeed, in reference to the wishes of the old gentleman he even struck out a number of sentences that were not exactly flattering to the imperial government, and besides, had the courtier Spalatin tone down his vigorous style somewhat to the level of the courtly manner. He could do this without being in the least untruthful. The situation was exactly as he declared it to be in the improved version: "without the knowledge, will, aid, permission or pleasure" of his lord he had come back to Wittenberg.

On the ninth of March, Luther then again for the first time appeared in the pulpit of the parish church. As though he wished by his dress to evidence how little such externals mattered to him he again wore the black robe of the Augustinians. He began his discourse as though he were merely going to expound the prescribed scriptural lesson. Then, however, he dropped the text and took up " the present business." He avoided all direct polemics and mentioned no names. He always spoke purely as the advocate of the weak in faith to whom so much offense had been given by the uncharitableness of those who deemed themselves strong. That they had proceeded blindly and in a disorderly manner, and that they ought first to have consulted the government, *i. e.,* the Elector, he only mentioned in passing. In this same strain he continued to preach daily for a whole week. The effect was tremendous. In the whole town "there was great gladness and jubilation among the learned and simple over his arrival and preaching." Even Zwilling confessed that "he had erred and gone too far." Only one person, Karlstadt, held himself sullenly aloof. Thus the spirit of unrest and the disorder in the city and the university was subdued.

Did not Luther, however, go a step further? Did he not at once "formally reinstitute the Catholic ritual"? In reply it will suffice to point to two documents already familiar to us. The one is the "Order of Mass for the City of Wittenberg," presented on the thirteenth of February at Eilenburg by Karlstadt and his associates. It reintroduces essentially the Catholic forms. The other is the letter of the Elector, of the seventeenth of February, which demanded outright the abolition of all innovations, that is, also the German consecration and communion in both kinds. It follows from this that the "apostolic mass" had already been abolished by consent of Karlstadt when Luther appeared in Wittenberg.

But the Catholic ritual had by no means herewith been "formally reinstituted." Private masses and the canon of the mass, compulsory confession, and fasting remained undone, and communion in both kinds quietly remained in force. Only at communion services for large numbers at Easter the participants now again received only the host. These wholesale communions were, however, so distasteful to Luther that even now he began to take steps for their abolition.

Much less did anyone contemplate doing away with the rest of the innovations of the last months. The new poor law and morals police remained in force unchanged. The monasteries were not restored. The assertion that the Wittenberg movement was replaced by a blind reaction is therefore simply a mistake. Only in the matter of cult was there a backward step, but what did this retrogression signify over against the progressive reforms which had been achieved along these same lines, the permanence of which was now definitely assured through the influence of Luther! For we must not give way to any doubt on the point that Luther's presence alone induced the Elector and his councillors to again let affairs take their own course in Wittenberg and thus to clear the path for further reforms.

That, according to the sources, is the history of the "Wittenberg Unrest" of 1521-22. Evidently it was not merely a question of disturbances in Wittenberg, but of a movement which took hold also of quite a number of smaller places in the neighborhood, such as Dobien, Lochau, Eilenburg, Schmiedeberg, Dueben, Herzberg and Jessen. Furthermore, it was not a revolutionary rising in which everything was turned topsy-turvy but an earnest attempt to reform the cult, the ecclesiastical law and the care of the poor in accordance with Luther's principles. In the course of this endeavor, it is true, dangerous excesses and disorders resulted in Wittenberg and Eilenburg for a time. That this attempt was only half-successful is the fault neither of Luther nor of the principles he represented. It was solely due to the incapacity and stubborn narrowness of the men who set themselves up as leaders of the movement without even recognizing that a reform without Luther's knowledge and against the will and wish of the Elector was impossible. That this was clearly established, that there could be no further doubt about how little could in these matters be done without the aid of the "government," as Luther says, this was unquestionably also a success of the "movement."

Is this not giving too little credit to Karlstadt? Was he really no more than a blind zealot? Can he on good grounds be designated as the "Calvinist" among the Wittenberg group and as the real father of Puritanism? No. Of the foremost characteristic of Calvinistic and Puritan piety, the zeal for the purification and sanctification of morals, neither he nor Zwilling afford any trace. The energy of both is rather absorbed altogether by the struggle against idolatry in the forms of worship. That which constitutes the greatness of Puritan piety they lack entirely, only its weakness, the legalistic and fanatic strain, we already find clearly expressed in them.

One might rather be tempted to call the framers of the Articles of December 9, 1521, Puritans. For they were earnestly concerned about the purification and sanctifying of morals. But, after all, they ask only what Luther had long ago demanded, they were merely zealous Lutherans. The fact that they were laymen is by no means a sufficient reason to characterize their proceeding with the weighty appellation of lay-Christian Puritanism. There have been such zealous Lutherans at all times among the laity and the fact that a number of them are found also among the laymen of Wittenberg after Luther had preached there so long is hardly cause for wonderment. At most one ought to feel surprised that the Wittenberg laity began to show signs of awakening so late and that they so quickly sank back into their accustomed lethargy after they had used up their enthusiasm in a few riots. However, anyone who knows this land and its people will not feel surprised at this but always be amazed again over the fact that Luther was able at this place and from out of this center, in whose cool temperature the germs of a higher life thrive with so much difficulty, to exert such a mighty influence. This he himself felt very strongly and stated very frankly. For Luther never took part in the catering to the "small man" which was so in vogue at the time. He justly shook his head over the affected rusticizing with which Karlstadt as the "new layman," after the fashion of Tolstoi, tried to ingratiate himself with peasants and craftsmen. Even before the Peasant Revolt he told this "small man" the plain and unvarnished truth. The fact that he is to-day still criticized for this does not prove that he was wrong, but only that in place of the "small man" as he really is people are wont to exhibit for public reverence an abstract personification of all citizen and peasant virtues, such as one never encounters in real life.

CHAPTER VI.

Luther as a Scholar and Author.

SINCE the appearance of Janssen's "History of the German People" no historical work has caused such a stir in Germany as Heinrich Denifle's "Luther and Lutheranism in its Earliest Development Presented on the Basis of the Sources," of which the first volume appeared in Mayence in 1904. Both Catholics and Protestants were at first equally astonished over the book. Then there followed on the Protestant side a veritable storm of indignation, a flood of counter-treatises, a lively debate in the scientific journals, in the weekly and daily press. However, in Catholic circles also the work met almost nowhere with undivided approval. Individual scholars unqualifiedly repudiated it, others let it pass only after sharp criticism. No reader who was able to judge for himself was wholly in accord with it.

When we pick up the book, which meanwhile has been continued in a loftier strain by Grisar in his "Luther" we are at first somewhat surprised at the excitement caused by its publication. Like Grisar's work it is not at all a sensational piece of writing after the common understanding of that term. Indeed, it is not really a book at all but a collection of very learned and ofttimes very poorly arranged essays on various problems of research concerning Luther. The specialist can learn a great deal from these papers. However, the opinion of the specialist never decides the success of such books but rather the manner of presentation and the tendency they serve. With Denifle this leaning is sufficiently evident from the emphatic closing words: "Away from Luther, and back to the Church." In Grisar's work it appears more from the grouping and treatment of the facts, from the interpretation and the at times incomplete use of the documents. Both authors, nevertheless, have the honest conviction that they have proceeded in their work in a strictly historical and psychological manner, and that at last they are able to place before the eyes of the long misguided public the "true Luther."

The portrait of their true Luther, however, especially in Denifle, differs decidedly from that hitherto presented by the "unscientific" old-Catholic investigators. Before the judgment-seat of "science" Luther in the first place reveals himself as a crass ignoramus, further, he also appears as a glutton and inebriate of the lowest type, as a bestial profligate, ribald and buffoon of the worst sort, as a literary dirt slinger worse than Zola, as an audacious forger, liar and cheat, in short, as an individual dangerous to society, unequalled for "moral degeneracy."

To the specialist this portrait is in its main features not very new. He is quite familiar with it from the Catholic polemics of the sixteenth to the eighteenth centuries whose preliminary labors the learned Father has thoroughly and thankfully used. Only the crass ignoramus is a new discovery made by Denifle. For the rest the learned father has been content merely to put on the colors a trifle more heavily and coarsely, to bring out the detail somewhat more fully, and in this wise to freshen up the old picture so as to make it look as imposing as possible. Grisar evinces much less temperament. He endeavors to do justice also to the "good sides" of his subject, and he discards a number of the exaggerated verdicts of the old controversialists. For this very reason, however, his book fell short of making an impression commensurate to that of Denifle's work. At any rate, the latter's crude woodcut in the style of Murner has so far not been supplanted by Grisar's much fainter pencil drawing which in spite of its more than a thousand pages fails after all to make up a clear picture. Hence it is still advisable to cite the Luther of Denifle who lives in so many minds before the "judge's bench" and to determine which features have been correctly or falsely observed. In most cases the result furnishes an estimate also on those points in which Grisar has further developed Denifle's materials.

We fittingly begin with Luther, the crass ignoramus whose unmasking cost the learned Dominican so much effort and time and over the discovery of whom he is so extraordinarily proud. We therefore inquire directly: Did the Reformer really pass so unsatisfactorily the many tests to which he was subsequently subjected? O. G. Schmidt has quizzed him on the classical literature of the Greeks and Romans. In this examination the Reformer stood well. Truly, he is not familiar with the Greek poets and prose writers though he procured an edition of Homer as late as 1523 "that he might become a Greek." Instead, he was very well versed in the favorite Latin authors of the day: Vergil, Terence, Ovid, Æsop, Cicero, Livy, Seneca, Horace, Catullus, Juvenal, Silius, Statius, Lucan, Suetonius, Sallust, Quintilian, Varro, Pomponius Mela, the two Plinies and the Germania of Tacitus. In addition he, of course, knew the very popular Neo-Latinists Baptista Mantuanus, Filelfo and others. In a similar manner Schaefer and W. Koehler investigated his knowledge of General History and Church History. This test also he passed creditably, for it appears that he was very much interested in history and at times pursued very serious historical studies.

Finally, Father Denifle examined him in Scholastic Philosophy and Theology. The result: Failure! The candidate knows only the pseudo-philosophers and theologians of the declining Middle Ages. The Prince of Scholastics, St. Thomas of Aquinas, he did not study at all at the university and later on for controversial purposes only. To make the situation worse the accused has the front to assert: "I have been brought up on Scholasticism, I know Scholasticism," and boasts shamelessly: "I have read thousand and all doctors." This indeed sounds very badly. But is the severe examiner right? Not at all. As regards the bragging statement—made in a marginal note—Denifle for once (*interdum dormit Homerus*) has permitted himself to be misled by a misprint. In the original manuscript we read not legi, "I have read," but lege, "read thousand and all doctors, no one will solve the question better."

Also it has been proven that Luther as a student did read the "Prince of Scholastics," and not only his commentary on the Sentences but also the large and small edition of the Summa. (See Veit Dietrich, No. 280.) Furthermore, he studied Peter Lombard, Bernard of Clairvaux, Duns Skotus, Okkam, Gregory of Rimini, Pierre d'Ailly, Gerson and Biel so assiduously that he knew, for instance, d'Ailly and Biel almost by heart. Therefore he really knew Scholasticism, whereby we do not mean to say that he always correctly understood, for example, Thomas Aquinas. However, occasional errors in interpretation by an author are certainly not a sufficient basis for the verdict "crass ignorance." If that were the case we would also have to call the learned Father Denifle a crass ignoramus because he so often misinterpreted Luther.

But the Reformer is not only familiar with Scholasticism, he also "had read most everything" by Augustine; furthermore, if not all, at least considerable portions of Irenaeus, Cyprian, Eusebius, Athanasius, Hilary, Ambrose, Gregory of Nazianza, Jerome, Cassiodorus, Gregory the Great and Anselm of Canterbury. In addition he had made quite a close study of Tauler and the Frankfurt Anonymous and among Humanistic theologians of Lefevre, Erasmus and Pico della Mirandola. He was also quite at home in the exegetical literature of the Middle Ages, in the Canon

Law, in Aristotle and Porphyry. Finally, he was one
of the first German professors who learned Greek and
Hebrew and zealously and successfully, as his last lectures still prove, endeavored to gather information
about rabbinical literature and exegesis from Jews
and Proselytes. All this Denifle ignores because it
does not fit into his preconceived opinion. Indeed, he
is inclined rather to reproach the "crass ignoramus"
because he failed to use original manuscripts, and did
not think of correcting the misprints in the poor Basel
edition of the Church fathers to which alone he had
access.

Upon close scrutiny the crass ignoramus, therefore,
reveals himself as a very sound and respectable scholar,
However, as is well known, mere learning alone does
not produce a good professor. A good professor results only if to erudition be added something higher:
the faculty of plain, clear, correct and independent
thought, resourcefulness, acumen, in short, scientific
talent. Did the Reformer also possess these quali-
ties? He himself would perhaps not have answered
this question in the affirmative. As a scholar and
teacher he appeared to himself always as weak, poor
and small, a mere "prattler" over against the remarkable little man, Melanchthon. However, he had no
cause for such a poor estimate of himself. True, he
was not a Humanist like that "doctor above all doctors." Just as his hand in the "ductus" and in the
form of the letters never quite lost the stamp of the
monkish script of the fifteenth century, so also his
Latin, vivid and natural though it be, ever retained a

monkish tinge. He also never acquired in the same measure as his younger friend that facility of expressing an idea "neatly and tersely" and yet "clearly and fully." But since 1513 he gradually learned from the Humanists for his scientific labors on the Bible all that they could teach him. And as far as critical acumen is concerned he was at least the equal of the renowned Erasmus and considerably superior to Magister Philippus.

Already as a young professor, Luther ventured for linguistic and internal reasons to designate as spurious five treatises which had been handed down under the name of St. Augustine. Thereby he excited unpleasant notoriety in Wittenberg, in one case at least, in fact, he made enemies for himself. Later investigation, however, has completely confirmed his judgment. Equally apt and surprising are his famous remarks about the style, provenance and historical value of the biblical books. Though he in this respect followed in the main the verdict of the great scholars of the ancient church, Eusebius of Cæsarea and Jerome, he yet added a mass of striking observations and acute suppositions of his own. What is most important, he at once without lengthy parley draws from the critical results the correct conclusions. He limits the canon of the Old Testament to the writings of the Hebrew Bible and in the New Testament allows the four old "anti-legomena," James, Jude, Hebrews and the Apocalypse henceforth to count only as an appendix.

Even as an interpreter of Scriptures, however, Luther achieved a great deal more than is usually suspected. He is, if not the first, at least one of the first professors who in their work of expounding the Bible as a matter of principle followed the original text. Further he as early as 1520 from principle tabooed all the ecclesiastical methods of interpretation and supplanted these falsely famous arts by "natural, grammatical and historical" exegesis. In his opinion it is not the Church which ought to determine what Scripture teaches, but the Word of God ought to fix the doctrine of the Church. These are deeds which for all time assure him a place in the history of scholarship.

Even in the more minute interpretation, however, one is again and again astonished at the amount he was able to accomplish with his poor auxiliaries. We wonder also at his fine ear for the linguistic peculiarities of the text and marvel over the assurance with which he not only knew how to develop the religious ideas but also the theological concepts. If, besides, we add to the picture the ease and dexterity with which he moved amidst the most abstract philosophical and theological distinctions, the rapidity with which he worked into not merely the theological but also the political, legal, social and economic problems with which he was brought face to face by the progress of the Evangelical movement, and note how quickly and without effort he always found for his ideas a striking and original expression how easily, thanks to his enormous memory, he retained in mind whatever he had read, seen or heard, we will be forced to confess that even regarded purely as an intellectual character he was a phenomenon without equal.

Only one gift had been vouchsafed him in a relatively small degree, the very talent which he so much
admired in Melanchthon and would have admired still
more in Calvin had he become more closely acquainted
with this greatest scientific force of early Protestantism. This was the faculty of mastering, syste-
matically organizing and condensing into brief formulas the prodigious wealth of fertile ideas which
poured in upon him unbidden from all sides while he
was at work and even when engaged merely in light
conversation.

These considerations alone raise some suspicion
against the modern attempts to set down the Reformer as a powerful but uncouth bit of primeval
nature which, suddenly rising up from out of the
depths of nationality, all at once broke in upon the
blooming fields of culture with destructive force. Nor
do we for the reasons given above take kindly to the
other suggestion that he was at the very least a "simple
soul," a "northerner" deficient in culture, "who had
thus far vegetated on in snow and fog and amidst
the inclemencies of nature without any great need for
scholarship and without a glimmer of art."

This primordial man, this simple soul was after all
not quite so uncouth, one-sided and northern as it
seems to the outsider. To be sure, when Luther
wishes to state the value of science and art in life
he is unable to say more than that the former is indispensable for the secular and ecclesiastical government and that art inculcates valuable lessons in a
visual form. But utilitarian considerations like these

are in the sixteenth century found even with really scientific natures like Melanchthon and in very great artists like Albrecht Dürer. They only go to prove how naïve and natural the relation of this age still was to science and art, but not that people at this time did not yet possess a true understanding of these branches of culture. This is especially manifest also in the case of Luther. Though he in other things tenaciously holds to the Okkamist theory of knowledge he has already quite overcome the view of Okkam that there is but one science, logic, and has also thrown aside the indifference of the Okkamists to the languages, history and the exact sciences. Quite to the contrary, he values and recommends these sciences as noble arts and disciplines and himself works in the field of language as energetically as he can.

While Luther thus manifests a distinct need for scientific activity he also possesses more than a mere glimmering of art. Music he loves and practices with great zeal, not because it is useful, but because it is the greatest earthly pleasure and the finest gift with which God has adorned this miserable life. Further, he is also fond of the art of poetry and exercises it, not alone because Poetry is an able preceptress, but also because poems more profoundly move and delight him personally and remain more deeply impressed upon his soul than all common speech, be it even that of a Demosthenes or Cicero. Therefore Luther not only derived great pleasure from proverbs and the fables of Æsop but also from poems not directly of a didactic nature, as for instance, the songs about Diet-

rich of Bern and "other giants." For the same reason
he himself greatly loved to write little verses even
while engaged in so prosaic an occupation as the keeping of his household accounts. And though as a com-
poser of hymns he mainly followed pedagogical purposes he is at times, though but seldom, overcome by
the impulse for once to let his powerful emotions flow
forth freely in song. At such times he always sings
like a really great poet in strains the like of which had
never been heard before him in the German tongue.

Luther was less interested in the plastic arts and in
architecture, though he appreciated the beautiful also
if he met it in this form. In Rome he viewed with
wonderment the splendid palaces of the cardinals, the
Pantheon, the Colosseum and the Baths of Diocletian.
His interest was also aroused by the delicate manner
in which the Italian painters were able to reproduce
nature and expression, and by the beautiful coloring
employed by the Flemish artists. For plastic art
alone he seems to have had no sense, though he frequently enough praises the beauty of the human form,
and lauds the Italian tailors with great warmth because they know how to fit the clothes to the human
body, whereas the Germans made all trousers after one
model so that their customers strut about like tum-
bler pigeons. Considering all this one can certainly
not assert that he lacked "even a glimmer of art,"
though on the other hand it, of course, does not justify
the claim that he possessed a fine artistic appreciation.
Nevertheless, we can well say that the naïve pleasure
in art which is so characteristic of the whole age is

shared also by Luther, especially the delight in pretty pictures. Otherwise the busy man would hardly have gone to the trouble of personally selecting the wood-cuts for the so-called September Bible.

While thus not devoid of a sense of artistic appreciation, the Reformer also did not confront nature with "clouded and fettered sensibilities." Though in his belief devilish forces infested river and forest, the regions above and below the earth, this fact did not make nature as such seem un-canny to him, much less render it a waste gray chaos of snow, fog, and formless northern night. In spite of Satan it always remains in his eyes a green garden of pleasure, full of sunshine, clear songs of birds and thousands upon thousands of great and small miracles of God, like his native land Thuringia, where the timid boy first learned to look cheerfully about himself and grew up to be a nimble and happy young fellow.

As in his conception of nature so also in his feeling for nature we can detect the true Thuringian. The song-birds, especially, have grown dear to his heart as they are loved even now by all true children of the forest. Ever again Luther watches with solemn de-light the playing of the "gentle" deer and roe, and as frequently as possible he makes trips into the open, or goes into the woods for the happy hunt, not to murder innocent animals but quietly in the green soli-tude to observe God's wonders, or amidst the troating of the deer to meditate upon the psalm: As the hart panteth after the water brooks.

Whoever wishes rightly to understand Luther must seek him not only in church, in the lecture-room or in his study, must observe him not alone when speaking and writing, he must watch him when chaffing with wife and children, arguing with his companions at table, or when in a quiet moment with his own hands he repairs his trousers by sewing on patches from the jerkin of his son "Haensichen"; he must follow him also through woods and fields and accompany him into the garden and courtyard of the Black Cloister. There he will see the mighty one who perhaps a moment ago, crude "as with a peasant's ax," had struck vicious blows at the Pope, very peacefully, like an old country parson, sowing and weeding, grafting and inoculating, or studying with solicitous eyes his giant radishes from Erfurt and his "strange" mulberry and fig-trees. He will further notice him in childlike innocence playing with his little dog Toelpel or musingly regarding the comfortable ease of the hogs in Frau Katie's stable-yard. Again, he will see him at the hive attentively watching the bees gather honey, or in the bushes observing the birds building their nests; or perchance he will discover him wandering out into the green woods singing and shouting like a student. One who has thus seen him will henceforth not be in the least astonished at the fact that "the naïve barbarian" understood so "clearly and roundly" in flowing description and in fleeting banter to reproduce impressions of nature. He will recognize rather that this "barbarian" in his own way was a poet and an artist, though he was far from being able in emulation of his critic Dilthey to give definite information on what "the poet" and "the artist" may, can and should do.

Despite all this, it would appear as though the uncouth "barbarian" Luther were not an arbitrary invention of polemic writers. As a writer and speaker Luther even according to unbiased witnesses deserves no other characterization. Indeed "uncouth barbarian" is seemingly still an altogether too timid expression. A whole army of passionate judges assures us that we will strike a great deal closer to the mark if we call him: Champion boor, dirty fellow, pig, buffoon, bawd, literary dirt-slinger, lubber and pornographer. It is claimed that the literary legacy of Luther sufficiently justifies these honorable epithets. It is, however, hardly necessary to go to the trouble of hunting up proofs in his writings and letters. A widely known source, which is read a good deal even in popular editions, offers them in lavish profusion, a source which seems to present the Reformer to our eyes in his every-day garments without pose or coloring—the famous Table Talk. Modern research has very thoroughly studied this source also and has solved many, though unhappily not all of the riddles which it offers to the historian. We are here interested in the results obtained only in as far as they help us to answer the question: Do we really learn to know the genuine Luther best in the Table Talk?

Ever since the end of the second decade of the sixteenth century a regular Round Table of companions collected about the Reformer in the Black Cloister late every afternoon at five o'clock for the evening meal.

Truly, the Knights of this Round Table bore no high-sounding names. In the main they were poor, older students, who had their board and rooms in the house. Some belonged to the wider family circle as *famuli* of the Doctor, others as teachers of the children; the rest were boarders whom Luther's spouse had taken into the house in order to help out the family exchequer. One of these latter, Conrad Cordatus from Weisskirchen, in Austria, first hit upon the idea of immediately noting down then and there the remarks made by Luther at the table. That was in the summer of 1531. Since Luther raised no objections his example was immediately followed by others.

The company at table consequently sometimes resembled a lecture, so assiduously were John Schlaginhaufen, Veit Dietrich, Anton Lauterbach, Jerome Weller, the melancholy private tutor of little Hans, and since the early forties John Mathesius, Caspar Heydenreich, Jerome Besold, John Aurifaber and many others engaged in copying down into their memoranda the conversation of the Doctor and of other table companions.

Very soon, however, these men ceased merely to take notes. They carefully copied their jottings, supplemented the brief catchwords from memory and converted their notes into well-written reports. These copies they then frequently exchanged. Indeed, individual collectors, who were especially zealous, as, for example, Anton Lauterbach, began even during the lifetime of the Doctor to arrange their collections topically. Nevertheless, none of the older table companions thought of publishing these *collectanea*. They were proud of their treasure and willingly furnished information from it to admirers of Luther, but in the correct feeling that the Reformer himself would not have approved of it they made no attempt to give the larger public access to it.

Only John Aurifaber, the last *famulus* of the Doctor, who otherwise also, trafficked in relics of Luther did not regard it out of place to acquire glory and money by means of these copies. His large edition of the Table Talk, which appeared in 1566, was indeed such an immediate success that soon other enterprising literati published similar and equally valuable collections. Was this success merited? The answer can only be in the negative. Aurifaber was able to use his own notes only for the last two years of Luther's life. Even these he did not reproduce accurately. He transposed the mixture of German and Latin which was spoken at Luther's table into his own broad and wordy German, and since he was himself a very crude person he did not neglect to emphasize the strong terms occurring in the original. In the same fashion he thereupon edited the notes of several older associates. Where did he get these? Not from the original manuscripts or from the first copies, but from collections of the second and third hand, in which the chronological sequence of the remarks had been altogether destroyed and the utterances themselves more or less retouched. Besides, he was a very hasty and wholly uncritical editor. His edition of the Table Talk is therefore a rather turbid fountain from which no one who is accustomed to the fresh water of genuine tradition can drink without reluctance.

However, is access to the true tradition in these matters at all open to us? In the last decades the collections of a number of the older table companions have been made accessible, the notes of Cordatus, Lauterbach, Schlaginhaufen, Mathesius, Veit Dietrich, Weller and others. However, none of these, not even that of Veit Dietrich, always faithfully offers the original version. Even the three best are merely copies of those modest little memoranda by means of which the table companions rapidly fixed the utterances of the Doctor. In addition, the ablest among the many industrious fellows: Roerer, Dietrich, Lauterbach and Mathesius were despite their facile pens at the very first writing not insured against errors of hearing and misunderstandings. Above all, they were frequently unable to follow the rapid speech of the Reformer. Under these circumstances they were wont, even when the conversation had been in German, immediately to translate into Latin what they heard, for a species of shorthand was at the time known only for Latin.

The upshot of it all is that the chief witnesses cannot be accounted absolutely safe authorities. However, though we must constantly apply criticism when using them, it is certain by this time that they have preserved for us an unusual amount of valuable information about the life, deeds and views of Luther. They offer evidence in strict chronological sequence which in its essentials is genuine, and indeed brings the true Luther if not closer, at any rate as close to us as his own letters and writings.

If we join the Round Table in the Black Cloister in the company of these good witnesses, we may indeed sometimes be seized with the feeling of having blundered into a guard room, so rude, harsh, cynical, in fact, coarse seems the tone of the conversation. If we are not deterred thereby from further investigation, but follow the Doctor also into his study and quietly watch him while he is at work writing books, our astonishment is perhaps even changed into mild amazement. It seems that the old man waxes cruder in proportion to the ease with which he is able to work. He writes against the Papacy at Rome, founded by the devil, in a strain which is a reproach to good manners. He composes verses to go with satirical pictures against the Papacy which to-day would certainly cause the police to make him an object of their paternal solicitude.

If thereupon for the sake of recapitulation we page through his treatise against "Jack Sausage (Hans Würst, *i. e.*, clown) of Brunswick, we perchance begin to feel more uncomfortable still. The aged Reformer employs vulgar expressions so frequently and unconcernedly that it makes our head swim. Besides, for purposes of controversy, he keeps a whole menagerie in which he mercilessly incarcerates his adversaries. He delights in unexpectedly transforming them with the magic wand of Circe into hogs, donkeys, wolves, bears, he-goats, dogs, monkeys, sheep, oxen, cows, etc. Besides, he treats them quite like dumb animals. He does not fight them like a gallant author of the twentieth century, he stabs them like wild boars, or mauls them with a flail like an uncouth peasant, without mercy and without tiring.   In short, when his ire is up Luther is, as it seems, a "smut" without equal.   But he behaves thus rudely and coarsely not only within his own four walls, in his living room or study.   Even in the pulpit he uses very rude expressions and figures of speech.   He talks very "medicinally," in fact, "medicynically," about things of which everyone knows but at present no one speaks publicly.

This is all the more striking when we note the simple-hearted Mathesius asserting that the Doctor never indulged in shameless speech, and observe the well-known Humanistic historian Sleidan, describing those obscene pictures by Cranach which satirize the Papacy so calmly and cheerfully, as though he were dealing merely with one of the innocent satires on professors in the Fliegende Blaetter.   It would seem after all that in order to appreciate this tone we must again take to heart the word about the spirit of the times.   If we do that, if we transport ourselves three hundred and fifty years into the past, we will soon clearly see that the tone at Luther's table and in his writings is not at all at variance with polite manners in German, or in French, English, and even Italian society of the day.

The well-known adage: "What is natural is not shameful," was rarely if ever followed so verbally even by persons of high and highest rank (see, for instance, Pope Julius II) as in these rude times.   People evidently felt that what everyone knows, everyone may openly discuss with anybody, even in the presence of the "delicate" ladies. This latter class at the time possessed the delicacy of the Hamburg fish-mongress of to-day. The Humanist Scheurl upon entering the office of Rector at the university ventured an address before the ladies of the court to which in our time the coarsest woman would not listen without resentment. The polished and pious Queen Margaret of Navarre wrote novels which at present no respectable woman can read without blushing. And the virgin Queen of England in her day still relished immensely Shakespeare's very coarse comedy, The Merry Wives of Windsor. In fact, she permitted her jacktars to hail her with a not exactly incorrect but nevertheless very impolite greeting.

As for the men! When the famous preacher Geiler of Kaisersberg compares the perfect Christian with a well-contrived sausage, when he praises Christ as our sumpter mule who bears away our sins in a manure bucket, we can, if need be, even to-day stomach such comparisons. But the nonchalance with which that same Geiler and other noted preachers of the time, as, for example, the Westphalian Gottschalk Hollen, in the pulpit discussed intimacies of married life, the very strange jokes and anecdotes with which they spiced their sermons, after all strike us as rather peculiar.

And yet, these preachers seem almost prudes to the reader if thereupon he turns to the so-called polite letters of the sixteenth century. The popular books, the miracle plays, the satires of Thomas Murner, are not merely coarse but filthy, the Humanistic belles-

lettres not only filthy but wanton. If we remember
this, we will not be surprised to find even the honorable
Master Dürer inserting such extremely coarse jests
in his letters to Pirckheimer, nor that a family chronicle with so fundamentally serious a purpose as the Zim-
mern Chronicle positively swarms with indecent anecdotes, nor, finally, that the main Latin school book of
the day, the Familiar Colloquies of Erasmus of Rotterdam, is tuned to this same pitch. Even the polite
tone of the sixteenth century was therefore in our esti-
mation not at all polite. Uncleanly as the people in
general were in their habits of eating and drinking—
forks and handkerchiefs had not yet come into common use—indulgent as they were toward fleas, lice
and other vermin, toward the itch and other filthy diseases, so unclean according to our standards they still
were everywhere in their literary usages.

From a generation so rude and coarse Luther had
sprung, to such a generation he spoke, and against it
he was continually forced to do battle. His literacy
antagonists—Prierias, Alveld, Eck, Emser, Cochlaeus, Usingen, Mensing, Sylphius, Conrad, Koellin,
Karlstadt, Zwingli and whatever else their names may
be—are not a shade more delicate than he. Indeed,
some of them, as, for instance, Cochlaeus, are downright filthy and frivolous, while he, despite all coarseness, never descends to frivolity.

There is, besides, another factor which must be
taken into account in the case at hand. As soon as
a violent fit of anger rouses Luther's blood the humor-
ous poet in him begins to stir. It is quite impossible

for him to show his fists to his opponent without continually taunting him and making fun of him in the most unrestrained fashion. At such moments Dr. Emser, whose coat of arms exhibits a he-goat, directly himself becomes Dr. Billygoat, the very learned Cochlaeus (spooner) suddenly appears as Rotzloeffel (snotnose), Dr. Eck becomes Dr. Geck (dude) or even Dreck (dirt), the knight Schwenckfeld is transformed into Sir Stenchfield, Dr. Usingen becomes Dr. Unsinn (nonsense), Dr. Crotus is Dr. Toad (Kroete), the Franciscan Schatzgeier appears as Schatzfresser (devourer of treasures), while his brother in the order, Alveld, is the gray miller's beast which always brays *ika! ika!* Duke Henry of Braunschweig-Wolfenbuettel is presented as Hans Würst (clown), as a sausage devil, as a cow in the hickory tree, as a pig jingling a harp. The jurists are introduced as Ignorists, Knownothings, Beamdoctors, since they cure all with the beam of the gallows. Finally, the book of Dr. N. is presented as a poodle, whose hide swarms with fleas, to wit, not errors of print but errors of thought. However, the Doctor was particularly fond of perennially introducing "Her Serene Highness, the White Beast," the hog. He has well observed how the dear animal wallows in the mud, smacks and routs, how it grunts and grumbles, how it softly, securely and tranquilly snores and upon its "bed of down" lives on without a thought of the morrow, how through its snout it smiles pleasantly at its litter of grunters. For controversial ends, however, Luther seems sometimes almost to have trained the beast. It appears as a clown, at times with a lemon in its mouth, sometimes with a necklace of pearls, once in armor, then again with a spinning-wheel or a harp.

No person, therefore, who lacks a feeling for the humor of the sixteenth century can comprehend Luther as a contraversialist. This humor was not delicate. Luther frequently enough turns it very rudely against his own person. He refers to it repeatedly as "the fat Doctor," the "rotten, stinking wormbag," the "bundle of diseased flesh." But despite all such wild somersaults he never becomes indecent as Emser, Cochlaeus and Lemnius, for instance. Indeed, he may well be cited as a good proof of the fact that a German may be rude and crude to the point of coarseness without ever becoming obscene and frivolous.

On the other hand, did not Luther on one occasion request a melancholiac to cheer himself up with smutty jokes? Does he not on the twenty-third of May, 1534, write to Joachim of Anhalt: "Joy in the company of good pious people, in the fear of God and in all decency and honor, though there be a word or jest (Zötlein) too many, is pleasing to God." Indeed, this is the literal reading of the letter. But the very context permits the surmise that "Zötlein" here is not equivalent to our modern "Zote," i. e., smutty jest. If for purpose of information we open a German dictionary, for instance, the well-known work by Daniel Sanders, we not only see this surmise amply confirmed, but find also a whole list of proof passages showing that the term was used by Luther in the sense of joke, anecdote, droll story, idle excuse. This single experience teaches us that we must operate carefully with citations from Luther. His German must always first be translated into the German of our day. For not only the meaning, also the timbre of words has materially changed in the course of time. Certain vulgar terms were in the sixteenth century not regarded as indelicate and expressions like, you ass, you donkey, were not regarded as serious insults even by polite society. Luther, for instance, calmly publishes the words "I am a sheep and will remain a sheep," "I am a goose as compared to the cardinal, and a miserable sheep over against the jurists"; while he praises his Elector, the corpulent John Frederick, before the whole company at dinner, by saying: "He works like a mule."

However, even after we have become quite accustomed to the literary taste and habit of the sixteenth century and make due allowance for the humor of Luther, we can, nevertheless, not suppress an occasional feeling of astonishment over the tone of his polemics. And this sensation is not merely the result of modern prudishness. We meet it here and there also with Luther's contemporaries. Not alone Melanchthon who was not altogether free from the squeamishness of the closet scholar, but also Catharine von Bora, who certainly cannot be accused of being too finical, sometimes thought the Doctor too crude.

Much more frequently we hear friend and foe complaining about his ungovernable violence. Mosellan emphasizes this trait as early as 1519 in an otherwise very kindly report on the Disputation at Leipzig. Spalatin is, since the beginning of 1520, again and again commissioned by the old Elector to take Luther to task for this, and Wenzel Link in August, 1520, induces the Reformer to confess personally that "almost everybody criticizes my mordacity." This shows that he was conscious of this failing. He at times complains about his vehement nature and his biting style. In fact, he even went so far as to openly confess before the Emperor and the assembled Estates at Worms that in his writings against private persons he had been more violent than was proper. However, this self-knowledge did little good. In spite of all, Luther ever remained a typical choleric. In fact, in the tremendous excitement and tension of the endless struggle, he finally even felt a good violent fit of anger as a beneficial relief. "Then my blood is refreshed, my intellect becomes clear and sharp and temptations leave me," he once confessed.

Every highly temperamental person will be able to sympathize with Luther on this point. However, in this characteristic after all lurked an element of danger. Every such period of excitement immediately engendered an extraordinary desire for work and conflict. As though he were rejuvenated even the aged Luther would, while still fired by fresh resentment, pick up his pen in order to work off the anger of his heart in one sitting. Besides, he mostly did not await a more tranquil moment and once more calmly revise what he had written, but as soon as he began writing he also commenced printing, so that the new book was in most cases pretty nearly ready by the time he had written the last letter and drained to the dregs the cup of his wholesome anger.

This peculiar method of work to a considerable degree explains the incomparable freshness and the ravishing temperament with which the Reformer, even in the products of his last years full of suffering, astonishes the reader. On the other hand, it is responsible also for the exceeding violence of his polemics. Sentiments and opinions which a more even-tempered writer at once suppresses Luther instantly permits to gush forth without consideration or forethought. To be sure, he mostly also gives free rein to his sparkling wit, and plays with his adversary in a bearish humor like a wild and bellicose giant of the old sagas, while at the same time he is dealing out blows right and left with his peasant ax like a rude woodcutter. At other times, however, even he sees blood, and words of fiery hatred crowd to his lips. "If the fury of the Romanists continues in this wise," he writes at the end of May, 1520—though in Latin and in a hasty preface to the epitome by Prierias— "nothing will remain but that the Emperor, the kings and princes attack the pest by force of arms. . . . If thieves are punished with the gallows, robbers with the sword and heretics with fire, why do we not with all our weapons assail these cardinals, popes and the whole Roman Sodom and wash our hands in their blood"? More savage still, perhaps, are the pictures in which he revels in the last treatise about the Papacy, and in the verses accompanying the satirical woodcuts of Cranach of 1545. These latter, by the way, he himself regarded as too coarse. In them he quite outdoes himself like a blustering lansquenet in grotesque fancies and comparisons about His Hell-ishness, St. Paul the Third, the little daughter Pauline, the saintly virgin Paula and the "Epicurean Hogs," the cardinals.

Naturally one is not justified in interpreting into this reveling in forcible expressions and grewsome images which follow and neutralize one another any specific threats, as little as we directly take the scold-ing of an angry person as a menace. It must also not be forgotten that an access of rage like this, which spends itself at the writing desk, but never permits itself to be carried away to corresponding deeds must not be placed on a par with the cold-blooded hatred which slowly torments its victim to death.

In spite of all, however, this hatred was genuine and honest, just as real as the delicate affection, friendliness and paternal mildness which the power-ful man otherwise exhibited toward so many worthy and unworthy persons. For it was, in the last analy-sis, rooted in the notion derived from personal impres-sions and the reports of other pilgrims to Rome that the Roman Curia was the breeding place of the most criminal vices and of complete atheism, and that it was at the same time an organized robber band against which one ought to proceed with the same regard-lessness as against the robbers, murderers, whores, adulterers and Sodomites in one's own country. This must always be kept in mind in the presence of these outbreaks of titanic anger, for otherwise it is impossible to appreciate the feelings of the old man in such moments, or one will even consider the continual storming against the Pope as merely the product of a childish partisan hatred.

It is a well-recognized fact that persons of such colossal temperament are never capable of judging their opponents coolly, objectively and justly. But it is contrary to all experience that in the case of Luther, passionateness should continually increase with his years, so that his last polemics are also his rudest and most wrathful. As a rule, the vehemence of youth subsides with advancing age in such a marked degree that the effervescent youth can hardly be recognized again in the quiet, mild and clarified old man. The aged Luther, therefore, in this respect presents a psychological problem which calls for an explanation. This might perhaps in the first place be found in the fact that from the end of 1517 to his death the Reformer stood in the midst of one of the most bitter, spiteful and personal conflicts known to the history of the world, a controversy in which the honor of his wife, his children, his parents, his friends and his ruler were as little spared as his own person. Such ceaseless warfare to the knife makes the tenderest soul hard, irritable, rude and even coarse.

In this instance, however, where we have to deal with a robust fighter a much more trivial explanation has greater probability. From his fortieth year on Luther was a sick man. After having suffered for six months from severe digestive ailments, as early as

1521, he two years later became the victim of nervous headaches which never again left him. In 1526 he developed a serious attack of renal colic with all manner of complications, rheumatic fevers, sciatica and furuncles. In addition he frequently suffered from obstinate catarrhal and digestive disturbances, temporarily also from hæmorrhoids (1525), dysentery (1536), middle ear disease (1537), which robbed him of hearing and sleep for weeks, with toothache and frightful nervous pains in the chest (precordial pains).

Already, in 1530, Luther presents the typical picture of a "completely nervous, prematurely aged man" who despite ever more frequent and longer periods of rest nevertheless continually subjects himself to new hardships and excitement and thus makes himself always more ill. It consequently seems almost a miracle that he was able to keep himself up tolerably well for fifteen years more until he succumbed to a stroke of paralysis on the eighteenth of February, 1546. Evidently "God gave to him," as to his father, "a firm and enduring body," otherwise he would certainly have broken down earlier. His increasing illness fully explains the growing irritability, violence and ill-humor of the Reformer. However, it also shows how advisable it is to first hear the opinion of a medical expert before passing judgment on an accused person, even though that person has long been resting in the grave.

CHAPTER VII.

Personal Habits and Character of the Reformer.

WE have just seen that during the larger portion of his public life Luther was a sick man, and that a fair estimate of his person and character is impossible unless the verdict of medical experts be taken into account. Had this always been done, the current talk about the glutton and toper, Luther, would also have finally ceased. It is well-known that even Goethe scoffs: "Acquiring a paunch by fasting, like unto Doctor Luther." Is there good cause for such mockery? At the time of the Leipzig Disputation the Reformer was still so lean that every bone in his body could be numbered. After returning from the Wartburg, however, he already showed a "befitting plumpness," and he gained somewhat more in weight after his marriage to Catharine von Bora. Therefore his "paunch" is an incontrovertible historical fact. But this late acquisition was in his case as little a result of overindulgence as with most of the poor elderly men who are at present seen thus afflicted. It is merely the result of an anomalous metabolism brought on by a uric-acid diathesis, for it is an established fact that Luther was in no way a gormandizer. Though in the letters to his spouse and to his friends he occasionally praises facetiously the splendid hospitality of the princes and great men, he himself preferred

"a wholesome, common home diet" to all delicacies.
Even game was for him too "melancholy" in its effect.
However, even this ordinary home diet was by no
means always partaken of plentifully. At times Luther would for extended periods content himself with
a herring and a little bread for an entire day. In
fact, once, while in good health, he touched no food at
all for four whole days. Melanchthon, who during
almost twenty-eight years as neighbor and colleague
was in intimate intercourse with him, therefore, often
marveled how little meat and drink Luther required
in spite of his ample physique.

However, even though the Reformer was no gas-
tronomist and "glutton," did he not indulge more
than necessary in drink? Was he not an ever-thirsty
"hop-brother, wine-barrel, drunkard," or, to use the
milder terms of the present, an alcoholic and habitual
drinker of the most doubtful sort? One who knows
the people of the sixteenth century will indeed be
easily tempted to apply to him all these honorary
designations, for at no time, perhaps, was hard drinking so much in vogue in Germany than in these days.
Charles the Fifth was not exactly regarded as a tip-
pler for he took only "three draughts" with his meals.
But with every one of these he emptied, without drawing a breath, a crystal beaker containing probably one
and one-half pints, that is, about a bottle of wine.
The beautiful Philippina Welser was famous for her
delicate complexion, but, nevertheless, she was able
at Castle Amras to drain the "Welcome," a goblet
holding two full liters of wine. On the basis of these

instances one can approximately compute the quantity of wine which notorious alcoholics like the Elector John Frederick of Saxony, or the Dukes William IV and Albrecht V of Bavaria, were capable of consuming. The bad habit of heating the mouth with pepper, generally the excessive use of pepper, cloves and sharp spices, as well as the immoderate eating of meat, certainly increased considerably this astonishing craving for drink. But it would scarcely have assumed such dimensions had not, since 1520, excessive drinking become practically a sport, and drunkenness through ridiculously pedantic drinking regulations quite the fashion in high society. These facts also enable us to comprehend why the contemporary verdict on this vice was so very lenient. To us it seems an unheard of thing that the Protestant Mathesius and the Catholic Eck, while in the pulpit they energetically combat intoxication, should nevertheless find an "honest drunk" excusable. Their hearers were undoubtedly not offended by this attitude, indeed, very probably they even regarded such preachers as apostles of temperance.

Luther in speech and writing fought drunkenness more vehemently than any German of that day. He privately and publicly spoke his mind on this point also to princes and even censured his own Elector openly on this account, while he very drastically rebuked the members of the electoral court for the same reason. Nevertheless, he also judges a "good drunk" very mildly. He believed that people who grew violent and vicious from the effects of alcohol ought by all means to avoid drink like poison, but, on the other hand, he held that men who are engaged in dangerous work all week, as, for example, the miners, ought not to be judged harshly if on Sunday they permitted themselves a goodly quantity of liquor. Courtiers also ought not to be grudged a "drunk" after hard physical exertions, though he says that by no means must it be tolerated that they appear every morning as though their heads had been pickled in brine. This indulgent attitude will scarcely meet with approbation to-day. But in the sixteenth century even such a differentiation was looked upon as narrow-mindedness, pedantry and philistinism.

Theory in such manners is almost always the result of personal practice. Therefore, the question arises: Did Luther himself at times allow himself a "good drunk" like his father, the old Hans Luther? Indeed, was the Reformer not perhaps a regular toper? It seems advisable that we first consult the physician also on this point. Medical experts teach us that alcoholics are wholly incapable of any fatiguing and continuous mental work. How about Luther in this regard? Let us pick out at random the one or the other year from the various periods of his life in order to determine exactly his working capacity. The year 1521 may be considered first, for it is in that year that, according to Father Denifle, he began drinking. In spite of this he wrote twenty larger or smaller treatises in that period, which in the Weimar edition fill 985 pages. In addition he translated a book by Melanchthon into German, and began the translation of

the New Testament and the composition of his *postil,*
besides writing a great number of letters, of which
seventy-two are still available. And yet, he was in
this eventful year forced to be idle for five weeks owing to travel and on many days was sorely hindered
by illness. In 1523 the first attacks of the above-
mentioned headaches began to impair his well-being;
also he traveled about two weeks. Nevertheless, in
this twelvemonth he wrote twenty-four treatises of
varying size, preached one hundred and fifty sermons,
gave a course of lectures on Deuteronomy which takes
up two hundred and forty-seven pages in the Weimar
edition, completed the German version of the Penta-
teuch and began the translation of the remainder of
the Old Testament. Besides this, we still possess one
hundred and twelve letters of this year—"of course
only a fraction of his correspondence." During the
five and one-half months he spent at the Koburg in
1530 (April 25 to October 4), "he was so sick in his
head" that, as he himself says, he had to rest and remain idle. Despite this fact he in this interval completed twelve works of varying size, finished the translation of Jeremiah, partially translated Ezekiel and
all the lesser prophets, edited a number of Æsop's
Fables in German, and furthermore, wrote quite a
series of opinions and letters, some of which were of
considerable length and of which one hundred and
twenty-three are still preserved. Finally, we still
have the year 1545, of which he spent two months in
travel, and when he was already completely exhausted,
broken and tired of life, a number of long treatises

and a few short ones, also the concluding lectures on Genesis and more than sixty letters and arbitraments.

All told Luther published about three hundred and fifty treatises, among them, it is true, a series of translations and a great number of pamphlets. In literary productivity at best the Jesuit Gretscher (two hundred and sixty-eight treatises), Augustine (two hundred and thirty-two) and Origen can vie with him. And this fertility is with Luther not merely quantitative, as in the case of Gretscher. The Reformer appears almost inexhaustible in expressions as well as in ideas. He certainly is the first great German man of letters, and at the same time among the writers of all ages one of the richest in form and thought. These observations for the medical expert do away with the "alcoholic" Luther. A drunkard would, alone from the point of view of physical endurance, not have been equal to such a tremendous burden of work, much less would he have been able to bear the excitement of the colossal battles which the Reformer had to fight.

Of course, this does not exclude the possibility that the great fighter occasionally indulged in a "good drunk." We may say that whole generations of investigators and inquisitors have been at pains to collect evidence to substantiate this charge. Their great labors have, however, so far been futile, for all their proofs have later been shown to be invalid. If Luther, for instance, writes: "I am now not drunk nor indiscreet," this is only a forcible mode of assertion, for in the same sense he writes: Christ was not drunk when he spoke the sacramental words of the Holy

Eucharist, God is not drunk, the Evangelists are not drunk. When Wolfgang Musculus, in 1536, at the time of the Wittenberg Concord reports: On May the twenty-first we accompanied Luther home after the meal, he was wonderfully hilarious (*mire hilaris*), . . . during the evening potion in his home he again was wonderfully hilarious and very amiable, and when just prior he says of Melanchthon: Wonderfully exhilarated he discussed astrology at the table, this all does not prove that the two Reformers were intoxicated but merely that they were cheerful. For "*hilaris*" in this connection signifies only cheerful happy and not hilarious. When in March, 1523, Luther at Schweinitz vomited before the meal, this does not prove that during the meal he had become intoxicated from Grueneberger wine, but that at the time he suffered from digestive derangement. And if in this period the vomiting recurred daily it does not show that Luther every day drank until he became nauseated but merely that he was ill.

However, did not Luther once sign a letter with the significant words: Doctor plenus? (the "full" Doctor). Fortunately the missive has been preserved in the original. The word we find is naturally not "plenus" but "Johannes," the name of little Hans Luther, who is sending greetings to his sponsor. The situation is the same in the famous confession in the letter of the second of July, 1540, to his "Gracious Lady of Zuelsdorf at the New Hog Market," in which he says: "I am guttling like a Bohemian and toping like a German, thanks be to God, Amen." The tone of the whole document, and one must, of course, read it in full, shows that we have here a playful exaggeration. This is, besides, proven abundantly from a similar letter of the sixteenth of July to the same address. The message is also extant in the original and we read there: "Thank God we are here cheerful and well, glutting like Bohemians, though not very—and guzzling like Germans, though not much, but we are happy."

So these proofs, also, lead us nowhere. There remains the "notorious verse": *Who loves not wine, woman and song, remains a fool his whole life long.* This is, indeed, perhaps the most frequently cited utterance of Luther. However, it is not by Luther but very probably originated with Johann Heinrich Voss. The latter first published it in 1777 in the Wandsbecker Bote, and when pressed for the exact source of his citation was not able to give it. It is possible that he merely translated a rhymed Italian saying: "Who loves not wine, women and song (*canto*) is either a fool or a saint (*santo*)," and as a sworn adherent of Enlightenment suppressed the saint. It may also be that he made use of one of the Table Talks of Luther which, however, was meant in quite another way. It runs: "One must bear with the weaknesses of every country: The Bohemians gluttonize, the Wends steal, the Germans drink immoderately. For how would you now excel a German, except it be in drinking, especially one who does not love music and women?" These "proofs," therefore, all of them do not bear up under criticism, and others which are adduced besides have about the same value, as, for instance, the evidence about the supposed illegitimate son of Luther, Andrew, who in reality was his nephew.

Luther never says that he had been intoxicated, and no one ever saw him drunk, otherwise we would surely know about it, for if ever a man lived in a glasshouse it was Luther. This again naturally does not prove that the Reformer was an anti-alcoholic. In fact, Luther, as an advocate of prohibition would be as much an unhistorical fantasy as Luther the drunkard. When in August, 1540, he says: "I drink also, but not every person ought to try and imitate me," when he says that God ought to give him credit for occasionally taking a good draught in his honor, and when he writes to a melancholiac: "I frequently drink more copiously in order to vex the devil," this all proves sufficiently that Luther was by no means averse to a good drink. Without doubt he was very fond of good wine, either the Jueterbock, Grueneberg, Franconian, Rhenish or Rinvoglio vintage. Furthermore, he liked Torgau and Naumburg beer very much though he was given this pleasure very rarely, ordinarily he had to be satisfied with the murky and not very excellent home brew of his severe spouse.

However, there were times when in the Black Cloister there was a dearth not only of beer but also of money. Under those circumstances the Reformer was, willy-nilly, forced to forego his accustomed beverage for forty days or more. And it really seems as though this privation was not an easy matter for him. For Luther valued beer in the first place as a diuretic, secondly, as a remedy for his bad digestion—he made medical observations about it at times—and finally, as a narcotic. In his last years he suffered greatly from insomnia so that "he had to seek his pillow and bolster in the tankard." This explains why some particularly conscientious investigators assiduously endeavored to determine the amount of alcohol he imbibed daily, and the maximum quantity which he on special occasions was capable of consuming. However, all such investigations and computations have so far brought no results. This problem of research on Luther will hence perhaps always remain unsolved and will vex many an inquisitor in much the same manner as the devil vexed Doctor Luther.

Luther the drunkard and toper, therefore, never existed, and no one ever saw him intoxicated. Of all these accusations only the one fact remains that Luther regularly drank his beer and was fond of good wine, that on special occasions he loved to have a good drink, and that in his age he was wont to combat insomnia by taking "a more copious draught" in the evening. We may fittingly doubt, however, that this by no means overdue indulgence in alcoholic beverages was always good for his health. According to present-day opinion, at least, only the alcohol which they do not drink is beneficial to people who are nervous and suffer from the stone. But the medical art of the sixteenth century was still in the stage of complete scientific innocence. It had not the least notion as yet of the harmful effects of this poison. Therefore, it also did not make the slightest effort to curb the use and abuse of spirituous beverages. On the contrary, it advised copious drinking, without distinction as to materials as a remedy for the stone.

Intemperance is, as a rule, combined with unbridled sexual passion. This observation again is confirmed by the Germans of the fifteenth and sixteenth centuries. Adultery was at the time so common in Germany and was judged so leniently that even at Luther's table a companion dared to broach the question, whether *fornicatio simplex* were a sin at all. Venereal disease was for that very reason not held to be a stigma, but was looked upon as a thoroughly respectable ailment, indeed, as the disease of prominent people. Popes and kings, princes, cardinals and bishops were thus afflicted without feeling ashamed. Humanistic literati unhesitatingly called upon the protection of the Virgin Mary against the danger of infection. In fact, Hutten unconcernedly dedicated his treatise on the symptoms and the cure of the disease to the Cardinal Archbishop Albrecht of Mayence; while the physician Fracastaro inscribed his famous poem of like content to the papal prelate Bembo, and neither of the two high church officials made any objections.

It is generally known how much the priests, monks and nuns contributed to this corruption. The fact that Luther came up from monastic ranks is therefore in itself no proof at all for his moral integrity. But it is also not permissible to reckon him among the great number of black sheep without documentary evidence. And Father Denifle does not make this mistake. He believes himself in possession of a sufficient number of proofs for the contention that Luther was a wanton and at the same time a "urist," that is, a person chronically afflicted with lust.

One of these confirmatory documents is the letter of Luther to Spalatin written on the sixteenth of April, 1525. In it he says: "As for your remarks about my marriage, do not be surprised that I do not marry, seeing that I am such an exceedingly skilful lover. It is still more remarkable that I who write so much concerning marriage and in this way have so much to do with woman (*sic misceor feminis*) have not become a woman long since, not to mention the fact that I have not married a long time ago. Still, if you want my example, you have the very best reason. For I have had three wives at one time and loved them so desperately that I have lost two of them again who will now get other bridegrooms. As for the third, I am hardly keeping hold of her by the left arm, she too will perhaps soon be snatched from me. But you, you are a slothful lover, you do not even venture to become the husband of one wife."

An unbiased reader of these lines will immediately see that here again the humorist Luther is speaking. We know that the Reformer at this time already harbored thoughts of marrying. Several chances were open to him but he cared to accept neither. In this sense he speaks jestingly of his three wives, in much the same manner as Uncle Braesig of his three brides. Pater Denifle, however, does not appreciate the joke. He pins Luther down to the words: *tres uxores simul habui,* and concludes therefrom: The dissolute person

prior to his marriage lived in concubinage with three
nuns at the same time.   This interpretation, he feels,
is justified by the expression *misceor feminis* a few
lines above, for five years earlier Luther uses the same
words in the sense which would, taken literally, lend
color to Denifle's interpretation.   However, the strict
critic in this case did not carefully scrutinize Luther's
words.   The Reformer writes: I who write so much
concerning women, *et sic misceor feminis*.   This "sic"
shows clearly what Luther means: "I write so much
concerning marriage and *in this wise* have to do with
women."   This evidence therefore does not fulfill what
it promises.

However, there is seemingly a better proof, the letter of Melanchthon to Camerarius of the sixteenth of
June, 1525, which is known to us in the original only
for about three decades.   "Luther married Bora unexpectedly without informing any of his friends of his
purpose.   In the evening he invited only Pomeranus
(Bugenhagen, the city pastor of Wittenberg), the
painter Lucas Cranach and Dr. Apel for supper and
celebrated the wedding with the customary formali-
ties.   You will, perhaps, be surprised that at this unhappy juncture, when upright and right-thinking men
are everywhere being oppressed he is not also suffering, but to all appearance leads an easy life and en-
dangers his reputation, notwithstanding that just now
Germany stands in need of all his wisdom and authority.   It appears, however, that the occurrence can
be explained as follows: The man is very easily led,
and so the nuns who pursued him with all manner of

cunning have ensnared him. Perhaps all this close association with them has rendered him effeminate or influenced his passions, noble and high-minded though he is. He seems in this fashion to have been drawn into the untimely change in his mode of life. It is obvious, however, that the gossip concerning his previous criminal intercourse with her (Bora) was a falsehood. Now that the thing is done it is useless to take it amiss or to find fault with it, for if I see the situation aright nature impelled him to matrimony. Even though this mode of life is low, yet it is holy and more pleasing to God than the unmarried state. And since I see that Luther is somewhat sad and troubled about this change in his way of living, I seek very earnestly to encourage him by representing to him that he has done nothing which in my opinion can be made a subject of reproach to him or which he could not justify. Besides, I have no lack of proofs of his piety, so that a derogatory judgment about him is out of place. In reality I had always hoped that he would experience some humiliation rather than that he should be granted advancement and honor. For the latter are dangerous not only for priests but for all men. Since well-being gives opportunity for base sentiments to crop out, not only, as the orator (Demosthenes) has said, in the case of the unlearned but also with the wise. Also I am in hopes that the married state will make him more dignified and that he now will lay aside the buffoonery which we so often have criticized. For, as the old saw is, a different life brings about a change in the mode of living. I am

writing you so much in detail about this that you will
not permit yourself to be too much disconcerted by the
unexpected event. I know, of course, that you have
Luther's good name at heart and that you will be
pained if it is in any way besmirched. I exhort you to
bear this matter with patience, seeing that Holy Writ
says that marriage is to be highly esteemed. Very
probably nature impelled him also to marriage. God
has shown us by the numerous mistakes committed by
the saints in earlier ages that he wishes us to prove his
Word and not rely upon the reputation of any man
but only on his Word. He would indeed be a wholly
godless person who on account of a false step of the
teacher condemns his teachings."

This letter mirrors a peculiarly discordant frame of
mind. The married state is low, but it is holy, nevertheless. Luther by marrying has abased himself, committed a blunder, but, on the other hand, he has done
nothing worthy of censure and must not be condemned. What follows from this? The writer is in a
passionate state of excitement; Luther's marriage
completely surprised him. He was never favorably
disposed toward it, especially not now in these trying
times of the great German Revolution. Besides, he
feels deeply hurt personally, because Luther undertook this important step without first saying a word
to him about his intentions. In this condition of mind
he speaks in hostile terms of Luther, scornfully of
Catharine von Bora, and permits suppositions about
the earlier history of the union to escape him which
are equally insulting to Luther and to Catharine von
Bora.

Therein lies the verdict on the historical value of the letter. It is of interest as documentary proof of Melanchthon's excitable frame of mind in that eventful month of June of the year 1525. It is further significant as a new piece of evidence on the high tension existing at the time between Luther and Melanchthon on account of the controversy with Erasmus. The suppositions about the previous history of the marriage of Luther, which Melanchthon himself stamps as mere suppositions, carry no more weight than conjectures by impassioned and malevolent critics otherwise. Had Melanchthon himself taken them at face value it would be difficult to understand why his attitude changed so soon that he not only himself took part in Luther's public wedding festival on the twenty-seventh of June, but on his own responsibility in a note of the twentieth or twenty-first of that month invited Wenzel Link to attend the ceremony, even inserting a jest about Jerome Baumgaertner, Catharine's old suitor. Besides, we have very peculiar proofs from other situations of what Melanchthon was capable of in moments of excitement. They are his letter to the papal legate Campeggio from the days of the Diet at Augsburg, and his missive to the Saxon Minister von Carlowitz from the period of the Augsburg Interim. The letter cited above must be placed on the same level with these, for it certainly is not evidence of spiritual greatness.

Hence we will do well not to employ Magister Philippus but Luther himself as crown witness for the earlier history of his marriage. He not infrequently spoke also about this episode of his life with his characteristic frankness. He wished to marry, in the first place, in order to fulfill a wish of his aged father, secondly, that he might honor holy wedlock by personal example on his part also, thirdly, in order to anger the Papists. All these ends he fully achieved. That he was not "wood and stone" over against the fair sex he openly confessed in a letter to Spalatin of the thirtieth of November, 1524. However, this feeling was not so strong that for this reason alone he felt a desire to marry. This he directly declares to be out of the question in that same letter. And since at the time he was already forty-two years old there is no reason whatever to doubt his testimony. It is more likely that he was partly impelled to this decision by a "longing for a regulated home life," which at his age is a much more natural feeling than youthful infatuation. For his bachelor existence in the Black Cloister was not exactly an enviable one. In the last year before his marriage, for instance, he had no one to take care of his bed. He therefore always slept in an unmade bed so that finally, the bedclothes and the straw began to decay. "I knew nothing of this, for I was tired, having worked hard the whole day, and simply dropped into bed," he himself tells his table companions in 1540.

Luther also did not fail to answer the question why he finally decided on Catharine von Bora. Catharine had for nearly two years harbored a sincere affection for a young Nürnberg patrician, Jerome Baumgaertner. But since she was desperately poor the practical young man finally dissolved the relationship. Luther, who had zealously furthered the match now tried with his characteristic energy to persuade the deserted young lady to marry Pastor Glatz of Orlamuende. Catharine vigorously opposed the project, in fact, one day she told Professor Amsdorf in so many words: Him or Luther she would marry, but Glatz never. This very frank declaration, as far as we know, first gave Luther the idea of paying court to the not very sympathetic Saxon noblewoman, and as he drastically enough says "to take pity on the deserted young woman."

There is, therefore, absolutely nothing romantic about this marriage which has created more of a stir than any other union of which we know. Hence it is ridiculous when even to-day the forty-two-year-old bridegroom is represented as an infatuated student of twenty, and the bride who was twenty-seven and had just overcome the effects of an unrequited love is set down as an enthusiastic young girl of seventeen. Romance ever remained absent from the wedded life of this mature couple. The prematurely aging and always ailing husband and the very active, energetic, prudent and not uneducated wife were soon sincerely attached to each other and lived in very harmonious and faithful wedlock. But one seeks in vain in their wedded life for the sickly sentimentality and extravagance of feeling which later ages regarded as the indispensable sign of a successful marriage. If the "wholesome philistinism" of the German national character, which strikes the foreigner as so strange and yet was always a source of strength for Germany, becomes manifest anywhere it is in the wedlock of the Reformer.

That a monk like Father Denifle should be shocked by Luther's naïve utterances about his wedded bliss, and that he sees in the concubinage of the celibate priests "a less serious transgression" than in this "stable relationship" (liaison), which the Protestants call Luther's "married life," is not surprising. A monk is not quite competent to judge such matters; he is likely to be without the candor toward that which is natural and thus unable to give an objective opinion. Anyone who reads the naïve confessions of the married Luther with an unprejudiced mind discovers nowhere the Luther whom Denifle has branded as a "urist" and will detect in the annals of this marriage which has been maligned in such an unutterably base and vile manner absolutely nothing exceptional. Furthermore, he will be unable to regard the incredible "jokes" of the priest Cochlaeus and of his fellow in spirit, the writer Lemnius, as merely "crude realism" but will look upon them only as the product of a hopelessly degenerate imagination.

All this, however, does not yet exhaust the catalogue of the sins of Doctor Martinus. The urist, pornographer, ribald, drunkard, glutton and crass ignoramus lastly reveals himself besides as a common forger and liar. In this guise also the Reformer is not now presented to the world for the first time. Even during his lifetime he was frequently branded as a falsifier of the Bible. He personally answered this charge briefly in his telling "Open Letter on the Art of Translating" of the year 1530. Father Denifle does not take up this accusation. From the point of view of confessional polemics this point is so thor- oughly settled that it is hopeless to say any more about it or bring about an understanding between the parties.

Denifle, however, believes that he has caught the "rogue" at a considerable number of forgeries. He, in fact, does prove that Luther occasionally cites ec- clesiastical writers incorrectly, and that he sometimes draws far-reaching conclusions from wrong quota- tions. He might have considerably increased the number of these proofs, so large is the list of incorrect citations in the works of the Reformer. What fol- lows from this? In the first place only the fact that Luther worked rapidly and ofttimes did not take the trouble of verifying his references. At times also he was forced to depend altogether on his memory, as, for instance, in the treatise "On the Monastic Vows" of 1521-22, which Denifle has particularly torn to pieces by his criticism. For this work was written at the Wartburg where Luther had no library at his com- mand. That also his memory was not always ac- curate, that at times he erred greatly, that occasion- ally he altogether misunderstood the writers whom he consulted is a weakness which he shares with very famous scholars, for instance, with Father Denifle. As little, however, as anyone now would designate the errors of Father Denifle as forgeries, so little is any- one justified in denying that the erring Luther possessed the bona fides, especially since Luther had to work much more rapidly and commanded a much poorer scientific apparatus than a modern scholar.

If then the Reformer was not a forger, did he not assume an equivocal attitude toward the behests of truthfulness, and did he not himself flagrantly transgress this commandment? Indeed, he did not hesitate to declare that "white lies" were theoretically permissible, and in one famous case he directly demanded such a white lie. These are facts which are fixed beyond a doubt. But let us in this instance also first hear the accused before we indulge in the supreme enjoyment of a sensation of moral indignation.

Luther terms those lies "white lies" which are told in the interest and for the love of one's fellow man, as for instance the false statement made by the Egyptian midwives for the benefit of the Hebrew child which Pharaoh had commanded them to throw into the Nile. (Ex. 1: 18, 19.) Some of the theologians of the primitive church, as, for instance, Hilary, John Chrysostom and Cassian, had in their day declared such falsehoods to be unobjectionable. Augustine, however, followed by Thomas Aquinas (Summa II, 2, 110) and his school, asserted that they were sinful. However, these latter teachers always regarded this type of falsehood as a light sin, and on the other hand held the prudent concealing of the truth, the act of dissimulation, to be permissible.

Other theologians believed that under certain circumstances it was a greater sin to say the truth than to tell a "white lie." For according to their view God unconditionally forbids only the lie which works harm (*mendacium adversus proximum prohibet*), while he merely curbs the white lie. (*Pro proximo cohibet.*) Luther joined this latter view but in so doing he went his own way in some respects though he employed almost the same examples to make his point clear. He noted that the holy patriarchs in the Bible occasionally made use of this type of falsehood without being censured by the sacred writers for their conduct. In fact, it seemed to him as though even Paul, Christ and God himself had at times not said exactly what they meant. To Luther this proved the admissibility not of the common emergency lie (*Notluege*), but of the utility lie (*Nutzluege*), that is, the falsehood which is told for the benefit and good of one's fellow man.

No Protestant of to-day will further sanction this method of proof. That, however, does not prove that the Reformer was wrong in the matter itself. In fact, most ethical writers even now think substantially as he did, if we except a few rigorists. These latter, however, are, because of their principles, only too often in the greater and lesser troubles of this life placed in a dilemma. This is shown by the example of their leader, Immanuel Kant, who in theory solemnly condemns every kind of falsehood as base, but in practice was himself "base" enough to permit himself such a "baseness" —namely, an amphiboly, a mental reservation, that is, a common, ordinary white lie. What is more, he did this in a "most solemn" declaration to King Frederick William II of Prussia whom he greets "most devotedly." (The Conflict of the Faculties, Introduction, ed. by Rosenkranz, vii., p. 257.)

However, notwithstanding the fact that the Reformer exhibited a more correct judgment on this point than the great sage of Koenigsberg, it is still very much an open question whether in the one famous case where Luther demanded a white lie he was morally justified in so doing. For in this renowned instance it was not a question of averting, but of hushing up "a manifest crime," namely, the keeping secret of the "Turkish marriage" which the Landgrave Philip of Hesse had on the fourth of March, 1540, at Rothenburg on the Fulda contracted with Margaret von der Saale. The only question is, did Luther regard this Turkish marriage as a manifest crime, and did he not perhaps even look upon its concealment as necessary for moral reasons?

As far as the first part of this question is concerned it has long ago been determined that for many years prior to the affair of the Hessian marriage the Reformer held bigamy to be permissible. As early as 1520, in the treatise on the Babylonian Captivity, Luther publicly avows that he would sooner give his consent to a double marriage than to the severance of a union legally existing before God. And in keeping with this attitude he, since 1520, ever again confesses, not only in confidential arbitraments but also in some pronouncements intended for the public in general, that polygamy is not forbidden to Christians by the New Testament. He holds that in serious emergencies,

for instance, if the wife contracts leprosy or is in some
other way taken from her husband, he cannot be hindered from taking a second spouse.   However, this
permission ought always remain confined to such serious emergencies.   The idea of legalizing polygamy
ever remained foreign to the Reformer.   He always
considered monogamy as the regular form of wedlock,
though he did not until later emphatically state that
it alone was fully and completely in accordance with
the divine order of the universe.   Only on one point
did Luther change his opinion in the course of time,
namely, on the question whether a husband in the
emergencies mentioned ought to enter upon a second
union publicly, or whether he ought to do so secretly.
In September, 1531, Luther still regarded it as permissible that King Henry VIII of England should
marry Anne Boleyn as his second wife and queen.
Later he would have dispensation granted for such
a secondary union only if the same were kept a strict
secret.

Luther never left his hearers or readers in doubt as
to how he arrived at these views, which to us seem so
strange.   Abraham certainly was a true Christian and
a man filled with the Holy Spirit who, nevertheless,
lived a polygamous life.   Hence this form of marriage
cannot be directly contrary to divine law.   Furthermore, the gospel, since it contains revelations of God
which have reference only to the inner life, has not
cancelled the permissions of the law of Moses in this
respect.   Therefore, even to-day the Christian laity
cannot be prohibited from making use of this conces-

sion but only, and Luther emphasizes this point, the Christian laity. The clergy have, according to I Tim. 3:2, been expressly bidden to be content with one wife.

These statements of the Reformer roused attention very soon. His old adversary Cochlaeus assailed him on this account as early as 1528, and the authors of the Catholic Confutation intended to protest openly against these views at the Diet of Augsburg in 1530. However, did Luther stand alone in this matter? By no means. Melanchthon, Butzer, Karlstadt and Capito shared his opinion, while the Anabaptists even legally introduced polygamy in Muenster on the twenty-third of July, 1534. In the Catholic camp itself there was by no means a dearth of men who held similar opinions on this question. Cardinal Cajetan, for instance, believed that the Pope could grant dispensation for bigamy, and in the marriage negotiations of Henry VIII, he expressly advised Clement VII to make use of this power in order to obviate more serious trouble. The Pope, accordingly, in the consistory laid before the cardinals the question whether a dispensation of this sort were permissible or not. They replied in the negative. From all this it is evident that the discussion on the admissibility of bigamy was not broached for the first time by the double marriage of the Landgrave. Quite to the contrary, it had been in progress for a long time when Philip entered upon his Turkish marriage. Indeed, it was this very discussion which first gave him the idea of seeking a remedy for moral and domestic misery in this unusual manner.

Philip had married in 1523 when he was nineteen years old. The wife selected for him was, however, unable in the least to gain his affections. In fact, she was so repugnant to him that he seems to have conceived the plan of a second marriage as early as 1526. However, Luther's faithful admonition and advice induced him to give up the idea for the present. But his physical antipathy toward his unamiable spouse rather increased with the years, and his hot blood again and again seduced him.   The results did not fail to appear. At the beginning of 1539 he fell seriously ill. In this condition he "meditated on many things."   It became clear to him that he would ruin his body and soul if he continued his former mode of life. Also it had become plain to him long ago that he lacked the moral strength to remain continent, and that much less could he again become interested in his wife. He deemed it necessary, therefore, after all "to make use of the permission in the law of Moses which neither Christ nor the Apostles had abolished" and to take unto himself another wife, and thus "before God and his own conscience to improve his position."

However, he did not firmly make up his mind until in September, 1539, in the "woman's apartments" of his sister, the Duchess Elizabeth of Saxony, he made the acquaintance of the seventeen-year-old Fraülein Margaret von der Saale from Schoenfeld in Masovia. This young lady he chose as his second wife. Though after the custom of the day he acquainted her with his purpose, he in the beginning entered on serious negotiations in the matter only with her mother, the "Hofmeisterin" Anna von der Saale. After some hesitation she acceded to his wishes but imposed upon him a number of rather inconvenient conditions. She deemed it best that the new marriage be immediately recognized publicly. If this were found to be impossible, the prince was at least to acquaint a number of noblemen, a few "scholars," the Elector and the Duke Maurice of Saxony with the fact, and to see to it that the marriage ceremony was performed in the presence of the electoral and ducal emissaries and of no less than two theologians of note, be they Luther, Melanchthon or Butzer. Under all circumstances the Landgrave was to procure for her a testimony from several scholars to the effect that his project did not conflict with divine ordinance. While the Duchess felt that Luther's consent would be desirable, she did not regard it as absolutely necessary.

Philip might hope to reduce these demands somewhat by further parley. But unless he wished at the very outset to give up his plan, he would at least have to try to comply with the wishes of the "Hofmeisterin." Therefore, all his actions in the next months are dominated by the desire to fulfill the conditions proposed by the prudent and ambitious woman. It is possible that he never frankly confessed this to himself. At any rate he maintained absolute silence about the affair even toward his most confidential advisers, and from the first, without any indication of his real purpose, he endeavored in a roundabout way to win over all those persons who had been named to him by the "Hofmeisterin." First he addressed himself to

Butzer, then, while this theologian was on his way to Saxony, he approached his wife, and finally, after she had on the seventeenth of December, 1539, consented and the reply from Saxony had arrived (after the middle of this month), he turned to his own theologians and jurists.

What was the nature of the representations made for him in Wittenberg by Butzer in order that he might win over Luther and Melanchthon and what did these two reformers reply? In the first place, Philip gave an impressive account of the inner misery from which he was suffering because of his unhappy union with the Landgravine and because of the immoral life which that union conditioned. Further, he asserted that in order to free himself from this mire and the toils of the devil "he would feign make use of the means" which God had permitted and marry another wife. In view of these premises he then requested from the reformers, wholly in keeping with the wishes of the Duchess von der Saale, a public testimony in favor of bigamy. Should this be impossible, and should the step he proposed to take for the present have to remain a secret, he asked that he be at least given a "testimony for his personal use" to the effect that his project was not contrary to divine ordinance.

What of necessity were the Wittenberg theologians led to conclude from this and from the affecting account of his troubles of conscience in the first part of his instructions? Certainly this, that he was in need of such a certificate in order to definitely assure himself whether his plan was contrary to God's will or not. But was this really the case? Not at all. Personally he had thrown aside all scruples, and was so firmly convinced that it was permissible for him to wed the bride he had chosen that early in November, even before he had consulted Butzer, he sent his own physician to Württemberg to purchase wine for the coming nuptials! He was therefore in reality no more in need of a "testimony for his personal use." He required such a document only for the purpose of getting the final consent of his prospective mother-in-law. Of this, however, he prudently said not a word nor did he mention the fact that he had long ago chosen his new wife, and that he had for months been negotiating about the terms of the marriage. Hence he consciously deceived Luther. He deluded him, because he knew very well that Doctor Martinus "was difficult to lead and more difficult to drive, but that he was set in motion automatically whenever he was told that the matter in question was one of danger to God's Word, or dealt with troubles of conscience." However, Philip practised deception on Luther not only in this regard. He also withheld from him the fact that he had once before kept a concubine, and that consequently, according to Luther's opinion, which he knew perfectly well, he was bound and not in a position any more to make a free choice.

The answer of the Wittenberg theologians, given the tenth of December, 1539, is entirely in accord with the impression which they necessarily derived and were meant to derive from the propositions of Philip. They grant him no public certificate, but merely "a testimony and memorandum for himself," that is, a confessional advice. Therein they set forth at great length that, though the contracting of a second marriage was permissible according to God's Word, it was possible only in serious emergencies and solely under the confessional seal and upon dispensation by the competent pastor. They leave it to the Landgrave to decide whether he is in such an emergency. "They do not at all mean to incite or urge him on." On the contrary, they earnestly admonish him to be patient in his present wedded life and to avoid giving offense. Nevertheless, in order that he might occupy a better position before God and his conscience they finally, in very guarded terms, granted him dispensation under the confessional seal to enter upon a second marriage. This second marriage is, however, always to remain a secret. The prince is merely to have the right under the confessional seal of advising the bride and a few intimates that the union is a regular marriage and not mere concubinage.

We can readily understand why the Countess von der Saale was "sorely troubled" over this confessional counsel, and that the Landgrave was put to no little pains in order to calm her. He was forced to send emissaries to Saxony twice after this before she was satisfied. The confessional advice therefore failed of its purpose. Not this counsel, but Philip's assurance that "bigamy was to be permitted also to others," finally moved the valiant "Hofmeisterin" to give her consent. Now for the first time, in February, 1540, also Margaret von der Saale was told about the resolve of her mother and the Landgrave.

Philip was even now still very solicitous of carrying out the wishes of the "dear Hofmeisterin." In accordance with his promise he under some pretext lured the unsuspecting Melanchthon to Rothenburg on the Fulda that he might be present at the wedding. Thereupon on the fourth of March in direct violation of the confessional advice he had his union with Margaret solemnly blessed by the Church. Lastly, in order to ease the mind of his new mother-in-law he handed over to her, together with other important documents, also a copy of the confessional advice. The ambitious lady, therefore, had due cause to be satisfied with him.

Detailed information about all these occurrences did not reach Luther before the end of May, 1540. Not until then, too, did he find out that the prince had once before contracted an irregular union. This latter fact enraged him so that he declared: "Had I known this not even an angel from heaven could have induced me to give such advice." He now saw clearly that Philip had gained the dispensation surreptitiously by a misrepresentation of the facts, and he was quite willing to admit his "error" publicly, that is, to pronounce the confessional advice null and void.

But, despite all this, how could Luther consistently assert that this counsel had in itself been correct, and further, adhere to the conviction that every Evangelical pastor was empowered in case of emergency under the confessional seal to permit a secret second marriage? How in general did he hit upon the peculiar notion so downright intolerable for Protestant

feeling that a clergyman might secretly permit a
thing which in secular and ecclesiastical law is rightly
prohibited; that a pastor in the confessional had the
right of determining what a layman might or might
not do, and that in this wise he had the duty, as mentor
of consciences, to guide his parishioners? This attitude is indeed more than peculiar. At the first glance,
in fact, it is absolutely unintelligible, especially in the
case of the father of Protestantism. He himself has,
in a measure, solved the riddle for us.

In July, 1540, Luther candidly acknowledged to
the Elector of Saxony that in his opinion this affair
was not the business of a public secular court, but per-
tained purely to the confessional, and that for this
reason he had in his advice followed exactly the same
procedure which in similar questions of the confessional he had observed in use while he was still a member of the Papal Church. He contends, furthermore,
that his preceptor in the monastery, who had to deal
with many such cases, had also employed the same
methods.

Luther, therefore, formally justifies himself by
pointing to mediæval confessional practice and
would have his action judged according to the rules
and principles familiar to him from his monastic career. But was he, as he claims, really guided by these
rules and principles? In all his utterances on the
question of marriage he always presupposes the difference between natural and divine law on the one
hand and positive law on the other. That is good
mediæval doctrine. Further, he takes it for granted

that there are certain "concessions of God" which are contrary to natural law but which, because they are testified to in Scripture, ought, as permissible actions, still be respected in modern times. This again is truly mediæval. Thirdly, Luther concludes from this that the father confessor has the right to secretly grant dispensation for acts which are forbidden by secular and ecclesiastical law. The sole condition is that such actions must be "permissible" either according to natural law or in the sight of God.

In substance this is nothing more than the mediæval doctrine of the *dispensatio in foro interno tantum*. And on the basis of this point of view Luther himself grants to the Landgrave such a *dispensatio in foro interno tantum,* thereby assuming the right of guiding the conscience of the prince quite in the manner of a Catholic father confessor. That is, his confessional advice is, in truth, a product of the mediæval logic of the confessional, or, putting it in other words, the father confessor of former days in this grave affair won out over the Reformer.

A single phase of his proceeding is noteworthy and viewed from the angle of the present-day Catholic attitude objectionable, that is, that Luther felt empowered to grant such a *dispensatio in foro interno tantum* even in case of bigamy. However, we have seen above that at the time also a cardinal of the Roman Church, Cajetan, regarded such a dispensation as permissible and that even a pope held this view to be open for discussion. The confessional advice of the tenth of December, 1539, is, therefore, nothing more than a classical proof for the continuance of the mediæval Catholic confessional practice within the confines of Lutheranism.   And it is by no means the first evidence of this kind.   Luther himself tells us that he repeatedly gave such dispensations to others also. Thus, for example, he says that he had advised several clergymen in the Duchy of Saxony to secretly wed their housekeepers in first marriage, a thing they had no right to do according to the laws of the state.   Luther consequently strangely enough never deemed it wrong to act as "father confessor," to counsel and guide the consciences.   Furthermore, in doing so he unhesitatingly followed the rules which he had been taught in the monastery as though such practice were as self-evident for an Evangelical pastor as for a Catholic priest.

Small wonder, therefore, that throughout his life he defended with equal unconcern also the mediæval Catholic teaching about the inviolability of the confessional, and regardlessly asserted its consequences under all circumstances.   Proof of this is again the Hessian marriage.

The secret of Rothenburg did not long remain a secret.   The sister of the Landgrave, quite naturally incensed over the lies her brother had told her, soon revealed the affair in March, 1540.   The court at Dresden instantly and eagerly took up the matter, seeing therein a chance to make a good bargain, and on the second of June had the new mother-in-law of Philip arrested forthwith.   In the course of these proceedings several of the incriminatory documents which the lady had received at Rothenburg came to light. In these sore straits Philip requested permission from his allies to announce his new marriage in due form, and in order to render them amenable he plainly threatened to publish the Wittenberg confessional advice. Luther, however, was not for a moment intimidated by this threat. He opposed the wishes of the Landgrave with all his might. At the Eisenach conference in July, 1540, he unconditionally demanded from the Hessian mediators that the prince make a public and straight denial of the existence of his new union. Indeed, he requested that in order to silence the gossipers, Philip tell a straight untruth, or a utility lie (white lie). Should he, in spite of all, persist in making public the confessional advice, he would write against him and confess openly that he, Luther, had erred, that is, he would declare the counsel invalid.

Philip has often been praised for answering to this demand which was made upon him also by Butzer and by the electoral court of Saxony: "I will not lie, for lies sound badly; besides, no Apostle ever taught a Christian to speak untruth, indeed, Christ has explicitly forbidden it and said that one ought to abide by Yes and No." However, the Landgrave certainly did not deserve this commendation; for how often and brazenly had he not in this affair lied to his own sister! Furthermore, was he in reality ready to abide by Yes and No? "If some one should ask me about the matter," he says in the same breath, "I will make him a dark answer," that is, putting it in plain English, mislead the inquirer.

However, though we have no right to set up the Landgrave as a model of virtue over against Doctor Martinus the fact remains that Luther counseled him to tell a falsehood. The only question is: How did Luther come by this "criminal idea"? He personally always replies briefly and laconically: Because we have to deal here with a confessional advice. He holds that just as it is not permitted the father confessor to divulge any part of what he learns in the confessional so also the penitent is in duty bound to observe silence about the advice obtained in the confession. Likewise, as the father confessor may, under certain circumstances, be forced to swear a false oath in order to guard the sanctity of the confessional, so also the confessing penitent is under certain conditions held to protect this secrecy by a "straight white lie." Is this point of view after all as unusual as it is ordinarily represented to be? No. At present still Catholic theologians teach: "Also the penitent is obliged to observe natural secrecy on all those matters, which he cannot divulge without inflicting an unjust injury upon the father confessor." At the very time of Luther, in fact, the theologians in whose views he had been brought up, the Moderns or the Okkamists, claimed that whoever tells tales out of confession commits a mortal sin. This, self-evidently, for confessional practice, led to the conclusion: Therefore one ought sooner advise the confessing penitent to tell an untruth than to break the sacredness of the confessional. For the white lie is merely a venial sin and consequently is

directly advisable in such a case in order to avoid a
greater evil. What follows from this? Luther's demand for a white lie is merely a result of the doctrine
of the Okkamists about the inviolability of the confessional, to which he always adhered.

However, this does not yet fully clear up the situation. We may ask: Had the Landgrave really confessed
to Luther, and was the latter therefore in reality empowered over against him to call upon the old Catholic tenets about the confessional seal? Indeed, a "sacramental confession" had in this case not taken place.
But, according to Catholic doctrine, this was not and
is not now at all necessary in order to furnish a basis
for the plea of sacramental secrecy. "If any person,
merely for the purpose of securing confessional advice, reveals to the father confessor the state of his
conscience the duty of sacramental secrecy is thereby
imposed."   (Gury: Moraltheologie II, 648, 3.)

All these facts help us to understand why the Reformer never felt any qualms of conscience about the
affair of the Hessian marriage. It was very hard for
Luther to grant dispensation for bigamy to the Landgrave, but he was convinced that he was empowered to
do so, since bigamy in case of necessity was allowed by
God. Furthermore, deceived by the false statements
of Philip, he believed that his case was one involving
such a necessity. Later on in order to guard the confessional seal he advised a white lie. Here again, however, he felt that he had a moral right to do so. For
he looked upon breach of confessional secrecy as a
serious crime, to avert which he deemed a white lie

just as permissible as for the avoidance of murder or
homicide. Consequently, Luther did only what otherwise also he regarded as his right and duty as a confessor.

Unfortunately, as the documents show, he never
took into account the political phase of the affair, and
as usual never even dreamed of the consequences
which his actions might have for his own reputation.
Unhappily, he judged the whole matter only from the
narrow perspective of the confessional, and from out
of an honest desire to assist a seemingly despairing
man to a better standing before God and his conscience. He utterly forgot, as so often, that he had
long ere this laid aside the cowl of the priest. If this
be taken into account one may still deplore the stand
Luther took in the Hessian marriage tangle, but one
cannot condemn it, much less use it to prove the moral
inferiority of his new religious principles. For with
these new tenets it has nothing whatever to do. On
the contrary, it is an after effect of the old mediæval
Catholic teachings, and the classical proof how
strongly at times still his earlier habits of thought and
the pastoral methods of the old faith influenced Luther's actions even after he had long broken away from
them in principle.

The Reformer himself often emphatically declared:
"My person anyone who wishes may attack, I do not
pose as a saint." Both his contemporaries and the
later world eagerly accepted this invitation, as though
humanity had no more urgent concern than to burn
this heretic in effigy after his death, at least, since un-

fortunately neither Pope nor Emperor were able to
bring him to the rack or the stake during his life. And
what are the net results of the heresy trial which has
now been dragging on for three hundred and ninety-
five years? The proceedings must be quashed. For
most of the charges brought against the defendant
have turned out to be crude falsehoods, others cannot
be upheld because the accused manifestly acted in
good faith. This is above all true of the Hessian confessional advice and of his insulting remarks about
the Papacy.

Does this close the case of Luther? By no means.
So far it has only been proven that the advocate of the
devil has no claim upon this man even though he was
not a saint, and that the accused during his whole life
labored under the hindering influences which education and environment exert upon the thought and action even of the strongest, most mature and most
independent human beings. But by no means have
we thus gained a clear picture of the whole, the real
Luther. For the whole Luther one never learns
to know if one permits his accusers to prescribe
the course of observation. The complete Luther reveals himself only to him who meets him face to face,
and undeterred by friend or enemy permits the personality of the Reformer to act upon himself in all its
fullness and strength. Therefore, the negative result
of almost four centuries of trial necessitates a positive
supplement. The supplying of this missing phase,
however, may be left to the reader. Only this must
still be pointed out that only if one makes an unbiased

study of the whole Luther do the failings and weaknesses which his accusers play up so vividly appear in
the proper projections.

This is especially true if, for the sake of justice, all
the other members of that chosen race, among whose
number by his talent and historical effectiveness he
must be counted, are placed side by side with him,
those great prophets and heroes of Christian history
whose lot it also was in continuous struggle against a
world of hindrances to assist to victory new understanding or a new order of things: Paul and Athanasius, Bernard of Clairvaux and Savonarola, Calvin
and John Knox, Cromwell and Bismarck. All these
men, exactly like Luther, inclined to explosions of
passion and to a certain intolerance of the opinion of
others, and with all of them this hyper-irritability is
explained by the tremendous tension of their emotional life resulting from the exclusive devotion to a
purpose which could only be achieved by dint of continual wrestling with hostile powers.

Only one family characteristic of this august race
which was, for instance, particularly strongly developed in Bismarck: The often rather brutal lack of
consideration toward persons about them, seems not
to have been so sharply expressed in Luther. But it
was present, nevertheless. This is sufficiently evi-
denced by the energetic manner in which he tries to
compel Catharine von Bora against her will to marry
Pastor Glatz, and the tenacity with which he attempted to force Melanchthon into the theological
faculty. Luckily Catharine was herself a very forceful

nature. She not only opposed him, she also understood later on so nobly and firmly to maintain her ground as Doctoress in the Black Cloister that half in jest, half in admiration Luther referred to her not only as his "Kette" (=Chain—Katie) but also as his "Master Katie."

Though Melanchthon also possessed the courage of passive resistance when the imputations of Luther became too exacting, he never once found the courage to openly challenge the mighty Doctor. On the contrary, he purposely avoided any discussion of the theological differences which separated him from the aging "Pericles," kept his peace, was pliant and submissive like a timid pupil who is at all times in fear of a blow from the teacher's rod. No wonder, therefore, that his life by the side of the master whom in spite of all he heartily revered, finally seemed to him downright slavery, and that he breathed as one liberated when the powerful dark eyes which had made him tremble had closed forever. But the blame for this martyrdom rests not with Luther but with Melanchthon himself. Magister Philippus himself confessed that he was by nature somewhat subservient and behaved like a slave. One who has such tendencies, however, must, if he is chosen as the helpmate of one greater than he, either wholly give up any pretensions at independence, or he must in time make his escape from the oppressively rare atmosphere in the heights where genius thrives to the plains where the great herd grazes in comfort. It is truly tragic that the timid Magister Philippus could not make up his mind to either course.

Even more tragic after all is the fate of Luther. Already many of those who had worked with him and fought by his side since the opening of the year 1522 had turned away from Luther to become his most bitter enemies, first, Thomas Münzer and Karlstadt, then Balthasar Hubmaier, Zwingli, Oecolampadius, Schwenckfeld and Sebastian Franck. Now at the end of his days he also lost spiritual contact with the most gifted and oldest of his personal pupils without finding a new friend who might supply what he now lacked, namely, the truly fruitful intimate intercourse with minds at least in a measure his equal. For the greatest of his spiritual sons, who seemed more than any other destined to supplement him, John Calvin, in spite of a cordial admiration for him, ever remained strange to Luther. And though among the loyal group which swore by him there were many excellent and learned men of strong character, there was not one who had the gift of overcoming the one-sidedness of the master, and thereby to regain for Lutheranism the leadership of the Evangelical movement.

CHAPTER VIII.

The Background of Luther's Life and Religion.

L UTHER wrote several thousand books and booklets. All of them, however, more or less bear the character of occasional pamphlets. Not one provides a complete much less a systematic survey even of his religious and theological ideas, let alone a clear presentation of all the conclusions he derived from these for the ordering of personal and communal life. Not a single one furnishes a clear view of the premises regarding the theory of knowledge with which he starts out, nor of the fundamental tenets and practical ideas which determine his judgments on economic, social, political and pedagogical problems.

It was not Luther but Melanchthon who first undertook the obvious task of briefly summarizing the basic ideas of the Evangelical message. Considering that it is the first attempt of its kind this survey is unquestionably a splendid achievement. Nevertheless, the systematist finds in it much, indeed very much, that is faulty. To Luther, however, it seemed wholly adequate, indeed, it was in his eyes an unsurpassable classic, canonic achievement, transcending all his own works in value and usefulness for the public. This is proof sufficient that his demands in this respect were not very exacting. It also shows that he by no means regarded "the fine coiffure of the system" as a superfluous decoration, but quite to the contrary as an indispensable requisite of theological thinking. It further indicates that only because he felt unequal to the task he refrained from personally shouldering this useful and necessary burden.

In truth, Luther appeared to be much less fitted for just such work than the little Magister Philippus because of the very peculiarity of his early training. As a pupil of the "Moderns" he had learned to think and criticize, but he had never been trained to pay attention to the connection between religious and theological concepts, to organize and bring them into relation with one another, or even merely to collate them. Indeed, whatever inclination of this kind he may have had had been driven out of him in his youth by the purely critical methods of the Moderns, which dissolved the dogmas of the Church into innumerable individual problems.

To be sure, the claim has recently been made that the traditional verdict on the unsystematic character of his thinking does not comport with the facts. It is said that though he did not start out with the intention of formulating a system he, nevertheless, did possess one, and at that a system "which in characteristic doctrines is distinctly noteworthy for its strict logical consistency." Furthermore, it is asserted that this system is in closest relation to that of the Moderns, for the idea, they say, which must be regarded as the organizing principle of his theological thinking, the idea of the veracity of God, is derived from Okkam. To men holding this view the difference between Luther and Okkam consists merely in this that the latter, standing on the veracity of God, demands absolute submission to all utterances and teachings of Holy Writ, while Luther, following Augustine, is content to designate the clear and distinct statements of the Bible as the unquestionably trustworthy revelations of the veracious God.

However, is it really possible to derive even the fundamental concepts of Luther's theology in a clear-cut manner from this idea? No; at least not the basic tenet upon which he himself always looked as his fundamental article, the article on justification. This could never have assumed such a singular importance for him had he always consistently followed in his theological speculation this purely formal principle before which all clear and definite passages of the Old and the New Testament are altogether equal in value and importance, whether they treat merely of the waters that were above the firmament of heaven, or of salvation through Christ. Besides, he really did not arrive at this article through this principle at all. On the contrary, he did not gain his peculiar doctrine on Scriptures until, through "divine inspiration," the significance of the texts about the righteousness of God had become clear to him. This result is not nullified by the fact that Luther personally at times termed "justification" an effect of the veracity of God, inasmuch as in this connection the "veracity of God" refers to nothing more than the faithfulness and reliability with which God fulfills his promise.

The Reformer, therefore, did not conceive the

veracity of God with absolute clearness and singleness of meaning, nor did it completely dominate his theological speculation.   Instead of continually operating with one principle or general concept Luther is actually always using two.   However, the determining one for him was always the idea of justification.   Solely in his writings on the eucharist, in which he defends an old Scholastic view of the Okkamists, altogether in the style of Okkam, does the concept of the veracity of God stand in the foreground.   However, important though it may be for the understanding of these writings to keep this in mind, it would nevertheless be a hazardous undertaking to make just these treatises the basis for a reconstruction of his theology.   All would be harmonious and in order, notwithstanding, if Luther had carefully balanced these two concepts. But he never even made an attempt to do that.

Consequently, we are, even with the best of intentions, unable to discover a strict consistency in his system, indeed, we can in no way forcibly bind his views together into a logical structure.   Despite all endeavors of this kind the gulf remains between the two circles of doctrine which he developed: The dogma of justification in which his new religious thoughts are presented, and the dogma of the sacraments in which in many respects he is merely carrying on the Okkamistic view.   In fact, while other thinkers in later years, as a rule, try to adjust the inconsistencies in their system, Luther, as a result of the conflict about the eucharist, was induced to bring out even more sharply the contradiction between the two phases of his teaching, so that it is much more apparent in his later writings than in the publications of the year 1520-21, or especially in the oldest classic presentation of his doctrine, Melanchthon's Basic Theological Truths of the year 1521.

Luther's matured point of view, therefore, even if one pays attention only to the "characteristic doctrines," is like unto a building with a peculiar mixture of architectural styles. Moreover, if one purposely seeks out inconsistencies, a pleasure Sebastian Franck allowed himself as early as 1531 in his "Geschichtbibel," it is an easy matter to run down a dozen or two of them. This is due to the unconcerned manner in which Luther both in polemics and sermons would stress the one or the other point, and also to his tendency of occasionally giving free rein to his penchant for paradoxes. By setting forth this fact one in no way impairs his greatness nor the world-historical importance of his teachings; on the contrary, only thus is the path to a really fruitful appreciation of his genius laid open. For only if we resolutely refuse to systematize his individual utterances, if we permit them to act upon ourselves wholly without qualification or dislocation, in the form in which he put them to paper, while still hot and glowing from joy or anger, do we gain a full impression of the inexhaustible power, fullness, audacity and originality of his intellect.

Undoubtedly this enormous facility in the production of ideas is most intimately related to his lack of system. The energetic endeavor to construct a closely knit organized whole naturally puts a decided check on the inclination to give room to new ideas and hence also on the ability of producing new ideas, in fact, it gradually kills this faculty, while in the opposite case the mind ever remains fresh for new concepts and always can give itself up without restraint to the impulse of forming new ideas. We consequently do not claim too much when we assert that the Reformer's lack of system is a necessary outgrowth of his tremendous intellectual fertility and to that extent also a necessary prerequisite of his world-historical activity.

The genuine systematists, one need only to think of Calvin, are mostly not creative thinkers, and vice versa creative minds, as a rule, lack the capacity for organization. And though this latter type is not very frequent, creative thinkers are even rarer, especially in the field of religion and ethics, though for that very reason they always exert a more powerful and abiding influence than the systematic minds. They alone really bring forth something new, release new forces and found new institutions of historical life, while the systematists have only the more modest task of organizing and concentrating the new forces and ideas. By this process, to be sure, as a rule their effect upon contemporary and later civilization is materially increased, as the example of Calvin again shows.

Where the inclination and ability of concentrating one's mind and shutting out new impressions is found in so small a degree the development and change which the content of knowledge undergoes in the course of time naturally leaves more definite traces than in the case of born organizers, who immediately test out every new idea critically according to the basic principles of their system. Hence childhood, youth and maturity, the heritage of the parental home, of the school and the acquisitions of later years are in the case of such thinkers ofttimes still recognizable in the completed "system" like the year rings of a tree. And despite all changes which occurred meanwhile, in spite of the natural dying off and the forcible elimination of certain groups of ideas, one can, nevertheless, in the final complete product still determine so accurately the gradual growth of the intellectual property that it is possible to attempt a genetic analysis of the entire system by pointing out the several strata of which it is composed.

Such an analysis, however, is in this instance not only useful but a downright duty. For, particularly in the case of Luther, the question has ever again been propounded: What did the Reformer derive from his contemporaries, and what did he give them in return? It is true, the sixteenth century did not yet set this problem, it admired or hated, but it did not analyze. All the more eagerly has the nineteenth century busied itself with this question. It no longer sees in the great individual a revelation either of divine or diabolic powers, but merely a problem, and it is prone to solve this problem like a mathematical proposition, that is, the great individual is conceived as merely the sum or product of already existing energies in which the law on the conservation of energy is verified also in the realm of intellect.

This attitude, of course, easily leads scholars astray

into a new mythology. Concepts, like heredity and environment, which are perfectly justified in zoology and botany, are employed for the solution of phenomena of historical life without further ado, while in reality they frequently serve merely to obscure these phenomena; and when these concepts prove inadequate it may happen that scholars like Taine, in his characterization of Napoleon, quickly affirm a case of atavism. For all manner of hypotheses are permitted, only the words mystery, incomprehensible, riddle, dare not be mentioned aloud! However, this point of view would not have found so many adherents if at the bottom of it there were not a correct observation, the observation that also the genius in a certain sense is a part of the mass, and that the mass in a measure participates in the achievements of the genius.

We have noticed how much Luther in his manner of speech, in his literary customs and habits of life was a child of his time. This recognition alone obliges us to investigate also in how far he was a product of his period with respect to his ideas. There is no lack of introductory studies on this point, indeed, apparently the investigation as such is already complete. When Harnack asserts that Luther was on the periphery of his existence an old-Catholic mediæval phenomenon; if Wundt declares: Luther did not give humanity a new religion but a new ethical structure which, however, is but a reflex of the powerful *lebensgefuehl* "sense of life" (*i. e.,* appreciation of life) of the Renaissance; if Wernle sets down the opinion that neither Luther nor Lutheranism possessed a system of ethics, and Troeltsch adds: "Primitive Protestantism in its essential features and expressions is merely the transmutation of the mediæval idea," one needs apparently only to combine and add these verdicts and the problem is solved, solved very simply at that! The extraordinary, incomprehensible and original elements in the personality of the Reformer are thereby completely done away with, the "prophet" has been degraded to the rank of a very common human being. Only one riddle is left over, but this in reality has nothing to do with Luther's person, it concerns the course of the general development, it is the question: How comes it that certain individuals become as it were the rallying point of the forces and ideas of their age?

However, this extraordinarily simple solution of the problem Luther presupposes the solving of quite a series of difficult individual propositions about which so far an agreement has not been reached by any means. Hence, to be on the safe side we will first closely investigate these separate problems and endeavor to answer the relatively easy question: What does the Reformer owe to his parental home and to the school, and in how far does he merely express ideas and judgments which others championed before him?

Let us, therefore, in the first place, transport ourselves four hundred years into the past, into the home of the miner Hans Luther at Mansfeld. Miners have from of old always been very superstitious. However, in Luther's home this superstition is denser and

stronger than to-day in the most out-of-the-way village in the Eifel. For here we find added to the superstition of the miner the equally strong superstition
of the Thuringian peasant. The good people, therefore, really lived in continual fear of all kinds of
monsters and goblins, sorcerers and witches, great and
small, wise and stupid devils. Even when a natural
explanation seems most obvious, as, for instance, when
her infant cried with especial lustiness, the greatly
distressed mother, Margaret Luther, forthwith sup-
poses that the neighbor woman is a witch and Father
Hans does not doubt that she is right and that the
little son must die because he has been bewitched.

This firm belief in devils and witches was transmitted to Doctor Martinus in the same undiminished
degree as the inexhaustible stock of popular sayings
and stories, abuse and ridicule, which his father and
mother had at their disposal. In fact, it was materially increased during his days at school and his stay
in the monastery. Hence as a mature man Luther
never merely postulates the possible instance: "If
devils all the world should fill," no, the world to him
is actually full of devils. These bad spirits are busy in
house and yard, wood and field, about man and in
man. In the shape of a he-goat they infest woods and
swamps, in the form of quivering flames or as dragons
they swish through the air, as water sprites they draw
bathers down into the depths of the rivers. Also their
supreme master, Satan, does not disdain occasionally
to appear in visible form. Men he preferably approaches in the guise of a beautiful maiden, to women

he reveals himself as a gay cavalier in a green hat with a blue plume. For the more Satan's "Mother" henpecks him in his "hostelry" below the bolder he acts on earth. It is reported that he has been seen also in the disguise of a gray monk, as hermit, parish priest, dragon, calf, he-goat and as a horned gentleman. Besides, it is very probable that cats, apes and parrots and the strange caterpillars whose posterior is suspiciously decked out with a little horn also have a bit of the devil in them.

As a rule, however, these evil spirits move and act about and inside of men unseen, ever ready to cause harm and to murder his soul. At one time they scare the good Christian by inundations, at another by terrible storms, then again they trouble him with deadly epidemics among his flocks or by frightful plagues. Worse still is the fact that they are not afraid to enter into human beings themselves, and to rob them of their reason or incite them to evil deeds. The lesser devils lead man into adultery, avarice, vain ambition and suchlike sins, the greater and more dangerous ones seduce to melancholy, unbelief, despair and heresy. The Pope and other enemies of the gospel have in this wise become altogether the tools of the evil one. Hence it is self-evident that human beings can enter into a formal pact with Satan. In this way, for example, Dr. Eck, Joachim I of Brandenburg and the notorious Dr. Faust of Kundling, who toward the end of the second decade of the sixteenth century was active in Wittenberg until a warrant of arrest issued by the Elector John forced him to leave, have given themselves over to him. In fact, once even a student at Wittenberg did this.

More frequently than men, however, women permit the devil to befool them. Then they become witches, "make cruel weather," paralyze peoples' limbs by sudden fits of rheumatic pain (Hexenschuss), stop the milk of cows, steal the wool from the living sheep and commit other shameful deeds. Such witches often pursued also Doctor Luther and his Katie. Small wonder, therefore, that the Doctor occasionally threatens these impudent instruments of the Devil even from the pulpit, and that he shares completely the common view that these women must be punished by death, though only if they prove impervious to pastoral admonition, and not because of the harm they inflict upon man but because of the persistent blasphemy of which they are guilty. For according to the prevailing laws blasphemy is a crime worthy of capital punishment. (Cf. page 305 sq.)

Happily Luther knows exactly not only the works and the tools of Satan but also his character and that of his servants. He knows that the evil one is a proud spirit, and that least of all he can bear contempt. Such scorn of the devil Luther, therefore, exhibits again and again, often with decidedly popular gestures. Fear of the devil is altogether foreign to him. The consciousness of having continually to fight with the master of this world, but of always being able to fell him with a single word, only serves to increase the Doctor's joyful feeling of strength. More than any other person he confirms the statement of Goethe:

"Superstition is the heritage of energetic and noble natures."

However, Luther believes that man does not stand alone in this conflict with the evil spirits. The beneficent spirits, the angels whose commander is St. Gabriel, come to his aid. For just as every human being, so to speak, has a private devil so also everyone has his guardian angel. And though Satan were closer to us than our shirt, indeed closer than the body itself, the angels are, nevertheless, still more powerful and wise. They are consequently always able in case of need to give man good counsel and sometimes in fact even to teach him the secrets of the future.

This popular belief in devils and angels which he had imbibed with his mother's milk the Reformer tenaciously retained during his whole life. Besides, he ever clung to the ancient faith in the evil omen of comets, eclipses of the sun or moon, and was prone to see in human or animal monsters a good or bad portent like all other people of his time.

In spite of all this, peculiar though such a contention may sound, Luther impaired the reign of superstition more than any one of his contemporaries and was personally more enlightened than the majority of the educated class of that day, especially more so than the Italian free thinkers who have so often been praised as ideal enlighteners, for instance, Gemisthos Plethon, Codro Urceo, Machiavelli and Guicciardini. All the confused pseudo-sciences which Humanism had once more brought to honor and which were assiduously cultivated even at the Curia, such as astrology, alchemy, geomancy, chiromantics, etc., Luther despised and ridiculed with all his heart, even though the good Magister Philippus himself, as a true Humanist, could not abstain from dabbling a bit in this nonsense.   He also would not hear of exorcising devils, a custom which was very popular at the time, and of a goodly number of other superstitious practices and conceptions, such as, for example, the notion that witches rode through the air on brooms and were able to assume the forms of all kinds of animals, the illusion that the dead sometimes came to life again, the belief in the magic wand, in the magic effect of love potions, in telling fortune from finger-nails and in the magic mirror.   Furthermore, Luther in his earlier years actively fought and later on partly abolished or suppressed very nearly all the either absurd or revolting atropean customs which were still in vogue at birth, baptism and burial, in times of plague, floods and conflagrations.

But did Luther's belief in devils not grow increasingly gloomy, wild and crude with his advancing years? No! This view of certain modern inquisitors is as profoundly erroneous as the oft-mentioned assertion that the belief in witches, which at bottom is nothing more than a survival of ancient Germanic paganism, was first naturalized in the Protestant world by Luther.   We must in this case again beware of ingeniously isolating Luther, that is, we must not view him as a phenomenon standing by himself without reference to the belief of his era.   Further, we must guard against severing his thoughts and concepts from their natural context, as Grisar does when he presents Luther's views about the devil and demons altogether without regard for the strong and joyful faith in God, for which after all these former views are merely the foil, and who thus utterly fails to see behind the superstitious Luther the believing Luther who did such a great deal to diminish superstition.

With the same distinctness as the heritage of his paternal home we can detect also the legacy of the school in the system of the Reformer. A number of very characteristic proofs for this have been cited above. (Cf. page 62 sq.) It will be sufficient, therefore, to note at this point the additional fact that the Reformer also, in his political, social and economic theories and proposals of reform, usually follows very closely the Okkamistic tradition or other mediæval authorities. For example, he follows Okkam when he declares that the care of the poor is a task of the secular communal and territorial administration, when he points out that it is a duty and privilege of the secular power to remedy abuses in the administration of public worship. Further, the Okkamists are his guide when he makes the assertion, which sounds so heretical to modern ears, namely, that the secular government is unquestionably bound only by natural law or divine law, and that it has a right, indeed has the duty, under certain circumstances to simply disregard written law.

Not from Okkam himself, but, nevertheless, derived from the common mediæval tradition is in this connection the distinction, self-evident to Luther, between written (positive) law on the one hand and natural law on the other. The same source is responsible for the view to which he consistently adhered and which held that "Christendom" is the great international organization of Christian society, which in material things is ruled by the secular power, in spiritual matters by the Word of God. Again, also, his peculiar division of this Christian society into three sacred orders: the Teachers (pastors and teachers), the Governors (secular lords and governmental bodies) and the Breadwinners (peasants, craftsmen, merchants) has this same origin. To the identical source we may assign his idea which conceives of the civic calling as an office in the service of society, and particularly the claim, which appears so strange to our modern feeling in this matter, that the division of mankind into governing and governed classes, and the whole order of society which is based upon this principle, is the result of the fall of man.

More mediæval still, to the present-day German, seem his judgments on questions of economics and conditions of economic distress. The Middle Ages are distinctly agrarian in tone. The craftsman is not highly esteemed; industry and trade are regarded as improper means of gaining a livelihood; all money transactions pure and simple, especially those in which money plays the rôle of a productive factor, it utterly condemns. Luther is at bottom of the same opinion. He frankly adopts the mediæval saying: A merchant can scarcely obtain salvation. He stamps all import trade as a great evil, all money transactions, in as far as they aim at gain, he holds to be unnecessary and objectionable, and he would fain damn every puny little money lender as an unchristian usurer.

Even where he follows no tradition or authority but draws wholly upon his own ideas Luther is not always as absolutely new as it would seem to the outsider. In these instances also he often merely voices doubts and thoughts which had long been discussed publicly in the "heretical" communities and pro-reform circles of the Middle Ages. Plenty of parallels can be adduced both from the heretical and from the Catholic oppositionary literature of the Middle Ages on what Luther has to say, for example, about the abuses of the papal régime, also on the moral deterioration of monasticism, the worldliness of the higher and lower clergy, the forced celibacy of the priests, on indulgences, the worship of saints, relics and images, the ecclesiastical system of enforced fasts, the excessive number of festal days and similar outgrowths of the Catholic system. Taken as a whole, therefore, the treatise in which especially he criticizes the external abuses in Catholicism, the "Address to the Nobility," offers very little that is entirely new.

Also in his strictures on Catholic dogma Luther had in many particulars been preceded by the Lombard and German Waldenses, by the English and Bohemian Wiclifites. It will suffice to call attention merely to the doctrines on purgatory, transubstantiation, confirmation and extreme unction. Even the assertion that the Pope is the Antichrist and Rome the Babylon of the Apocalypse of St. John we meet earlier with the adherents of Peter Waldo in Lombardy. Hence, the truly new elements in Luther's criticisms of the Catholic system are apparently only three in number: The strictures on the Catholic view of sin and grace, the attack on the Church's concept of the sacraments and on its view of the religious value of an ascetic life.

There is, however, no dearth of scholars who will not concede even this much without reservation. Indeed, some would not even recognize him as the first discoverer of the positive ideas and ideals which he always uses as a starting point in his criticism. And it does seem as though a number of facts justified this view. The extraordinary rapidity with which the burgher class joins the Evangelical movement, the wholesale accession of the Humanists to the Lutheran party, the erroneous opinion, at first shared by so many of the educated and partially educated, that Luther was merely the perfector, or simply the fellow combatant of Erasmus of Rotterdam, all this naturally leads to the question: Did not the new in the Reformer, at bottom, consist only in the fact that he expressed in an effective form the knowledge and the demands which had long passed current among the German burgher class and in the circles of the partisans of Humanistic reform?

It is claimed, for instance, that Luther was the first to once more bring to honor the Apostle Paul and to revive Paulinism. But previously the Humanist Marsilio Ficino, of Florence, and his pupils John Colet and Jacob Lefevre d'Etaples had given out the watchword: Back to Paul! Moreover, not Luther but

Lefevre published the first commentary based upon the original text, and first employed Pauline concepts for the purpose of criticizing the piety of the day.

It is further asserted that before Luther no one emphasized that there is but one religious authority for a Christian: Christ, or the Bible as far as it teaches Christ's views. But quite a while before Luther, Erasmus of Rotterdam had expressed the same opinion very vigorously and had earnestly demanded the return to the simple doctrines of Christ, a reform of theology, and, more significantly still, also the recasting of practical piety after the model of Christ's theology. The same Humanist further clearly recognized that a reform of this sort could be successful only if the simple teachings of Christ, which like the sun were intended to bring light to all, were made accessible to mankind as a whole. Pursuant to this idea Erasmus, as early as 1516, in the admonitory preface to the first edition of the New Testament emphatically developed the concept which sounds distinctly Lutheran, namely, the tenet that the Bible ought to be translated into all popular tongues and spread in every language, so that man and woman, young and old, nobles and commons, might read the gospels and the Pauline letters, and in the future the peasant in the field, the workman in the shop, the traveler upon the high road might pass the time with passages from Scriptures and with hymns.

Lastly, some insist that Luther was the first person to overcome the external, legalistic morality of the Middle Ages, who denied monasticism the right of existence, who first pointed to the family and community, the state and the civil occupation as the normal sphere for the fulfillment of man's moral duty. But apparently Erasmus had preceded him also in these reforms. As early as 1502 in his famous edificatory treatise, the Handbook of the Christian Soldier, he ever again points from the good works of the Church without expressly condemning them to that most difficult part of the law, the purification and sanctification of the mind. At the same time Erasmus expressly repudiates the customary distinction between the duties of monks and of lay Christians, and further, presents Christ in an impressive manner as the prototype and example for every human being.

However, Erasmus is by no means the sole witness to the fact that at the very beginning of the sixteenth century a change in the moral point of view is in progress. In the numerous pamphlets, denunciatory poems and apocalypses which preceded the Reformation, is revealed not only an ofttimes terrible hatred of the lazy priests and monks, but also occasionally an exuberant valuation of the pious, faithful layman and laborer, i. e., manual laborer. Indeed, "the laborer" is essentially the pet figure of this literature, his doings are explicitly praised as worship of God, the sweat of his brow thought to be as sacred and healing as the blood of the martyrs. Nothing characterizes the strength and the wide diffusion of this sentiment so much as the fact that even monastic preachers like the Leipzig Dominican Marcus von Weida made concessions to it,

Linked with the high estimate of the laborer we occasionally find an almost fanatical veneration of the "pious married folk." Thus, for example, the author of the Apocalypse of St. Michael declares that wedlock is the sacrament of sacraments, and requests pious married people to join in a fraternity of St. Michael in order to reform Church and Empire, while, on the other hand, he unqualifiedly condemns monastic life in all its forms. Here and there we also begin to hear open protests against the ascetic ideal. When about 1494 several distinguished citizens of Strassburg entered the Carthusian order, a number of "fools," as the pious Sebastian Brant complains, did not hesitate to assert: "God has not created us in order that we become monks or priests and particularly not that we should flee the world: . . . It is not God's will that one should renounce the world." Such opposition certainly was not frequent, but the feeling revealed therein already existed in wide strata of the population when Luther appeared before the public. And even where the world-renouncing attitude still dominated the soul, people frequently had lost all sympathy for monastic asceticism. In fact, as the Anabaptist movement later shows, they demanded the formation of world-renouncing communities after the pattern of the early Christians or the Taborites.

It would appear from all this as though Luther's message in truth contained no new or original elements, as though Erasmus had not been mistaken when he believed that the Wittenberg monk had ruined his whole reformation by his rude interference.

The criticism and the literary propaganda of the Christian Humanists, the mighty stirring up of the spirits would, as it seems, have led automatically to a reformation, indeed, would have brought on a reform in keeping with the wishes of Erasmus without any "tumult."

There are, in fact, still Erasmians who faithfully repeat this verdict of the old chieftain of the Humanists. Anyone, however, who does not view the history of the world from out of the perspective of his study certainly will find this assertion just as clever as the claim that the Napoleonic Empire would of necessity have come about even without Napoleon, and the unity of Germany been achieved without Bismarck. Critics and rhetoricians like Erasmus, fanatics like his counterpart, the author of the Apocalypse of St. Michael, may call forth and strengthen a world-historical movement, but they can never create a new order of things. This can be done alone by an heroic will which calmly and resolutely takes up the struggle with the forces of the old order of things and, by exerting to the full all the powers of intellect and soul, carries it through to the final end. The possession of such an heroic will, this most rare and most mighty of the creative forces of history, therefore, can certainly not be denied to Luther.

But is it true that besides this heroic will Luther possessed no characteristics which place him ahead of Erasmus and other similar partisans of reform? Is he really as a thinker nothing more than a sharp-eared and clever interpreter of the ideas of his time, only the speaking trumpet through which the soft murmur coursing through the land now gathered into one mighty wave of sound and finally made itself heard? Is Luther merely the "prophet" who serves the spirit of the day as Aaron of old aided the slow-tongued Moses, in that he, so to speak, snatched the word from the tongues of the millions?

A brief examination of Erasmus and his predecessors as well as of the spokesmen of the popular opposition, for example, the author of the Apocalypse of St. Michael, will suffice to elicit the correct answer. It is true, Ficino, Colet, Lefevre, Erasmus and his numerous sympathizers did enthuse over Paul in the most extravagant terms. However, not even the most Christian of these Christian Humanists, Lefevre, rightly understood the great Apostle, as Luther correctly remarked as early as the nineteenth of October, 1516. Much less did the wise Erasmus comprehend him. The first reformatory declaration after all which does Paul complete justice, if not in the letter at least in the spirit, is Luther's lecture of Romans of the year 1515-16, which was long lost and forgotten.

Since these Humanists failed to understand Paul they were likewise unable to appreciate the other representatives of the primitive Christian faith. What Erasmus, for example, praises as the philosophy of Christ with a great show of fine words, is not the Christianity of the New Testament, much less the "Christianity of Christ." It is merely a "Moralism" trimmed with Christian elements after the manner of Minucius Felix and other ancient Catholic apologists, for the basic ideas of which the same authorities must be held responsible which were followed by Minucius, namely, Cicero and Seneca.

What, according to Erasmus, were in the ultimate analysis the constituent parts of the "philosophy" or the "theology of Christ"? The new law, that is, ascetic morality, the belief in Providence, and the belief in a retribution in after life. Solely in this narrow moralizing circle of ideas does the great writer move with that calm assurance and confidence which personal conviction imparts. As soon as he ventures beyond these Erasmus begins to vacillate between skepticism and traditional faith, a striking proof of how little all the ideas lying outside of this sphere mean for his own inner life. If we keep this in mind we can understand why Erasmians like Zwingli and Capito, for example, later join the Evangelical movement, or why others like Erasmus himself, Julius Pflug, Gropper and Witzel more or less definitely offered their services to the Catholic Reformation. The meager religious rations upon which they subsisted might be very profitably employed for the criticism of popular religion and of the then immensely complicated theology of the Church; for a time also they might serve the educated classes, who began to feel more and more homeless in the Church, as a substitute for the seriously felt want of simple and clear religious ideas in the public worship of the declining Middle Ages, but they were much too general and feeble to permanently satisfy religious needs. They would inevitably loose their influence over the spirits as soon as they were confronted with an inwardly more powerful and richer conviction, be that Luther's "philosophy of faith" or the mysticism of Loyola.

Less mature still than the religious ideas of Erasmus appear his ethical concepts if we turn the light on them. To be sure, he occasionally protested against the differentiation between lay and monastic morality, and emphatically urged that a teacher of children is more highly esteemed before God than a monk, but in spite of his truly fanatic hatred of monasticism, as it stood revealed before his eyes, he never thought of striking at the root of the tree and denying that the old ascetic ideal had any justification for its existence. On the contrary, Erasmus during his whole life remained in theory an ascetic because of his dependence upon the eclectic Stoicism of Roman philosophy. Consequently, he absolutely lacks all understanding of the moral worth of the great moral entities: marriage, the family, and the state, and has no clear conception of the moral significance of vocational labors. Instead, he loved to indulge in communistic ideas and fantasies. However, even here one does not get the impression that he earnestly believes his own communistic views.

Generally speaking one must beware of taking Erasmus too seriously. At times, certainly, he talks in the style of the prophet, but even in that case he again and again drops his solemn tone as soon as a malicious witticism pops into his mind, for at bottom he is a skeptic, scoffer and rhetorician. With genuine and abiding enthusiasm he labors alone for the fur-

therance of linguistic studies after the ideal of the
Humanists, for the reform of the Latin style and
of the learned curriculum.   In reality the unadul-
terated optimist, prudent man of the world and wholly
unphilosophical scholar possesses no religious organ.
That despite all this he felt himself specially called
upon to be a religious reformer, and that he was most
willingly recognized as such by his contemporaries can
be comprehended only if we make clear to ourselves
how strong and general was the discontent prevailing
especially in the educated classes with the official religious practice.   Where such a feeling dominates
people are always ready to see in every critic a reformer and willing to venerate as a prophet every
teacher of morality who, while he does not do away
with the unintelligible teachings of the Church, at
least pushes them aside.

Much more earnest than the great writer who
frankly confessed that there was in his veins not a
drop of martyr's blood, much more serious also than
the other Christian Humanists seem to have been,
appear the spokesmen of the popular opposition. As
their classic representatives we may regard the anonymous author of the Apocalypse of St. Michael. Here
we meet a truly honest and laborious wrestling for a
new ethical point of view. But, how exceedingly confused, how indistinct, how wild and fanatical withal
are all these well-meaning world uplifters. More or
less all of them pay homage to the most absurd so-
cialistic dreams, refuse to recognize as real work anything but hard manual labor, and all are still in some

manner or other held in the bondage of the ascetic ideal of the Church. Thus, the author of the Apocalypse, for example, most energetically combats the overestimation of fasting, while at the same time he still persists in regarding fasting as such as a good work. He further looks upon celibacy as a serious crime, but deems the unmarried life of the priests so necessary that he recommends the most cruel measures for safeguarding this institution. Among other things he suggests that children of priests ought simply to be starved to death. Even the Strassburg "fools," who protested so vigorously against the flight of Brant's friends into the Carthusian monastery, must not be declared principal opponents of asceticism without further proof than the above-cited lines of the old Humanist.

In short, the whole lay opposition to the ethical views of the Church contents itself with the mere expression of sentiment or stops halfway, as in the case of Erasmus. Nowhere, not in Italy, either, does it lead to a clear grasp, let alone a conscious active assertion of a new ethical ideal. For, the few Humanists who, like Lorenzo Valla, ridiculed asceticism as unnatural nonsense, or like Machiavelli both in theory and practice overstepped all behests of morality, can be looked upon as prophets of a new ethical system only on condition that Cæsar Borgia, Ferrante of Naples and other "moraline-free" tyrants of the Italy of those days are also allowed to count as such. Certainly the majority of the Italian Humanists were far from harboring any conscious and prin-

cipal opposition to the ethics of the Church, even
though, in their personal life they paid absolutely no
attention to it whatsoever. Some of them, in fact, and
not the least famous, like the Neoplatonists of Florence, Leon Battista Alberti, Mantovano, Vida and
Sannazaro were Catholics by conviction, and all of
the great artists of Florence: Sandro Botticelli, Fra
Bartolommeo, the Robbia brothers and Michelan-
gelo were avowed and unqualified adherents of the
piety of Savonarola.

Thus the assertion that Luther's ethics are no more
than a "reflex of the mighty life-consciousness of the
Renaissance," or a clever presentation of the lay
morality of the period, is but a striking proof of how
little known at bottom, even at present, are Luther,
the so-called Renaissance, and the temper of the German laity at the end of the Middle Ages. For Luther
never was as "world open" and alive to the world as
many scholars incessantly assume even in our day; also
the "sense of life" is no general or exclusive characteristic of the Renaissance, but rather a phenomenon
which we meet at all times, and hence also in the Middle Ages, within circumscribed groups of the educated
and ruling classes.

If, then, Luther is not to be credited with originality
no other course remains open to us than after the
recipe of any philosophical mythology to make the
"idea" or the spirit of the time, or the genius of the
German people, or the joint will, or whatever else
we choose to call that wholly unknown and invisible
idol, responsible for the new ethical ideals of the Re-

former. However, that would mean conjuring up ghosts for the purpose of solving an historical problem, or would be tantamount to an interpretation of historical facts on the basis of a mythological text. We had, therefore, better leave spirits and ghosts, even the much-admired genius of the German people, alone and be content with simply setting forth the fact that Luther's ideal was his own discovery, at the same time, however, in a measure the fulfillment of a tendency and desire long present in the laity, though so far it had manifested itself very indistinctly and confusedly.

CHAPTER IX.

Luther as the Prophet of a New Religious and Ethical Ideal.

THE considerations just mentioned amply show
that the Reformer may with justice be called a
prophet of a new religious point of view and a creator
of a new ethical ideal, despite the fact that he exhibits traits of mediævalism. Many things passed
current as religion at the time when Luther stepped
forth: The veneration of God in the spirit and the
worship of the host, reverential consideration of the
life of Christ and the cult of saints, relics and images,
the purification and sanctification of the soul and the
most superficial fulfillment of the ordinances of the
Church, humble self-sacrifice in the interest of the
poor and sick, and the wholly mechanical completion
of all sorts of good works, such as fasting, saying the
rosary, pilgrimages, almsgiving, founding of masses,
donating pictures, candles, altars, soul-baths, entering
into an order or a religious fraternity, the purchase
and sale of indulgences, and untold others. Christian
and pagan, sublime and mean, holy and unholy, indeed, altogether, abstruse elements are found thrown
together in an ofttimes exceedingly strange mixture.
Piety was attached to so many things—acts, places,
buildings, customs, formulas, doctrines and institutions—the religious point of view so varicolored and

full of inconsistencies that the question as to the essence of Christianity can for this period scarcely be answered otherwise than: Christianity is everything the Church teaches, does, demands and tolerates. For just this was the most characteristic feature of the Christianity of the day that the Church suffered the most divergent kinds of religion within its bosom: The fact that it demanded the veneration of the supposed *præputium Christi* as well as the veneration of Christ himself; that it erected altars in the same manner to saints, often only in name distinguished from the ancient pagan gods, as to the true God; that it granted a place in the devotion of the faithful to the divinity of Plato and Plotinus as well as to the "Father of our Lord Jesus Christ."

Then Luther appeared, and directly the picture began to change, wherever he found a hearing. The saints toppled from their thrones, purgatory sank into the abyss, the god of Plato and Plotinus became silent. Thousands of altars vanished, divine service, in the old sense stopped entirely. Offerings, masses, priests and sacraments, the Church, all external means and mediators of which, according to the old faith, the divinity had need in order that it might impart to man the forces of salvation were now to be valid no longer. Heaven and earth, present life and future existence appeared altogether transformed.

However, if Luther thus recklessly with his peasant ax assailed the simple polytheism of popular religion, the sublime worship of many gods in the official cult and dogma, and the naïve pantheism of the Mystics

which had so long haunted also the theology of the
time, he did this solely with the purpose of giving light
and air once more to *religion* which threatened to die
of suffocation under the weight of its ancient trap-
pings.

What did Luther himself understand the term religion to mean? Nothing complex, but something
very simple, not a thing which is bound to external
means and mediators, but something wholly spiritual,
internal and personal, not a *knowing* either, but an
attitude of the heart which the individual first experiences as a solace of the conscience. This attitude of
the heart to begin with presupposes the recognition of
the truth: the greatest evil is guilt, the highest boon
abolition of guilt; secondly, the experience which can
always only be acquired personally by the individual:
that man is freed from guilt alone if he unconditionally trusts in the Holy God who reveals himself in
Christ as a merciful Father. This experience, however, is not materialized until this trust in the form of
a divine gift takes possession of the soul, since it is
nothing more than the faith in God as the all-govern-
ing and all-merciful Father.

Thus in Luther's opinion religion, the whole religion, consists in seeking and finding God in Jesus
Christ, who is the mirror of his paternal heart, of loving, fearing and trusting in him alone above all things,
attaching one's heart solely to him and letting it repose
in him alone. But how does man come to Jesus
Christ? Luther replies: With the help of the Spirit
of God through whom God is ever present and active

in the world for the purpose of gathering for himself
a people or a church. The medium which the Spirit
employs for this end is none other than the Word of
God, or the testimony of the benefactions of Christ.
This in turn confronts man in a threefold form:
orally in Christian preaching, visibly in baptism and
the eucharist, and in written form in the Bible as far as
it teaches Christianity, or speaks of the blessing of
Christ.

Thus Christianity as conceived by Luther is not
only a spiritual and inward factor throughout, but is,
in addition, thought of as depending on a medium
which operates only in a spiritual manner—the Word.
Moreover, the Church is not merely viewed as an institution working through purely spiritual means, but
also as an invisible realm governed by an unseen ruler,
Christ, through the invisible means of the Word. This
realm is only in so far connected with the visible
churches as they preach the Word of God and thus in
a sense serve as missionary institutions for the true
Church. For that which in the visible churches really
represents the Church is imperceptible, while the element which can be seen is not the Church but merely
an institution of human law determined in its character by place, time and changing circumstances.

The recognition that religion is an attitude of the
soul which can be awakened and nourished only by
spiritual means is Luther's most significant disclosure.
For all his later discoveries, the abolition of the "extra-
worldly asceticism," the destruction of the Catholic
conception of the mass, etc., are but logical conclu-

sions derived from this first fundamental tenet. Three of these deductions came to be especially important for the future. First, the knowledge that there is but one way of knowing God and of entering into the fellowship of God, namely, the way of faith. This principle invalidates the whole previous mechanism of theology. At the same time Neoplatonic Mysticism which until then had played such a large part also in private edification lost its title to existence. Secondly, the recognition that there is only one way of worshiping God, the way of faith—faith, in the first place, in the sense of trust in the merciful love of God for the sinner; secondly, as a living and bold confidence in that gracious guidance and providence of God which makes all things serve the best interests of man. As a result of these tenets, the entire earlier divine worship with its immense sacramental and hierarchical apparatus is rendered worthless. The service of God which remains is not, technically speaking, divine service any longer, but only a sort of pedagogical contrivance for the purpose of edifying and educating the congregation. Thirdly, since religion is an attitude of the heart, which must and can be proven by outward acts at all times and in every condition of life, it is an illusion to hold that man must fly this world and withdraw from it. Quite the contrary is true: God placed man into the world for the explicit purpose that he conquer the world in the world, in the position which Providence allotted to him. Not the monastery, therefore, but the secular vocation is the normal sphere for proving one's faith and one's love for his fellow

man. Self-evidently, however, mere vocational loyalty alone does not constitute fulfillment of the ethical
ideal. This qualification is met only when this loyalty
springs from obedience to the will of God as revealed
in the natural order of society, and, viewing the calling
as a means of salvation, if one serves his neighbor
in self-denying love. Thereby not alone an equalization of the secular vocations with the calling of the
monk is achieved, such as is occasionally already found
in the German Mystic, John Tauler, but world-renouncing asceticism, monasticism as such has been
overcome in principle and a new ideal of personal conduct in life set up. For not even the word vocation
had been previously in use in the sense which Luther
attributed to it.

Thus, Luther, by the simple discovery that religion
is an attitude of the heart which is spiritual, and hence
cannot be aroused by any material means and must in
its operations not be bound to anything material or
external, came to be not merely a reformer of religion
but also a reformer of ethics, for both religion and
ethics belong together. To be pious means at the
same time to be religious and also to be good. Faith
does not only comfort the conscience, it also fills the
soul with a joyous readiness which is the mother of all
virtue. As a "living, active" thing it causes in man
the desire for moral activity and remains as a never-
ceasing stimulus constantly operative in all moral
action.

Naturally the value of these basic thoughts of Lutheran preaching has been quite differently estimated

in the course of time and in accordance with the prevailing philosophical or religious point of view.
Hence, also, very diverging opinions have been voiced
about the relation of Luther to the Catholic mediæval
system.   We have already learned to know quite a
number of these valuations which are in themselves
more characteristic for their originators than for Luther.   (Cf. Chap. I.)   Consequently, it will at this
point suffice to discuss only the latest effort along this
line, the criticism of the Lutheran Reformation by E.
Troeltsch.

Troeltsch asserts: "The central religious idea of
Protestantism, hence also that of Luther, is the abolition of the Catholic concept of the sacrament.   This
idea, but this idea alone, is the undeniably modern element in Luther's message.   For in its essential basic
principles and expressions early Protestantism is only
a recasting of the mediæval idea."   This thesis must
in the first place be called into question for reasons of
simple historical logic.   Instead of starting out from
the positive fundamental ideas of Luther, Troeltsch
places an undoubtedly very noteworthy negative consequence of these positive tenets in the foreground and
labels it the central idea of Protestantism.   Had he
immediately considered the obvious question how
"Luther came to break through the Catholic system
just at this central point" he would scarcely have been
able to avoid recognizing that the so-called "central
idea" is a different one, namely, the new notion of
religion which was given doctrinal expression in the
phrase "justification by faith alone," that is, the con-

ception of "subjective religion" as an attitude of man, of "objective religion" as a revelation of the sentiment of God. From these premises the abolition of the Catholic concept of the sacrament, namely, the belief that salvation is a force which must be conceived materially, and in the communication of which to man God binds himself to specific material mediums, follows automatically.

Moreover, historically this view of the situation is the only justifiable one. At first Luther in 1515-16 gained his new view of grace, faith and justification. Only after this did he in the Address on the Babylonian Captivity of the Church take the offensive against the Catholic notion of the sacrament. It is perfectly true that of all his writings this treatise made the deepest impression on his contemporaries. But why did it have such a powerful effect? Because it struck the point at which the inner opposition of Luther to the Catholic system appeared outwardly in the most striking fashion.

Of greater moment, however, is the question: Must we see in Luther's view on grace, faith and justification in reality nothing more than a transformation of the mediæval idea, or, as Troeltsch expresses it, merely new solutions of mediæval Catholic problems? Judging only from the first surface impressions this claim does indeed not seem wholly without justification. In the Catholic system the doctrine of justification occupies the central position, in the Protestant body of dogma the same is true; in Catholicism the concepts grace, faith, good works play an important rôle, in

Protestantism likewise, etc. But at the very outset we are struck by the observation that Luther was not at all in need of the concept of justification in order to give clear and unabridged expression to his religious ideas: it does not occur a single time either in his large or small catechism. Furthermore, it is certainly not a negligible circumstance that all these concepts have quite a different meaning in Luther's message than in Catholicism. They have been completely de-catholicized, de-materialized, rendered more inward, more personal by the new fundamental view of religion. Grace ceases for Luther to be a supernatural force or remedy which through the sacraments is poured into man, but is nevertheless meant to bring about in him spiritual and ethical effects. It has become a "sentiment of God," which is made known in the "Word of God," and operates through this medium as otherwise also an attitude is made manifest and operates by means of the Word. Justification is not thought of as a sort of physical miracle by means of which the substance sin is suddenly driven out by the supernatural substance grace, but as a spiritual psychological miracle which is consummated in the soul of man wholly without material expedients and which consists of nothing more than the acquisition of a new point of view, namely, the unconditional faith in the gracious disposition of God. Faith is not pictured as the external submission of man to the doctrine of the Church which confronts him as a body of external legal ordinances, but again as an attitude, an attitude, however, which does not relate to something external, be it the Church or a dogma, but again to an attitude, the sentiment of God.

Thus, though we find everywhere the same concepts they have a totally different meaning. How anyone can find in this fact merely a transformation of the mediæval idea is difficult to comprehend. To men who employ the logic of this world the expression *transformation* is certainly in this case meaningless, unless we understand *form* to signify the essence of the matter, or, to speak with Plato, the idea, and not the form in the commonly accepted sense.

However, are we not at least justified in regarding these teachings of the Reformer as new solutions of mediæval Catholic problems? Catholic theologians, as we have repeatedly indicated, ever since the fourteenth century, manifest a desire to free religious thought from the bonds of ancient naturalism and substantialism. Duns Skotus, by conceiving God strictly as *will* and *person* attempts to do away with the vestiges of naturalistic pantheism in the concept of God. Further, he endeavors to kill off naturalism in the notion of sin and hereditary sin by viewing them purely as manifestations of the will. Through his doctrine of merit he is undermining also the old conception of religion as a private law relationship between God and man, and to a certain degree even endeavors to spiritualize the idea of grace by differentiating between sacramental grace and justificatory grace. Okkam and his school faithfully follow his footsteps. They carry out the criticism of these fundamental concepts of the Catholic system even more rigidly, and further, begin the attempt of uprooting the hierarchical concept of the Church. At the same time, however, the Mystics commence ever more and more to push aside for purposes of private edification the hierarchical-cultural apparatus of the Church in order to make room for an inward and personal acquisition of religion such as the earlier Middle Ages, at least among the laity, had not known.

While it is true that all these efforts did not lead to an abolition but only to a disintegration of the Catholic structure, it is, notwithstanding, incontestible that in and with these endeavors tendencies came to light which point forward, but break through fully only in the message of Luther. Does this prove that early Protestantism is in its fundamental characteristics merely a new solution of mediæval Catholic problems? By no means. It only goes to show that already in this period which, ever since Cellarius, has commonly been called by the unfortunate name Middle Ages, tendencies made themselves felt which by and by would necessarily have led to complete disintegration, and if consistently continued finally brought about the utter collapse of the mediæval Catholic system. Such tendencies and new ideas, deadly for Catholicism, are indeed noticeable at the turning of the thirteenth and fourteenth centuries almost simultaneously in all fields of civilized life, so that this period, the era of Pope Boniface VIII, can with good cause be designated as the real turning-point of the ages.

In this period for the first time, both in the political theories of the French publicists and in the political practices of the French monarchy, the Augustinian-Mediæval conception of the universal association of Christian humanity is opposed by the modern ideal of the sovereign national state which laid claim not only to complete autonomy but also to unrestricted control over all the fields of the material and spiritual life of its subjects. Simultaneously, with Duns Skotus and Okkam, begins the criticism and dissolution of the Scholastic system, with Mysticism the neutralization of the hierarchical-cultural apparatus of the Church as far as practical piety is concerned. And what is equally noteworthy, the landed and military nobility more and more recedes before the municipal burgher class which everywhere, also in the sphere of intellectual life, seizes the leadership.

All these factors, however, are customarily not regarded as specifically mediæval or Catholic, but rather as significant symptoms of the dissolution of mediæval culture and the forming of a new civilization. The Catholic Church professed this view of the matter with especial energy and very early. It did not dogmatize the "diseased" theology of Duns Skotus and the Okkamists, but the "healthy" religious teachings of Thomas Aquinas. All Mysticism which tried to emancipate itself from the Church it strictly disavowed, the modern idea of the state and the underlying cultural ideal it condemned, Conciliarism, Episcopalism, Gallicanism, in short, all the political, ecclesiastical and theological efforts at reform which in any way seemed to threaten the continued existence of its system it rebuffed. And there is no doubt that the Church from its point of view could not have acted otherwise. Had it given way only in a single point to these tendencies it would have given up its very self.

Hence, though Luther in his development proves in many ways to have been under the influence of Skotian and Okkamistic criticism of the existing dogma and of the edificatory ideas of Mysticism, this does not by any chance justify the assertion that his message was only a new solution of mediæval Catholic problems. In the first place, this criticism and these edificatory thoughts lacked the specifically mediæval Catholic stamp. Secondly, Luther was under the necessity of attaining the very most fundamental ideas of his new religious point of view: the new concepts about man, God, on the relation of man to God, in a bitter conflict with Okkam and Mysticism.

Though it is, of course, true that in this combat Mysticism materially aided him in overcoming Okkam, while the Invincible Doctor assisted him in clearing up his relations to Mysticism (page 107 sq.), yet the net result at which he finally arrived is, nevertheless, quite a good deal more than a mere crossbreeding of Okkamism and Mysticism. For in the third place, the problem which is uppermost in this struggle, the question: How will I, the individual, gain assurance of forgiveness? was propounded neither by Okkam nor by the Mystics, nor can it be arrived at from the premises of both by a process of deduction. On the contrary, both tried with all their might to engender and hold fast precisely that peculiar attitude of consciousness and frame of mind which Luther wished to overcome. In fact, they endeavored as far as possible to increase this disposition, this wavering 'twixt hope and fear; the Okkamists because under such conditions the pious person is more inclined to moral effort, the Mystics because only thus can he persist in that perfect humility which accepts from God tranquilly even eternal death and damnation. Neither can any of the other varieties of Catholic piety attain or grasp Luther's problem, in fact, it is to them even as a mere problem an impiety and wickedness from which the truly pious man turns away with disgust.

Consequently, if one wishes correctly to determine the relationship of the Reformer to the religion of the Middle Ages there remains no other way than to directly invert the formula of Troeltsch and to state that: Luther's message is the solution of a new religious problem on the basis of Okkamistic criticism of the Catholic system and the practical edificatory speculations of the late mediæval Mystics.

However, Troeltsch did not at all reach his conclusions by the usual historical method. He built up his whole structure not from the front but from the rear. Instead of first determining the content of the mediæval and the Lutheran systems and then comparing the two, he endeavored before all else to ascertain the difference existing between the culture of the present and *all* preceding civilizations of Christian history. Only after that did he pay closer atention to the peculiarities of these older stages of civilzation. This method is certainly a good one for the purpose of clearly presenting certain characteristic features of modern civilization. But these certain characteristics are thereby easily overaccentuated and others of perhaps equal importance are overlooked. At best, as remnants of older epochs of culture, they acquire the taint of illegitimacy and are thus not sufficiently appreciated in their significance for the picture as a whole. Above all, as is invariably the case in such retrospective treatments of history, present and past, are involuntarily placed over against one another from the angle of contrast and not from that of development. In that way the differences of the several cultural stages stand out sharply, while on the other hand, in viewing the steps of cultural growth in the past these differences are unwittingly blurred and weakened and the firm contours as far as possible dissolved, since in this wise the desired effect of contrast is more easily obtained. In short, right in the middle of the process of historical consideration the method of procedure is changed: First, the antitheses which have been noted are heightened and then they are with like energy equalized. It is obvious that no faithful general picture of the period can be gained in this way. The projections will, of necessity, always be somewhat oblique, the perspectives too short, the lights sometimes too glaring, sometimes too colorless even when the portrayer takes pains to work from nature as much as possible, that is, in this case, from the sources.

This peculiar "blunder," which is unavoidable if one employs the method described above has happened to Troeltsch precisely at the point where in his opinion the dependence of early Protestantism on mediæval concepts is tangible, namely, in his estimate of the reformatory concept of authority, of the ethics of the Reformation, and of its view of the Church.

The author explains that in the manner of the Middle Ages, Luther takes for granted that true religion is known, that the content of the revelation can be ascertained exactly and must be respected by everyone inasmuch as revelation is the self-understood authority for everybody. The only difference, according to Troeltsch, is that Luther refuses further to accept the teaching Church as the organ and vehicle of revelation and authority, and is willing to recognize as such only "God's Word," the Bible. This is quite true. But, is this concept of authority in fact characteristic only of the mediæval Church and early Protestantism? No! It is well known in primitive Christianity, because the same significance which for Luther attaches to the clear and distinct passages of Holy Writ, attaches for the primitive Christians to the writings in the Hebrew or Alexandrine Canon, the words of Christ and the instructions of the early Christian prophets. They are to both absolute revelation, absolute truth and unconditionally binding authority.

We are, therefore, in this instance dealing not with a specifically mediæval concept but with a concept common to all Christians. The distinctly mediæval and Catholic features, the belief in the revealing function of the teaching Church, and the externalization and materialization of the notion of authority which flows from it, Luther has overcome, and really *overcome, not* merely *transformed* by simply substituting

for the teaching Church the external authority of the
letter of the Bible as is still so frequently asserted.

In Luther's opinion the Word of God can become
revelation and authority actually only for him in
whom it has impressively proved itself as a Word of
God through direct action of God upon his soul.
Whether this correction of the old doctrine of authority is sufficient may well be a matter of contention. That the concept of authority itself, however,
is indispensable to Christianity and is also so regarded
by the "New Protestantism" is substantiated at every
step by the most recent Protestant theology. For,
what are the speculations about the idea of Christianity and about the historical Christ as medium of
the revelation and as authority other than attempts
to spiritualize the ancient doctrine of authority and
thereby to securely fix it for modern thought?

As a student of ethics and sociology Troeltsch tends
to place even greater emphasis on the second point, the
inner relationship of Lutheran and mediæval Catholic
ethics. He asserts: Luther's Christianity also is at
bottom still entirely ascetic. In his mind the Reformer differs from the Middle Ages only in that he
demands not an ascetic attitude toward the external
world, but an internal asceticism, no more an outward
but an inward fleeing of the world, that is, an inner
independence of the heart, ever active in the midst of
the world, from the world and its pleasures and suf-
ferings. This again is undoubtedly true. The spiritual dominion (*imperium spirtuale*) over the world
which the Reformer praises in such mighty tones has

indeed no connection with the modern cultural idea. It means nothing more than the inner freedom and independence from the world. But it need hardly be said that the striving for this inner independence is not characteristic alone of the Middle Ages and the reformers but of the Christianity of all ages and places, that consequently we have here again to deal with a common Christian trait of Lutheran preaching, and not with one that is peculiar to the Middle Ages. The specifically mediæval and Catholic phases Luther has abolished in this case also. Again, it is the "materialization of the religious idea," the notion that man can only then keep himself wholly undefiled by the world if he also externally severs completely all connection with the world, its gifts and its tasks, and the assertion that the ascetic's supernatural mode of life is the straight road to salvation.

The same in every particular is true of Luther's relation to the Catholic idea of the Church. The common Christian feature of this concept, the notion already current in primitive Christianity, that Christ through his Spirit is always present in the world in order to lead man to faith and thereby to a share in his kingdom, were retained by the Reformer. The distinctly Catholic elements in this idea, however, the conviction that the realm of Christ is visibly represented in the hierarchically constituted institution of the Church, and the belief that a fixed external organization is essential for Christ's kingdom, these again he wholly set aside.

However, did Luther hereby abolish completely all

claims of the mediæval ecclesiastical system, above all the most important one that the Church was appointed for the purpose of guiding, regulating and ruling the whole civilized life as supreme lawgiver, and that it was privileged as God's appointed administratrix of the doctrine and the sacraments, to permanently keep the faithful under its tutelage? Indeed not; he did not radically break with the Middle Ages in this respect either. He calmly retained the typically mediæval institution of the national church. But in so doing he not only recast it but really made it into something quite different. In the first place he attributed to it quite another significance for religious life. Henceforth, as far as it is an externally visible legal institution it does not count any longer as an institution of divine but as one of human law. It is, furthermore, not regarded as in itself a medium of salvation but only in as far as it teaches Christ. Above all, it is not any more accounted the only and exclusive institution of salvation but must permit all churches, religious institutions and associations, which in any way serve the cause of Christ to pass as such. For wherever Christ is preached there is Christ's kingdom, or the Church in the ideal sense, while the kingdom of God is not infallibly present where the external legal institution of the Church is found.

Pursuant to this view the Reformer also formulated in a different manner than the Middle Ages the task of the national church. It has no other call than that of preaching Christ. It has, therefore, neither the right nor the duty to order also the physical life of man, nor has it any occasion to hold mankind in guardianship through laws and prescriptions as though man were not able to attend to this himself with the aid of reason. Further, the Church must content itself with preaching Christ, that is, it is in substance nothing more than a missionary institution, a school for those who are not yet true Christians. Therefore, it is neither competent nor authorized to permanently lead, rule, or hold in tutelage the true Christians, or those who believe in Christ and who earnestly desire to be Christians.

Thus in the first place the mediæval cultural idea is done away with in principle. The Church is once more limited to its immediate vocation, the saving of souls. In fact, this most direct task has now become its sole function, for the day of judgment is near at hand, the number of those who must still be saved is still so great that in the eyes of the Reformer all other possible activities recede before this one.

For that reason also he never answered in principle the old problem "Christianity and Civilization," which his Reformation had set up anew. He was content to take a stand, in the affirmative, on the question whether a Christian could with good conscience be an official, soldier, prince or merchant, and, furthermore, emphatically reiterated that it was impious and immoral to lend money at usurious rates of interest. That is all! This much is certain, nevertheless, he did not regard a complete adaptation of Christianity to civilization and of civilization to Christianity such as the Middle Ages had striven to attain by subjecting the whole cultural life to the dominion of the Church either as possible or desirable.

The national church, however, had not only for Luther ceased to be the lawgiver and leader of the whole cultural life. It had also lost the right to permanently patronize the faithful. Actually the Church had nothing to say any more to the true Christians. They had outgrown its discipline. For that very reason they are now in a position to realize an ideal which the national church as an external institution of law never can realize by itself: the idea of a Christian association. True Christians, namely, can combine in so-called congregations and then in the first place in free private religious exercises edify themselves; secondly, they can mutually educate one another after the Christian ideal by means of strict discipline, and thirdly, they can jointly practice all kinds of good works of brotherly love. Only in this manner is the "true type of Evangelical order" achieved, for thus a form of religious organization is attained which corresponds to the Evangelical view that all Christian believers as priests are able and competent to decide on questions of religious and moral life by themselves.

At the very moment when he reorganizes the national church, in the Evangelical sense, the Reformer also considers the foundation of an altogether new kind of religious organization which is to take its place side by side with the former. And he certainly was quite serious in this plan, even though in view of the moral immaturity of the masses he as early as 1527 gave up the hope that he himself would in his own life-

time still be able to establish such congregations, and
though he was not in the position to voice approval of
the Hessian attempt to forthwith put this project
into execution in connection with the reorganization
of the national church.

Therefore, Luther did not simply retain the mediæval institution of the national church. On the contrary, in this instance also he abolished what was specifically mediæval and Catholic. He gave an altogether new definition of the tasks of the national
church, and already planned the founding of a completely new type of religious organization in which
for the first time the church ideal which corresponded
to the Evangelical conception of the priesthood of the
faithful—as far as this is possible on earth—was to
find expression. This plan, to be sure, remained a
mere plan for the present, but it is very noteworthy,
notwithstanding, that Luther's thoughts on the practical shaping of religious worship already centered
about the two typical forms of religious organization,
the co-existence and relation of which is just as characteristic for Protestantism as for Catholicism: the
co-existence and relation of world church and monasticism; national church and congregation. He also
fixed the relative value of these two types in such a
way that one can hardly say anything in criticism of
his scheme. Certainly the free association, as far as
it does not degenerate into mere forming of gangs,
i. e., sectarianism, is the true type of Evangelical order
and the ideal calling, but the limits of the national
church also can hardly be characterized more accu-

rately than by the predicates, missionary institution
and school.

In view of these considerations, we may justly assert that the path to an historical appreciation of Luther, but also of the mediæval Catholic system, is
closed to anyone who judges both after the formula:
"The message of Luther is in its essential characteristics only a recasting of the mediæval idea," or
"merely a new solution of mediæval Catholic problems." Exactly the opposite is true. The essential
characteristics and the problems are new with Luther,
the forms have in many respects remained the old. To
be sure, new though the problems and essential characteristics of his preaching are, the poet is right, nevertheless, when he says of him: His spirit is the battleground of two ages. The Middle Ages and modern
times, indeed, continually fought one another within
him, and Luther also like all others, even the most
eminent thinkers, naturally did not at all times succeed in wholly escaping the influence of older habits
of thought, and of prejudices which in principle he
had long ago overcome.

Not infrequently old inherited views cross wholly
new thoughts which Luther had worked out himself.
Besides, he is naturally, in the conflict with others,
prone to stress most sharply these vulnerable positions
in his system and to move them into the foreground
so energetically as though it were a matter of life and
salvation. The classic example for this is the controversy over the Lord's Supper. Perhaps more clearly
still, however, than in his doctrine of the Sacraments,

this peculiar two-faced character of his thought comes to light in his utterances on the nature and worth of marriage, and in his expositions on the tasks and the origin of the secular power, or the state.

There have been few men who thought so highly of marriage and who so ardently recommended it as Luther. He never tires of praising it as an institution of God and as a school of the most perfect morality, as the sweetest, loveliest and most chaste form of life. To be sure, the physical communion of married people is the basis for the normal conduct of married life, but it is not the only, let alone the highest purpose of wedlock. Its supreme end is the founding of a not merely natural but also moral life companionship between husband and wife which rests upon community of moral duties, especially in the education of the children, and upon community of religious conviction. However, these considerations are ever again crossed by an ascetic reflection of which the Reformer is never able wholly to divest himself. He, too, cannot help seeing in the furor of the sexual impulse something unclean, unholy, in fact, a manifestation of sin. Pursuant to·this fact Luther always looks upon marriage in the first place as a remedy prescribed by God against the tyrannical power of sensuality, through the wise use of which the unrest of passion is moderated and man and woman are enabled to enter a moral life companionship.

The same observations hold good of his utterances on the task, the purpose and the origin of the secular power. People even to-day speak of Luther's view,

indeed of "Luther's Doctrine of the State and Society." They would do well to forego this formulation at the very outset, for it rouses altogether false
expectations. As little as the Reformer knows the
expressions state and society, so little does he know
the thing itself. A state and a society in the modern
sense of these terms did not exist in the Central and
Northern Germany of his day. There were only a
great number of statelike formations which all, however, furnished a very incomplete view of the state.
Small wonder, therefore, that the Reformer also in
speculating about the state always centers his attention exclusively upon the strongest state-forming factor in those territories—the government. Moreover,
in accordance with the political development of his
surroundings he starts out from mediæval concepts in
fixing the duties of the government. Like the classical Middle Ages Luther uses as the point of departure
and presupposition of all political speculation the
idea of the universal state of "Christendom," or of
"the common order of Christian love." The preser-
vation and government of this body is to his mind
everywhere entrusted to the three sacred orders, or
the natural hierarchy: those who have the office of
providing, the laboring class; those whose duty it is
to defend, the noble and military class; those whose
function is instruction, the teaching class.

Like the classical Middle Ages he is furthermore
interested only in two problems of political science,
the question about the duties and purposes, and the
closely related one about the origin of the military

order, or the government. 'And at least this last question he, too, answers quite in the manner of Augustine
when he claims that the institution of a government
had become necessary only as a result of sin, and that
the ideal Christian really needed no government. For
he says: "If all the world were composed of true
Christians, no king, prince, lord, sword or law were
needful or of any use. What would be the purpose
of these, since Christians have the Holy Spirit in their
heart, who teaches and persuades them not to do anyone harm, to love all mankind, to suffer wrong, even
death itself, from everyone cheerfully and willingly."

From the foregoing we can understand that his
thoughts about the duties of the government are in
general very much like those of the Middle Ages.
The secular power must keep down the bad people
within its territories by a strict handling of the sword.
Further, should its subjects be attacked from without
it must defend them against external foes in necessary wars—for only this type of warfare is permitted.
The guarding of the external and internal peace,
therefore, is the true function of the government.

Notwithstanding, government, though it has come
about only as a result of sin, is still a divine institution and foundation. This is not only expressly stated
in Holy Writ, it is also told to everyone by the natural
right or the natural law which God in creation inscribed into the heart of man and which for that reason may also be called divine right or divine law. This
natural law is the aggregate of all those moral claims,
the validity of which every man recognizes without

question, because "his soul is fashioned and created according to them." It includes all those claims which have in the Ten Commandments once more been explicitly inculcated. At the same time, however, by this law, all those institutions are sanctioned as divinely ordained which are safeguarded by the decalogue: marriage, the family and government. For the government "belongs to the paternal order," hence it may, on the strength of the natural law, lay claim to the same rights as the parents, may by virtue of natural law demand from all subjects honor, taxes, tolls, all manner of services, and obedience even to the point of sacrificing life itself. Further, it may on these same grounds proceed against thieves, robbers, murderers and rebels with the sword.

But the concept of natural law is even broader in scope. Already Luther holds to the opinion that it legitimatizes, as divinely appointed, the whole agrarian and class organization of society in the era of the Reformation, and he stamps every attempt at subversion of this order as a crime. This is a view which was of the utmost significance for the whole future of Lutheranism but which at bottom is very ancient. The concept of natural law is a heritage of Greek philosophy, the equalization of this natural law with the decalogue is already known to the ancient Catholic theologians, and the thought of basing the whole secular legal and social order upon it is quite familiar to the Middle Ages.

Luther's political and social points of view are, therefore, in some very essential phases most anti-

quated, mediæval and un-modern. But here again
it becomes manifest that his spirit is the battleground
of two ages. Here also Luther victoriously broke
through the mediæval attitude at the decisive points,
for the classical Middle Ages regard the holder of the
secular power merely as the bailiff of the Church, secular law is held to be law only in as far as it does not
conflict with ecclesiastical law and is not protested by
the Church. To be sure, this idea is opposed by that
of the sovereign national state already in the writings
of the French publicists of the age of Boniface VIII.
But Luther is the first person who succeeds in de-
stroying its religious roots in that he dissolves the
dogma of the divine call of the Church to the government of the world and of the religious sanctions behind the Church organization. Not until the appearance of Luther, therefore, is the sovereignty of the
secular power established beyond a doubt also for
the religious consciousness, not until then was every
attempt of the Church to interfere in the political and
social life as giver of moral standards and of laws
demonstrated to be irreligious.

But Luther does not only declare the secular power
free from the guardianship of the Church, he also
destroys the view which had been made current by
Wiclif, Huss and their followers and which attributed to the Bible law-making authority for the political and social life. Thus he also freed the secular
government and the secular law from the tutelage of
the letter of the Bible. He did this by asserting that
all legal prescriptions of Holy Writ have lost binding

force for the Christians, and that they are important only as examples of traditional legislation.

At the same time Luther energetically champions an extension of the duties of the state after the modern theory of the state. Though he believes that the guarding of the external and internal peace is the proper function of government, he nevertheless demands further that the government through the erection of schools and libraries and by means of a certain measure of compulsory education provide for the upbringing of its subjects; further, that it promote order and decency in its territories by strict use of the police against idleness, beggary, drunkenness and luxury of dress; that it curb all abuse in trade and traffic by severe laws against usury and the large corporations; that it intercede with word and deed for the poor, widows and orphans, and that otherwise also it make the material welfare of the people its concern, inasmuch as it is a further duty of the government to instruct everyone how to manage his house and home and how to win money and goods.

Even Luther, therefore, sees the ideal state in his mind's eye as a "Kulturstaat." True, this ideal was not altogether new. It asserts itself already in the policies of the city states of the thirteenth and fourteenth centuries, and since the fifteenth is gaining influence also on the policies of the territorial princes. But no one before Luther conceived and portrayed the "paternal vocation" of the state so broadly and definitely. He also is responsible for the introduction into political speculation of the so-called patriarchal theory, according to which the governmental authority is considered as a developmental form of the paternal power, and it is he who established the notion that the prince is the father of his country and must rule as such. Thus, he paved the way for a new concept of the state and of political life, which though it is not identical with the modern view of the state, nevertheless prepared the path for the modern "Kulturstaat," at least in Lutheran Germany.

Is the view of the Reformer about the relation of the secular power to religion and public worship also part of those ideas which point beyond the Middle Ages? This question has recently been much discussed but answered very differently, depending entirely upon the degree of prominence given to the opinions of the young or the old Luther. For Luther in these two periods of his life holds somewhat diverging views on this question. Throughout his life the Reformer clings firmly only to the one principle: the government has no right to decide questions of belief, and also to the conviction that "thoughts are not dutiable." From this follows further that the old mediæval law on heresy which under certain conditions made also the private opinions of people the subject of an ecclesiastical criminal procedure must cease operating.

Did Luther always draw the same conclusions from these fundamental considerations? We must in this connection remember in the first place that the law of the time besides heresy recognized also another crime against religion: public blasphemy. This was generally regarded as a serious offense which the government was in duty bound to punish. The German imperial laws of 1495, 1512, 1530 and 1532, in agreement with the Roman law, provide for this crime "depending upon the circumstance and form of the person and the blasphemous act" in life and limb, at least, in case of relapse. Did Luther ever judge differently on this point? As far as we know, never. Only the question as to what was to be regarded as blasphemy was apparently not clear to him at the beginning. (Enders V, 117.) Not until 1530 was he moved to give this matter serious consideration, and thereupon he came to the conclusion, blasphemy is all public teaching and slander against a public article of faith, for instance, against an article of the Apostolic Creed. (Weimar Ed., XXXI, 1, 18.) Thus, a person who openly teaches that Christ is not God. but a mere man, that he has not atoned for our sins, but that this must be done by everyone personally, that there is no such thing as a resurrection, an eternal life, and a hell, cannot be tolerated by the government and must be banished from the country. Herewith no one is *forced* to believe, for *privately everybody* may *believe what he wishes,* only public teaching and slander against the "common articles of Christendom" is interdicted.

This shows sufficiently that the Reformer never thought of unrestricted freedom of teaching and religion. The mere possibility of such a thing was altogether foreign to the thought of this age. Nevertheless, Luther's definition leaves a wide range for teach-

ing and for blasphemy. Did he within this scope hold
unrestricted freedom of teaching to be lawful and
proper? For the first, yes! As late as the summer of
1522, he says, in writing about Münzer and his associates: "There must be some sects." (Weimar Ed.,
XV, 218.) "Let the intellects clash and meet in controversy. If as a result some are led astray, let them
go, such is the fortune of war. Where there is conflict and battle, there some must fall or be wounded."

This restricted freedom of teaching has only one
barrier: Rebellion must be preached under no circumstance whatsoever. Where this is done there the government must instantly interfere and straightway "interdict the soil" to such preachers, whether they be
Lutherans or adherents of Münzer. However, under
the impression of the great disaster which Karlstadt,
Münzer and their companions had occasioned "in par-
ishes whither no one had sent them" his attitude on
this point is changed. "Oppositionary preaching,"
he writes in 1530 (Weimar Ed., XXXI, 1, 209),
"engenders not merely sectarianism, but also discord,
hatred and jealousy in secular affairs." In case,
therefore, anywhere Papists and Lutherans publicly
preach and swear against one another, and if the Lutherans notice that their preaching is not meeting
with sympathetic ears, then they must observe
silence and recede. But if, for conscience' sake,
neither of the parties wants to give way, then
the government is to take a hand and to interrogate
the combatants. Whichever side then cannot prove
its stand from Scriptures the government must command to remain silent.

More intolerable still, however, than such public dissension are the secret machinations of the hedge priests. Anyone who without office or command teaches secretly must certainly be planning rebellion or something worse. Such an one must not be permitted to go on, even though he were the Angel Gabriel himself, but must be turned over to the proper master, whose name is Hans, that is, to the executioner. This same rule is applicable also to Lutheran pastors if they dare to secretly preach and teach in the congregation of a Catholic or heretical clergyman without his knowledge or permission.

Of whom is the Reformer thinking when he speaks these harsh words? In the first place of the apostles of the Anabaptists who both secretly and openly taught that no government ought to be tolerated, that no Christian be permitted to hold an office, that private property ought to be done away with, that wife and child must be forsaken and all things ought to be held in common. (Weimar Ed., XXXI, 1, 208.) But were these accusations against the Anabaptists altogether justified? Were not many of them peaceable, quiet and moderate people who were very far from harboring any revolutionary tendencies or intentions? Certainly, but by far the greater number were not harmless by any means, they were distinctly seditious in their opinions. That the existing government was an irreligious institution was the dominant opinion ever since the death of Hubmaier even among the moderates, who never thought of taking the sword themselves. Communistic ideas also were everywhere current in the congregations of the "children of God," and furthermore, the conviction that an adherent of Anabaptism might without further ceremony sever his marriage with a "heathen" and forsake his children in order to wed a "sister." The most radical exponent of all these views was the book-agent Haensel Hutt of Bibra, the most fanatical and bloodthirsty of all the Anabaptist apostles. And it was this wild Apocalyptic himself who gained the largest number of adherents in the Franconian and Thuringian possessions of the Saxon House.

It is therefore not surprising that the Wittenberg theologians in October, 1531, in an arbitrament answer the question whether the government ought to punish the Anabaptists with the sword in the affirmative and that also Luther adds his "placet" with the characteristic motivation that "though it may seem cruel to punish them with the sword, it is more cruel still that they condemn the office of the Word and suppress the true doctrine, and, besides, wish to destroy the *regna mundi* (the secular government.)" (C. R. IV, 740.) A like verdict Luther uttered in an opinion rendered at the time of the Anabaptist horrors at Münster on the twentieth of October, 1532 (DeWette VI, 151), and a similar one in a memorial addressed to the Landgrave of Hesse on the fifth of June, 1536. (Enders X, 346.) In this latter document he declares that the prince is empowered to punish the Anabaptists with the sword if for no other reason because they had, despite their oath, again secretly entered his territories and were seducing the people. He advises, however, that at all times, in accordance with the circumstances in the individual cases, mercy ought to go side by side with punishment. Finally, he once more briefly summarizes his attitude on this question in a Table Talk of September, 1540 (Mathesius, 378) : "The Anabaptists who rebel against the government the Elector lawfully punishes with death, the others, who harbor fanatical opinions, are mostly banished from the country." It is apparent, therefore, that in the matter of freedom of teaching Luther gave up his earlier attitude. Until 1525 he energetically champions a restricted freedom of teaching, later on he refuses to hear of it. Up to 1525 he merely pleads banishment, even when notorious rebels like Münzer are concerned, later on he deems the death penalty justified in such cases.

What were his views in earlier years about blasphemy is not clear. But later, in agreement with Melanchthon and in harmony with the current law, he evidently regards blasphemy, that is, every kind of public teaching and slander against the doctrines of the Apostolic Creed as a crime worthy of capital punishment. (Enders VIII, 163.) This certainly is a significant change in his opinions. But are we right if, in view of this, we assert: In his age Luther returned again to the old law on heresy? No. He neither knows nor desires an Inquisition, nor an ecclesiastical heresy trial, he knows only a secular punitive procedure exercised in disturbance of the peace of the Church through discordant teachings, in seditious agitation against the established political order and in public blasphemy, and he regards the death penalty as proper only in those cases where also the laws of the state demand it, in rebellion and blasphemy. Private religious opinion, however, is not interfered with either before or after. Personal convictions are never to become the subject of criminal procedure. If we compare with these principles and with the practice of the Lutheran governments based upon them the principles and the practice of the Papal Inquisition in Italy since 1542, we will not long remain in doubt about the difference between Lutheranism and Catholicism also with regard to freedom of thought and of teaching.

Very similar to his position on freedom of teaching is the Reformer's attitude on the freedom of worship. In his younger years he did not busy himself with this question at all, later on he always answers it on the basis of three principles which to him have the force of axioms: public worship is part of the municipal law, and is therefore part of the public order; the preaching of two divergent doctrines necessarily leads to sedition; true religion is known and it alone has any claim to public toleration. From these premises he draws the conclusion: The suppression of the public Catholic worship is a duty of the government, the suppression of Evangelical preaching, however, on the other hand is an unjustifiable tyranny over religious belief.

Hence Luther not only approves of the prohibition of Catholic worship but demands it, in fact, in his opinion, it is not religious coercion if the government forces gross slanderers into the Evangelical services and makes them memorize the Evangelical catechism, so that they, at least, learn the "economy," that is, learn how they ought to behave as citizens and heads of families. For in Luther's eyes the national church is not only a missionary institution for the kingdom of Christ, but also a public educational institution in which civic morality and decency is inculcated, and hence it has claim not only upon protection but also for material aid from the government. However, all this does not in any way touch the freedom of private worship: "In their chambers also those of other religious convictions may adore and worship whomsoever they wish and as many gods as they want to." Hence, if it pleases the monks behind closed doors to commit their blasphemous acts they must be hindered just as little as the Jews in their synagogues.

But what if Catholic princes retaliate in kind upon Evangelical believers and suppress the free preaching of the gospel? They are in that case doubtless tyrants, manifestly rebels against God's Word. However, may they be treated as such, is it allowable to rise and plot against them and put an end to their rule? By no means. If they do not wish to tolerate Evangelical preaching, they may do so on their own responsibility and at their own peril. But they are held to at least grant to their Evangelical subjects the free permission to leave their lands. Only in a single instance did the Reformer forsake this principle to which otherwise he adhered strictly. He conceded to the Evangelical princes, though not to the

Evangelical subjects the right to proceed with the sword against those who defend false doctrine and worship and who try to coerce others into the same.

Does it not follow from all this that Luther granted to the secular power the right to decide questions of faith and to determine the public worship in their territories? Not at all. The government has over against religion *only duties, no rights.* After the opinion of Luther it occupies toward the question of worship much the same position as that which the modern state in the opinion of the modern world occupies over against the task of fostering science. Just as it is generally demanded to-day that the state protect science and furnish it with abundant means, while, nevertheless, the state is denied any right to prescribe to the devotees of science their methods or the conclusions they must reach, so Luther also regards the relationship of the state to religion as one of reverence, from which there result for the political power only duties, but no rights whatsoever. It is the duty of the Emperor and the princes to check the evils in the Church by calling a council (Address to the Nobility, 1520); it is a duty of the territorial lords to institute a system of church inspection, to suppress Catholic worship, to prepare a free path for God's Word by calling Evangelical preachers. But even by the most loyal fulfillment of these duties the government never acquires the right to rule the Church and to decide on questions of belief.

Nothing is further from the truth, therefore, than the notion that the system in which the political sovereign controls the Church is the form of church régime which most closely corresponds to Luther's ideals. On the contrary, we may assert that this form of church government, as far as it is government at all, as the very name shows, is in direct opposition to Luther's principal concept of religion.

It is furthermore impossible to bring this form of church government into direct connection historically with the Reformation. For it is not a product of the reformatory speculation at all, but, as especially the development of the Church of England proves in a classical example, an outcome of late mediæval public law fertilized by ideas emanating from the ancient Germanic "Eigenkirchentum." This latter fact, of course, in no way decides its value for the present time, for the question as to how a legal system or an idea originated, is for the determination of its worth just as indifferent as the question whether its author was beautiful or homely.

Moreover, as little as the idea of the state church, so little can the modern natural law ideal of the self-governing congregation, made up of the payers of the church tax, be regarded as a legitimate development from Lutheran principles. It is true, the Reformer, in the first years of the Evangelical movement, frequently enough argued: Every Christian assembly or congregation is capable and empowered to judge on all doctrine and to install or depose its teachers, *i. e.,* its pastors; every Christian has the right to reprimand the preacher in a respectful and modest manner should he err. But on what fact is this competency based in the opinion of Luther? Self-evidently not on mere external membership in a congregation but on membership in the ideal community of the faithful. And why? Because this right presupposes the ability to "judge all doctrines," which, however, is found only in those people to whom God has given faith, and to whom he has thereby opened an understanding for his promises and commands, or his revelation.

It follows from this that all the utterances about the congregation from the years 1520-23 must be judged in accordance with the expositions about the assembly or congregation of the year 1525-27 with which we are familiar. Not until he gave these had the Reformer finished the difficult task of finding an organization which conformed to his religious ideals and which did not abolish or disturb the efficient operation of the national church. In these latter pronouncements for the first time all that is made clearly apparent after which Luther had always striven in obscure longing. In them also for the first time is distinctly shown that the ideal which he had before his eyes was not the autonomous congregation, but the self-governing community of the true believers. From out of this ideal, it is quite evident, one may possibly arrive at the autonomous congregation of the Independents, but never at the modern natural-law theory of the congregation.

Thus in the soul of the Reformer ancient and inherited, wholly new and novel, truly mediæval and unquestionably modern ideas and moods intertwine and permeate one another. Hence it is not an easy matter to characterize Luther as a thinker. One who considers him from the standpoint of present-day civilization will naturally always be struck especially by the "Old-Franconian" and mediæval elements of his character, and he will, therefore, be in danger of overlooking its undoubtedly modern phases. A person who approaches him from the Middle Ages, however, will, on the contrary, be most impressed by the undeniably modern features of his thought, so that he will be tempted to disregard the Middle Ages and to portray Luther as a modern man. In reality he is neither the one nor the other. He is not a mediæval man, for he burst the iron ring of the mediæval view of the world at just the point where so far it had most strongly bound even the most vigorous spirits. Nor is the Reformer a modern man, for he retained many genuinely mediæval concepts.

However, Luther can likewise not well be conceived as a so-called transitional type. For in the first place the transition which is connected with his name is not merely a transition, but a revolution, which attacked the very foundations of the cultural system as it had hitherto existed, a revolution through which cultural life was led over into entirely new channels. He is, secondly, not a transitional type because this revolution was not merely automatically consummated in his person, not merely experienced by him as an exterior occurrence, but because it was executed by him and made an event for mankind through him alone. Thus also as a thinker Luther is not a type, but a "man by himself," who belongs to no age exclusively,

and who for that very reason at the same time is a
"genius" in the classic sense of that term, *i. e.,* a man
who, as a productive force, exerted a most powerful
influence on the contemporary and later world.

Who wishes to do full justice to the Reformer, therefore, dare not attempt merely to portray him as a
product of already existing forces, but must depict
him also as a productive force by determining all those
manifold results which emanated from him. Only
in these does his tremendous productivity become
truly visible. Such a portrayal, however, would be
out of place at this juncture.

Only this one fact may still be emphasized: One
seriously underestimates Luther by considering him
solely as the founder of Lutheranism. That religious
group is only one of the world-historical consequences
of the powerful movement which he called forth.
Side by side with Lutheranism one must always name
also the other great and small church bodies which
owe their existence to this movement: the Reformed
Church, the Church of England, the Schwenkfeldians,
the Independents, and even the Anabaptists and
Quakers. His relation to these churches is much
like that of Augustine to the Catholic Church of the
Middle Ages. Just as Catholicism did not take up
the whole Augustine, so also none of these churches expressed clearly and exhaustively the Christianity of
Luther. In all of them, in a manner of speaking, it
suffered a mediævalization, in the first place already
in this wise that they allowed the remnants of mediæval thought which Luther had not overcome to con-

tinue on; secondly, in that they again accepted genuine mediæval ideas, and thirdly, inasmuch as they in the majority organized as compulsory religious organizations after the type of the mediæval national church.

As Augustine, therefore, did not cease operating when the mediæval ecclesiastical and cultural system dissolved, so Luther also did not stop being effective when those oldest organizations of Protestant Christianity were dissolved. Rather, his influence on religious development continued. It is even now in the Protestant world more vigorous and powerful than that of any other religious personality. But Luther never restricted himself—and in this respect he is again like Augustine—merely to the field of religion. He embraced the whole of cultural life. Mediæval civilization was altogether an ecclesiastical one, i. e., a civilization founded and dominated by the Church. By attacking the Church, therefore, Luther, without realizing it, at the same time provided the impetus for the abolition of the civilization, created and directed by it, and for the growth of a new civilization. To what extent he himself participated in this, and how far, in individual instances, the remoter effects of his religious reform reach, that, to be sure, is far from having been determined in detail. Solely about this there is no doubt: That he blazed a path for the new age at just that point from out of which the recasting of civilization, as things stood, could alone proceed, and that for this reason if for none other he may well be called and celebrated a hero of civilization.

A Pictorial Life

of

Luther

Being the First Publication of
the Collection of Rare Prints
in the Possession of

REV. WILLIAM KOEPCHEN

Who also contributes
the Descriptive Text and Titles

1916
THE CHRISTIAN HERALD
Bible House, New York

ing scenes from the life of Christ. In not a few instances what appeared to be a mere mechanical perusal of a book of pictures has proven a remarkably efficient medium of information and character-formation. But why dilate on something that everybody concedes and no one disputes?

Those were stirring times four hundred years ago. The world seemed out of joint. A battle was on, and the din of the conflict was reverberating through Europe, from the Grampian Hills to the Golden Horn, and from Madrid to Riga. Yea, they were telling in the streets of Jerusalem how a German friar had defied the Bishop of Rome. They were noting, some with plain satisfaction, some with amazement, some with feelings still undefined, that serious-minded men throughout Europe were siding with the monk against the bishop, and not a few persons of consequence and authority were either openly abetting the monk in his endeavor or secretly shielding him from the fury of his enemies.

It was a war different from the one which is now convulsing Europe. There was no clashing of arms, no brandishing of swords, no crackle of musketry, no endless columns of warriors marching to the beat of the drum to take up their positions in the serried ranks of battle. There was not heard the cannons' echoing roar, that shatters men's nerves and then, after a short shrift, sends them into the carnage of the bayonet charge. At any rate, no battle of this kind was fought in this war until a generation later. It was a battle of spirits. The war was in the hearts of men.

ii

THE PICTORIAL STORY OF LUTHER'S LIFE AND WORK.

By Prof. W. H. T. Dau.

NO person engaged in the work of instructing others or of conveying information to the general public will undervalue the aid derived from a good illustration. The pictorial art has a recognized mission in every department of the education of our race. In the study of historical subjects, in particular, there will be manifested by every healthy mind a keen desire to behold the likeness of the famous men who achieved great things in this world, to obtain a glimpse of the places where, and the physical conditions, under which, their work was performed; to have placed before one a suggestive representation of decisive moments in their lives, and to see the dramatic scenes in which they were the actors.

We do not realize, as a rule, how much knowledge is taken up by us unconsciously since our childhood days by looking at pictures. And not only knowledge is gathered in this way, but settled opinions are formed, aspirations quickened, preferences and aversions fixed. A young boy is turning in a seemingly listless way the pages in Doré's Bible Gallery, or sits musing over the quaint drawings of Schnorr von Carolsfeld, or over the Perry pictures, or the Tissot Collection, or Mastroianni's sculptural reliefs, depict-

i

Convictions clashed. Arguments grappled. Principles were pitted against principles, declarations defied by counter-declarations. Superstitions were shattered, and beliefs sustained. It was as if the plan of this battle had been formulated by the ancient prophet who said: "Not by might, nor by power, but by my spirit, saith the Lord of hosts." (Zech. 4:6.)

The story of that mighty conflict has been told by some of the ablest writers of the world. The historian, the novelist, the dramatist, the poet, have vied with each other to immortalize the actors and the scenes in that war. But the painter and the sculptor have not been behind their brother artists and scholars in zealous devotion to the stirring subject of this war: with more than ordinary prodigality and eminent skill they have reproduced to the eye the leading figures and the most notable events in that conflict. Luther's face, in particular, as that of the master mind of the reformatory movement, has become familiar to most men of our day who lay claim to some degree of culture. Artistic representations of scenes from his life adorn some of the most famous galleries of Europe.

We are on the eve of the four hundredth anniversary of that event from which the beginning of the Reformation is commonly reckoned—the publication of Luther's Ninety-five Theses against the sale of indulgences on the thirty-first of October, 1517. Able authors have in most recent times given us very creditable accounts of Luther's life-work. Some have enlivened the pages of their books with illustrations.

iii

Among these there have been reproduced some rare prints.

The volume which is here submitted to the reader has separated the narrative of Luther's life from the illustrations: it makes the pictures tell the story of Luther. The views assembled in this volume are the result of critical and painstaking research. Years were spent in getting them together. Rev. William Koepchen, himself an ardent and loyal Lutheran, and the pastor of a large Lutheran Church in New York City, has collected these views and written the informing and stirring explanatory remarks that accompany them. The patient labor which he has expended in the assembling of the various parts that make up this series has been ably seconded by the publisher of this memorial volume. No expense has been spared by The Christian Herald in the endeavor to make these views historically accurate and artistically adequate to the great subject which they treat.

May it achieve its silent mission of enlightenment and encouragement in many a Christian home, placing before the old at a glance many a scene that has dimly formed in their minds during hours of laborious reading, and attracting the inquiring youths who may draw an inspiration from the imperishable work of a plain man of the people and a loyal son of the church of Jesus Christ, who dared to obey God's Word rather than men.

W. H. T. Dau.
St. Louis, Mo., October 20, 1915.

MARTIN LUTHER.

There are men of whom the world will never be tired, and Martin Luther is one of them. It would be saying little to state that he is a representative man. He is one of the vital forces of modern civilization. Blot Luther from the sixteenth century and the historical development of the last four hundred years would have been impossible. By him the seething elements of progress were fused, forged into a thunderbolt, and hurled against that power which obstructed the march of civilization, and led mankind captive at its will.

3

LUTHER'S FATHER.

Hans Luther was a firm, straightforward, and pious man, endowed with an unusual portion of sound sense. He knew what he wanted and had no fear of saying what he meant in unmistakable terms. His integrity and sturdy common sense made him, in later life, a respected adviser of the princes at Mansfeld and a trusted magistrate.

4

LUTHER'S MOTHER.

Margaretha Ziegler of Eisenach had been known as a virtuous and pious girl. She retained her modesty and fear of God after her marriage to Hans Luther, and led such a virtuous life that she could be made a model for her sex. On her face, as preserved by Cranach's brush, the struggles of her early life are recorded. For many years, nearly every waking hour was spent in exhausting manual labor.

5

THE HOUSE WHERE MARTIN LUTHER WAS BORN.

It stands in Eisleben, Saxony, at the top of the street which bears his name. The house was partly burned in 1689, but was restored in 1817. The modern entrance is surmounted by a poorly executed bust of Luther with the following inscription: ''In this house Dr. Martin Luther was born November 10, 1483. God's Word and Luther's doctrine pure shall to eternity endure.''

6

LUTHER'S HOME IN MANS-FELD, SAXONY.

For Luther's parents worldly success came slowly. But in time the days of pinching poverty and narrow circumstances passed; industry, frugality and integrity ultimately triumphed. Hans Luther became the proprietor of two furnaces and the owner of this comfortable two-story house in the main street of Mansfeld. This home went, in later years, to Martin's brother James, who paid the four remaining heirs for their share in the estate. The illustration shows the house in its present condition.

7

MANSFELD.

Mansfeld is to-day a small town, with a church in the center and ruins of a castle on a high hill. In 1533 it had three churches and the castle was in its splendor, with high-roofed buildings, spires, and walls pierced by numerous windows. Here Martin grew up under the shadow of dark and wooded cliffs, crowned by the castle of the Counts of Mansfeld and pierced by the shafts of the mines.

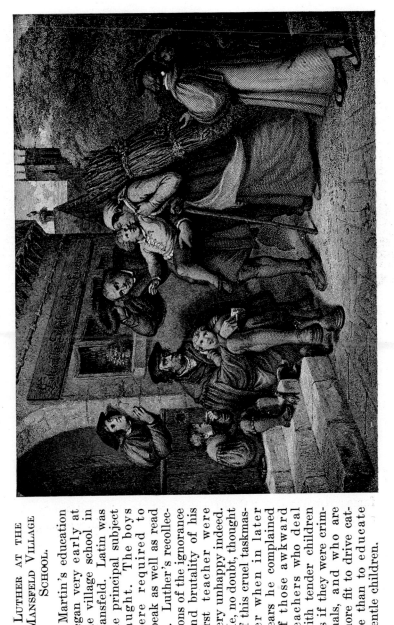

LUTHER AT THE MANSFELD VILLAGE SCHOOL.

Martin's education began very early at the village school in Mansfeld. Latin was the principal subject taught. The boys were required to speak as well as read it. Luther's recollections of the ignorance and brutality of his first teacher were very unhappy indeed. He, no doubt, thought of this cruel taskmaster when in later years he complained of those awkward teachers who deal with tender children as if they were criminals, and who are more fit to drive cattle than to educate gentle children.

9

COTTA HOUSE IN EISENACH.

In the congenial atmosphere of home and school in Eisenach, Luther developed rapidly and made such progress in his studies that, at the age of eighteen years, he said farewell to the generous Cotta family and their home to enter the old and famous University at Erfurt, at that time, perhaps, the most advanced of the higher institutions of learning in Germany.

LUTHER AT THE COR-
TA HOME IN
EISENACH.

The charity of this Christian woman worked a transformation in Luther. He could devote all his time to his studies, and was surrounded by the refining influence of a Christian home. The influence of Martin's new environment was life-long. His intimate friendship with this family of culture during the formative period of his life served to temper such roughness and uncouthness as he brought from the peasant's home and mining town, and fitted him for association with the world.

11

LUTHER RECEIVED INTO COTTA'S HOME AT EISENACH.

While attending school at Eisenach, Luther joined one of
the companies of singers who went from house to house singing
and accepting money. His beautiful voice brought him to the
attention of Ursula Cotta, the pious wife of a wealthy merchant. She took him into her home, spoke to him sympathetically and made him one of her family.

OLD ERFURT

It was the custom of the students who did not board
with one of the professors to live at the "Burse," a combination of dormitory and eating-club. Luther lived at the
Burse of St. George, which once stood on Lehmann's Bridge.
It was a building similar to the one seen on this Krämer-
brücke.

ERFURT UNIVERSITY.

The University at Erfurt was one of the earliest on German soil. It was founded in 1392, and reached its high-water mark in 1480, with an enrollment of 2,000. On the records, still preserved, though the university ceased to exist in 1816, may be read to-day the entry: "Martinus Luder ex Mansfeld."

14

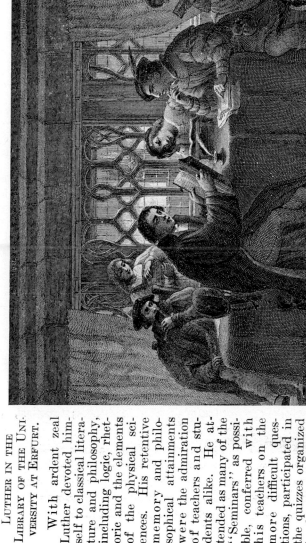

LUTHER IN THE
LIBRARY OF THE UNI-
VERSITY AT ERFURT.

With ardent zeal
Luther devoted him-
self to classical litera-
ture and philosophy,
including logic, rhet-
oric and the elements
of the physical sci-
ences. His retentive
memory and philo-
sophical attainments
were the admiration
of teachers and stu-
dents alike. He at-
tended as many of the
"Seminars" as possi-
ble, conferred with
his teachers on the
more difficult ques-
tions, participated in
the quizzes organized
by the most interested
students, and spent
many an hour in the
library of the uni-
versity.

15

LUTHER AS STUDENT AT ERFURT.

Luther was a sociable fellow, witty, talkative, fond of joke and jest, and devoted to music, for which he had a natural talent, and which he regarded as one of the most beautiful gifts of God, ranking it next after theology in importance. When he felt fatigued or otherwise indisposed with study and writing, he took his flute or his guitar and played some agreeable air. He often praised the art of music to his friends, saying: "Music is the best cordial to a person in sadness; it soothes, quickens and refreshes the heart."

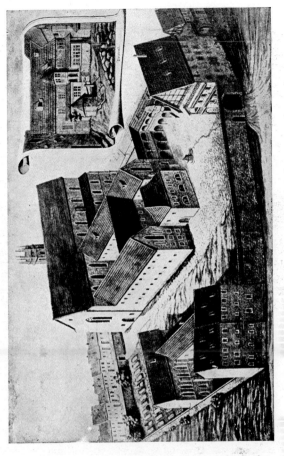

THE AUGUSTINIAN MON-
ASTERY IN ERFURT.

(As it was in 1560.)

Of the twenty monas-
teries in Erfurt in Lu-
ther's time, the Augustinian bore the highest rep-
utation for theological
learning and for public
service. This convent at
Erfurt was dissolved
after the Reformation
and converted into an
Orphans' Home, called
"Martinsstift," in honor
of the most illustrious inmate the building ever
held.

17

LUTHER AT THE AUGUSTINIAN MONASTERY AT ERFURT.

No exemptions from the humiliating duties in the cloister were made for this distinguished Master of Arts. He swept the walks, scrubbed the floors, washed the filthiest vessels, and, with a sack on his back, begged provisions in Erfurt and the neighboring villages. But the spiritual peace for which his heart craved did not come to his heart by this participation in the duties, drudgeries and humiliations of convent life.

18

LUTHER IN ROME.

Besides attending to the business of his mission to Rome, Luther at once began to gather all the "spiritual blessings", which his church had to offer in this city. In this church, Santa Maria del Popolo, Luther read his first mass within the city wall. The structure is said to cover the place where Pope Pascal burned to ashes the exhumed body of the wicked Roman Emperor Nero, who had Peter crucified, Paul beheaded, and many Christians put to death in the most brutal manner.

19

JOHANN VON STAUPITZ, D.D.

In this Vicar General of the Augustinian Order the monk
Luther found a sincere friend and spiritual helper. Staupitz
was of noble birth, of high scholarly attainments and with a
spirit of simple, unaffected piety and wide sympathies. His
judgment was sober, and his great tact in dealing with cases
of conscience made him pre-eminently a true shepherd of souls.
The portrait represents Staupitz as Abbot of the Benedictine
Monastery of St. Peter at Salzburg. He died there in 1524.

CONVENT OF THE AUGUSTIN-
IANS IN ROME.

During Luther's four
weeks' stay at this convent of
the Augustinians in Rome his
mind was filled with amazement. He had come to Rome
as to the throne of God's High
Priest on earth, but found it
filled with degrading vices.
Under Pope Alexander VI,
the Papacy had reached its
very lowest degradation. He
is about the only pope that
has never found an apologist.
Conditions under his successor, Julius II, were still un-
speakable in their vileness.

21

SCALA SANCTA.

One of the many shrines visited by Luther during his stay in Rome was the "Scala Sancta," or Pilate's Staircase, supposed to be the very stairway upon which our Saviour ascended to the palace of Pontius Pilate. Luther crawled up these steps upon his knees but failed to experience any spiritual satisfaction in this exercise.

22

MARTIN LUTHER, DOCTOR OF THEOLOGY.

Staupitz, wishing to be relieved from his duties at the university, had, with the consent of the Elector, selected Luther as his successor. Luther urged his delicate health and begged to be excused. But he finally consented, held the required disputation, October 18, 1512, and was with all due ceremony created a Doctor of Divinity on the following day, pledging himself to devote his whole life to the study, exposition, and defense of the Scriptures. This pledge gave him privileges and rights which his enemies could not deny, and it laid on him obligations and duties which he never forgot.

23

LEO X.

Reared amidst all the luxuries wealth could bring and enjoying the highest social rank, this pope recoiled from the coarse sensuality of Alexander VI, but he was no less a devotee of pleasure, according to the standards of his more cultivated tastes. In furthering his plans for personal pleasure, as well as in continuing the adornment of the Papal city in keeping with the artistic ideals of his age, Leo was the most prodigal of spendthrifts. Often in desperate straits for the ready cash, it was only too convenient for him to realize the necessary money by the sale of indulgences.

24

Friedrich, surnamed the Wise, Elector of Saxony, was a judicious capable ruler and pious according to mediæval standards. He loved peace, order and justice. This moved him to protect Luther, though he otherwise avoided all personal contact with the Reformer. The Elector was the most powerful of the princes of the Empire, and it is due to his passive aid, his guarding the inviolability of Luther's person, rather than to any public assent to Luther's work, that the Reformation was so successful in Germany. This noble-minded prince came at the close of his life to a fuller insight of the Gospel.

25

WITTENBERG. MAR-
KETPLACE,
CASTLE CHURCH AND
CASTLE.

Wittenberg is situ-
ated on the banks of
the Elbe, about half-
way between Leipzig
and Berlin. Towards
the end of the fif-
teenth century Wit-
tenberg had only 350
low, frame, straw-
thatched houses, an
old church and a town
hall. Friedrich, who
became Elector of
Saxony in 1486, chose
Wittenberg as his
residence and thus in

26

a way as the capital of his northern territory. He began immediately to ornament the town with public buildings, including a castle and a church. In 1502 he founded the university, which was later made world-renowned by Luther.

THE
BLACK CLOISTER IN
WITTENBERG.

This Augustinian cloister, where Luther had lived ever since he came to Wittenberg, is situated at the extreme southeast of the town, near the Elster Gate. It is a roomy building and had accommodated at one time as many as forty monks. Elector Friedrich made Luther a wedding present of the building with the court in front and

the gardens behind. The gift was legally confirmed seven years later, when the Elector Johann deeded this property to Luther and his wife jointly.

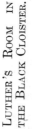

LUTHER'S ROOM IN THE BLACK CLOISTER.

Luther's rooms are now used as a museum, and are filled with interesting relics of the Reformer. In this, his study-room, the old writing table where Luther worked stands defiant of time, though its splinters and rough edges are beginning to tell the secret of its great age. The large iron stove that warmed Luther's blood can yet hold the flames of many fires; the same window-panes with a broken one here and there, still let in the sunlight; the same planks remain in the floor of his study.

28

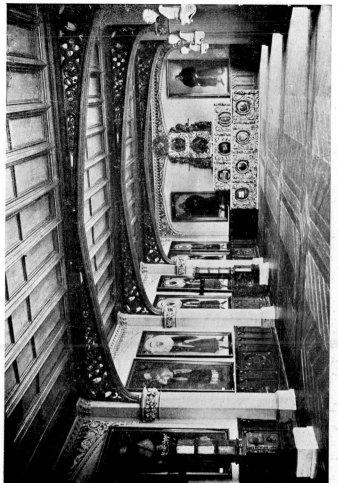

LUTHER'S LECTURE HALL.

On the south side of the second floor of the Black Cloister, or Luther Haus, was Luther's lecture hall, for Luther held his lectures here, instead of in the university building. The University of Wittenberg remained for many decades a noble monument to Luther's influence. It was the first European institution to teach the three ancient languages, Hebrew, Greek and Latin. In 1817 it was incorporated with the University of Halle. Luther gave his last lecture in this hall on November 17, 1545, completing his course on the Book of Genesis.

29

THE UNIVERSITY AT WITTENBERG.

Wittenberg, the electoral residence, was selected as the site of the university, partly because the income of the Castle Church could be used for its support, partly because there was an Augustinian monastery there, which could be relied upon for teachers of philosophy and theology. Martin Pollich, Doctor of Medicine, Philosophy and Theology, and physician to the Elector, and Staupitz were the Elector's chief advisers. To promote Friedrich's plan, they called to Wittenberg competent monks from other cities to aid in the work of instruction. Among those drafted was Martin Luther.

30

"STADTKIRCHE" IN WITTENBERG.

By urgent request of the town council of Wittenberg, Luther, in 1515, accepted the charge as pastor of the Town Church, whose pastor, Simon Heintz, was sickly and unable to fulfill his many duties. This edifice, surmounted by double towers, is large and massive, externally plain and without any architectural pretension. The interior is commodious and well adapted to Protestant worship.

31

INTERIOR OF THE STADTKIRCHE IN WITTENBERG.

Notwithstanding his other occupations, Luther found time
to preach constantly. Bugenhagen was pastor of this Stadtkirche. When in 1528 and 1529, 1530 and 1532, and again
from 1537 to 1540 Bugenhagen was away on missionary and
other duties, Luther preached in his pulpit, Sunday after Sunday, frequently also on Wednesdays and Saturdays.

PULPIT IN THE STADTKIRCHE, WITTENBERG, IN LUTHER'S TIME.

From this pulpit Luther preached most of those eloquent sermons that set the souls of his hearers aflame. His voice was sonorous and far-reaching, his large and dark eyes seemed to flash fire when under excitement, and when reaching a climax he bore down with the full torrent of his oratory. While indescribably powerful his preaching was always reverent and humble.

CASTLE CHURCH AT WITTENBERG.

To the door of this Castle Church Luther affixed his ninety-five theses, October 31, 1517. The wooden doors to which the theses were nailed were burned in 1760, during the war with Austria, but in 1858 Emperor Friedrich Wilhelm IV replaced them by iron doors, bearing the original text of the theses.

INTERIOR OF THE CASTLE CHURCH IN WITTENBERG.

Monday, February 22d, the Counts of Mansfeld arrived with Luther's corpse before Wittenberg. At the Elsterthor they were received by the whole University, the town counselors and citizens. The leaden coffin was carried into this Castle Church, against which he had nailed the ninety-five theses. Bugenhagen, as pastor of the town church, delivered a sermon in German and Melanchthon followed with a funeral oration in Latin on behalf of the University. The body was then lowered into a prepared grave near the pulpit.

35

PHILIP MELANCHTHON.

Melanchthon had entered Heidelberg University at the age of thirteen, had taken the degree of bachelor at fifteen and of master one year later. At the age of twenty-one he was called to the University of Wittenberg from Tübingen to become its first professor of Greek. One of the greatest scholars and teachers of the century, he not only immensely enhanced the fame of the university, but also proved himself a most efficient aide of Luther.

THE SALE OF INDULGENCES.

One of the commissioners appointed by Albert, Archbishop of Mainz, to conduct the sale of indulgences was the Dominican monk, Johann Tetzel, an experienced, aggressive and violent haranguer, who had been used very efficiently in similar enterprises. He was neither a model of virtue nor a person with particularly high ideals or sensitive conscience, but an arrogant and audacious salesman, who mingled with truth what was erroneous and uncertain.

37

THE POPULACE READING THE NINETY-FIVE THESES.

The immediate effect of these theses was startling. Their boldness and pointedness paralyzed both speech and action. They did not immediately call forth the enthusiasm which might have been expected at the sudden appearance of a leader for a cause for whose maintenance there was a crying need. Nor did they at once meet a storm of protest from those not ready to express their satisfaction. The statements were too true to warrant any indiscriminate attack,

38

Nailing the Ninety-five Theses to the Church Door.

Instead of thundering against Tetzel from the pulpit, or
publishing a polemic pamphlet, or issuing an open letter to the
archbishop, calling him sharply to account, as Luther was
quite capable of doing, he invited the theologians in Wittenberg
and the neighborhood to a discussion. Adopting the usual
method of announcing such a debate, he posted a notice on the
door of the Castle Church stating time and place of the proposed disputation and the theses he intended to defend.

VERA IMAGO IOHANNIS ECCII
THEOLOGIÆ D. ÆTATIS
SVÆ XLIII

ECK EIN GROSSER FEIND CHRISTI WAR
HAT SEHR VERFOLGT DIE CHRISTLICH SCHAR
MIT SCHREIBEN VND VNNVCZEM GSCHWECZ
BRACHT ER DIE EINFELTIGEN INS NEC Z
EIFRIG VND BÖS WAR ALL SEIN SIINN
VERNEBS IM GOT ER IST LANG HIINN.

JOHANN ECK, D.D., a professor of the University of Ingolstadt, was like Luther a peasant by extraction and a monk by profession, a theologian of no mean ability, and a man of energy and resource. He was, without doubt, the ablest and most persistent opponent Luther ever had. In Rome he painted Luther's "heresy" in such black colors that Leo finally decided that there was nothing left but to condemn Luther.

40

LUTHER BEFORE CARDINAL CAJETAN.

In his defense before the Cardinal, Luther declared that he held to all he had said as Catholic truth and could not retract unless convinced of error. Since he was but human and therefore fallible, he declared himself willing to submit his theses to a legitimate judgment of the Church, and to the learned Doctors of the Universities of Basel, Louvain and Paris. Cajetan, who was not a match for Luther in theology, dismissed this proposal and again urged him to retract, threatening him and all his friends with excommunication. Thus ended this formal effort to induce Luther to recant.

41

DISPUTATION BETWEEN LUTHER AND ECK IN LEIPZIG.

The debate was opened with much pomp and solemnity on the twenty-seventh of June, 1519. After Karlstadt had debated until the fourth of July, Luther himself took the floor. Though very careful and moderate in his utterances, he yet maintained that the authority of the Pope was of human and not of divine right, and that a Christian might therefore be saved, even if he refused to submit to it. This the sneering Eck at once declared sounded like the opinion of Johann Hus, who had been condemned by the Council of Constance and burned as a heretic a hundred years before.

42

BURNING OF THE PAPAL BULL.

On December 10, 1520, Luther invited all who adhered to the truth of the Gospel to be present at the solemn burning of the papal law books. At 9 A. M. he and a large number of students and teachers marched to a place outside of the Elster Gate, near the Chapel of the Holy Cross, where the clothing of those who had died of contagious diseases was wont to be burned. In the presence of the multitude Luther placed upon the woodpile the books of the Canon Law and when the pile had been lighted, threw into the flames the bull of excommunication issued against him by the Pope.

43

LUTHER SETTING OUT FOR WORMS.

The Imperial herald, Caspar Sturm, arrived at Wittenberg with the official summons, March 26, 1521. Granting the herald a few days for rest, Luther set forth on April 2 so as to afford ample time to reach Worms within the twenty-one days granted. The town council of Wittenberg provided the horses and the covered wagon for the journey, and the University voted twenty gulden to cover the necessary expenses. With Luther were Amsdorf, his life-long friend; Dr. Schurf, the canon lawyer; Johann Petzensteiner, a fellow monk, and Peter Swaṇen, a Pomeranian nobleman.

44

CHARLES V.

The election of Charles of Spain, on June 28, 1519, had been hailed with enthusiasm, but those who had expected much were doomed to disappointment. He was by temperament and training far more Spanish than German. Germany was hardly more than a pawn in his political game. When he needed the support of the Papacy he was quite willing to use his power to suppress Lutheranism, and though a devout Catholic, he permitted it to flourish when he wished to bring the Pope to terms.

45

LUTHER PREACHING
AT MOEHRA.

The towns through which Luther passed on his return from the Diet received him as warmly as on his way to Worms. On the second of May he entered his dear old Eisenach, where he had spent the happiest years of his boyhood. The next day he left the hospital town to visit his relatives in the nearby village of Moehra, about fifteen miles south of Eisenach. He spent the night with his grandmother, and preached a sermon to the village folks on the following morning, May 4, 1521, under a linden tree. After dinner he left, accompanied by Amsdorf and Petzensteiner.

46

LUTHER ENTERING
WORMS.

The news that Luther was approaching soon filled the streets of Worms with a surging mass of people. A number of noblemen had mounted their horses and gone out to meet him and now led the bold Reformer in grand procession into the city. Luther was greeted with prolonged cheers as he proceeded toward his lodgings at the inn of the Knights of St. John. The whole city seemed to have turned out to see Luther enter.

THE BISHOP'S PALACE IN WORMS.

On April 17th, the day after his arrival in Worms, Luther was cited to appear before the Diet that afternoon at 4 o'clock in the Bishop's Palace, where the Emperor Charles and his brother Ferdinand were staying. This Bishop's Palace was destroyed by the French in 1689 and, after being rebuilt, was again destroyed by them in 1794.

LUTHER BEFORE THE DIET AT WORMS.

On the seventeenth of April, at four o'clock, Luther was led into the assembly hall in the Episcopal Palace to stand before the Emperor and the realm. It was a brilliant spectacle which his eyes beheld. Upon a gorgeous throne sat the Emperor Charles V, whose dominions encircled the globe, upon whose realms the sun never set. Upon elevated chairs were seated the Electors of the Empire, and with them were assembled the chief princes of Germany, the representatives of the free cities, and many others of authority in German territory, in all 204 persons, including the seven ambassadors of foreign powers.

49

LUTHER AT THE ENTRANCE OF THE COUNCIL HALL.

When the hour had arrived in which this faithful witness of Jesus Christ was to stand before the great and mighty of the earth to make a good profession, the valiant and famous general, Georg von Frundsberg, touched him on the shoulder and said: "My dear monk, thou hast to-day a march and a struggle to go through, such as neither I nor other great captains have seen in our most bloody battles; but if thy cause be just, go forward in God's name; he will not forsake thee."

LUTHER BEFORE THE DIET AT WORMS.

All parties must unite in admiring and venerating the man who, undaunted and alone, could stand before such an assembly and vindicate with unshaken courage what he conceived to be the truth over against the deliberate, ancient and almost universal opinion of mankind, fearless of any reproach but that of his own conscience, or of any disapproval but that of his God. Luther knew of no authority in divine matters outside of the inspired Word of God. He recognized no conscience as enlightened except by this Word.

51

LUTHER BEFORE THE DIET AT WORMS.

"Since his Imperial Majesty requires a simple and straight answer, I will give him one: I do not believe in either the Pope or the councils alone, since it is certain that they have often erred and contradicted themselves. Unless I am therefore convinced by the testimony of the Scriptures, or by clear and forcible reasons, I neither can nor will recant a single word." This "No" may be said to have given back to the world a Church without a Pope and a State without an Inquisition.

THE CATHEDRAL AT WORMS.

Of all the buildings which existed at the period of the Diet, the cathedral alone remains. It is built of red sandstone, Romanesque in style. The interior, four hundred and seventy feet in length, lighted through stained windows, is very impressive. Services were conducted in this spacious church building during the session of the Diet. Here, on May 26, 1521, after divine service, Charles V signed the decree which made Luther an outlaw.

EIN FESTE BURG IST UNSER GOTT.

This hymn, "A Mighty Fortress is Our God," is Luther in song. It is pitched in the very key of the man. Rugged and majestic, trustful of God and confident, it was the defiant trumpet-blast of the Reformation speaking out to the powers of the earth and under the earth an all-conquering conviction of divine vocation and empowerment. The world has many songs of exquisite tenderness and uncommon trust, but this one is matchless in its warlike tone, its rugged strength and its inspiring challenge.

ERASMUS OF ROTTERDAM.

Erasmus of Rotterdam was a scholar of great talent, with more friends, reputation and influence than any other private person in Europe. Though once an inmate of a monastery, he abhorred the monks and exposed their stupidity and vices with terrible severity. His opposition to the scandalous condition of things in the Roman Church was sincere, and his place should have been at Luther's side in his conflict with Rome. But the waters were too deep and the storms too fierce for the wavering Erasmus.

LUTHER'S ARRIVAL AT
THE WARTBURG,
MAY 4, 1521.

Hans von Ber-
lepsch, commander of
The Wartburg, had
been entrusted with
the securing and safe-
keeping of Luther.
The removal of Lu-
ther to a place of safe-
ty and retirement was
certainly a wise pre-
caution, for on May
26, after the Saxon
Elector and other
supporters of Luther
had left Worms, the
Emperor signed the
bill which made Lu-
ther an outlaw in the
Empire. Luther was to be seized wherever found. His books were ordered burned; and to publish, sell,
buy or read any of his writings was strictly forbidden.

56

THE WARTBURG.

As the prophet of old was hid in a cave from the wrath of Ahab, so Luther was conveyed to this grim fortress, crowning the wooded heights two miles to the south of the town of Eisenach. The building is neither magnificent nor picturesque, but it exhibits Romanesque arcades which run back to the twelfth century. In this stronghold of the Elector, Luther was to enjoy a safe refuge from the storms that were now to break over him.

57

THE WARTBURG. LUTHER'S ROOM.

After Luther's arrival at The Wartburg he was led to the room where he was to spend months in retirement. This room, with its bay-window, is shown in the center of our picture. In 1847 the Grand Duke Karl Alexander of Weimar resolved to restore the castle as nearly as possible to its former architectural beauty, and the work has been carried out in excellent taste and skill, and in full harmony with the original designs of the twelfth and thirteenth centuries.

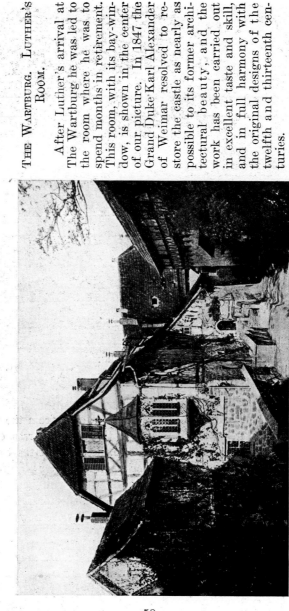

LUTHER AT THE WARTBURG.

Though outlawed by the Emperor, Luther was neither crushed nor silenced. From the height of this, his lonely retreat, from this, his castle in the clouds, he delivered blow after blow against the Papacy, and every blow meant progress. Men listened and wondered at the change caused by the thunder that crashed from The Wartburg, while at the sight of these repeated blows his friends and enemies with equal astonishment exclaimed: "He is still alive and in touch with all that is going on."

59

LUTHER AS KNIGHT GEORGE AT THE WARTBURG.

The identity of Luther while at The Wartburg was carefully concealed. He allowed his hair and beard to grow, put on the costume of a knight, wore a gold chain, carried a sword, and engaged occasionally in the sports and occupations of a young nobleman. He went by the name of Junker Jörg, and was supposed to be a knight living in temporary retirement. This picture of Luther was painted by Cranach during Luther's secret visit to Wittenberg in the early part of December, 1521.

KATHARINA VON BORA.

Katharina von Bora, Luther's wife, was the daughter of Hans von Bora and Katharina von Haugwitz, who died shortly after the birth of her daughter. When but five years of age her father married again, and therefore sent little Katharina to the convent school of the Benedictine nuns near Brehna, Saxony. When nine years old she was set apart for the religious life and put into the convent at Nimbschen. She was a pious woman, a vigorous and efficient housewife, and deeply interested in her husband's work.

THE BETROTHAL OF LUTHER TO KATHARINA VON BORA.

On a certain day in May or early in June, 1525, Luther, accompanied by his friend Lucas Cranach, wended his way to the home of Philip Reichenbach and made to Katharina von Bora the proposition of marriage, which was promptly and joyfully accepted. It is this scene the artist Scheurenberg seeks to present to us in the painting reproduced on this page.

LUTHER'S MARRIAGE.

Luther's courtship was brief. Constantly under the eyes of the world, with enemies and friends observing his every movement, he naturally wished the matter conducted as speedily as possible. The marriage took place June 13, 1525, more than two years after the nun had renounced communion with Rome. Luther had invited the two chief pastors of Wittenberg, Bugenhagen and Jonas, Dr. Apel, a colleague of the law faculty, and Lucas Cranach and his wife. Pastor Bugenhagen officiated at the marriage.

63

PUBLIC CELEBRATION OF LUTHER'S MARRIAGE.

June 27th was appointed as the day for the formal and public celebration of Luther's marriage. On the appointed day, a service was held in the Stadtkirche and a wedding feast given at Luther's home. A large circle of guests were present at that eventful ceremony; among these was Leonhard von Koppe, who had assisted Katharina in her escape from the convent. Wedding presents were sent by the University, the Elector, Cranach, and also from the Archbishop Albrecht of Mainz, who had been the frequent object of many of Luther's most merciless attacks.

ELECTOR JOHANN, SURNAMED THE CONSTANT.

The Elector Friedrich was succeeded by his brother
Johann. Except on rare occasions the Elector Friedrich took
no active part in the work of the Reformation, but with the
accession of his brother the period of hesitation was over.
Johann was devoted heart and soul to Luther's cause and was
glad to let it be known. He died August 16, 1532, and was
buried in the Castle Church at Wittenberg, Luther officiating.

LUTHER'S FAMILY LIFE.

Luther's greatest happiness, next to that of the Word of God, was to be with his family. The home life of Luther was touching and beautiful. Here we see him in his truest self. Luther's home was his Bethany, where in innocent joy, love and peace he recuperated for life's fierce battles. Few of the world's greatest men have been privileged to enjoy for many years the solace and comfort of home and family as he did.

66

LUTHER AND HIS CHILDREN.

Besides his own children, Luther and his wife brought up no less than eleven of his orphaned nephews and nieces. This reprimander of Popes and Kings was loved by the children, and the great champion was as playful among them as though he were himself again a child. He could fight fiercely all day for his cause and in the evening take his lute, gaze at the stars, sing psalms and muse upon the clouds, the fields, the flowers, the birds, dissolved in melody and devotion.

MAGDALENA LUTHER.

Magdalena Luther was a child of singular depth of character, amiable, affectionate and deeply religious. Without the ordinary failings of children, her father testifies that she had never done an act requiring parental reproof. A profound impression was made upon all of Luther's acquaintances as they saw or heard of a man of such rugged strength overcome with emotion by the side of his dying child. At the age of thirteen she fell asleep in her father's arms.

THE PEASANTS' WAR.

The most disastrous blow to Luther and his work was the Peasants' War. Luther was neither responsible for it, nor did it begin among his disciples. It was only a repetition, on a larger scale, of many similar attempts of former years, and the interests underlying all of them were not religious, but economic. These and a misinterpretation of certain of Luther's utterances precipitated and gave impetus to the revolt. Never found wanting in the hour of danger, Luther sought by every means in his power to make the princes and lords see their wrong policy toward these unfortunates, and when this was of no avail he tried to persuade the peasants to peace. Had Luther's advice been followed at the outset, much bloodshed would have been avoided and many of the demands of the peasants would have been granted.

LUTHER TRANSLATING THE OLD TESTAMENT.

The warm reception given the translation of the New Testament induced Luther to continue his translation of the Old Testament. In this work he gladly availed himself of the learning of Aurogallus, the Professor of Hebrew at Wittenberg, and of Melanchthon. Other Wittenberg professors and pastors were called in for consultation, among whom were Ziegler, Rörer, Jonas, Bugenhagen and Förster. For a time a weekly "Collegium" was held, beginning a few hours before supper, in which the various texts and translations were faithfully compared.

ARRIVAL OF LUTHER AND HIS COLABORERS AT MARBURG.

Luther expected little good from the conference which Philip of Hesse had arranged between Zwingli and himself, and frankly informed the Landgraf of his attitude. He finally yielded, however, and promised to be present. Zwingli, with Œcolampadius, Bucer, Hedio and others, arrived September 27, 1529. Three days later came Luther, accompanied by Melanchthon, Jonas, Cruciger, Myconius, Brenz, Osiander, Stephan Agricola and others. The tireless Landgraf provided accommodations for all in his castle and entertained them in truly royal fashion.

LUTHER ARGUING WITH ZWINGLI AT MARBURG.

Taking his stand upon the literal interpretation of the words: "This is my body, etc.," Luther refused to compromise with the Zwinglian party. As often as Zwingli appealed to reason Luther appealed to the immutable Word of God, declaring that one word of Scripture was more to him than heaven and earth. When he realized that Zwingli would not yield he closed the colloquy with the words: "You have a different spirit than ours."

LUTHER AND
ZWINGLI AT MARBURG.

It must have cost
Luther much heart-
ache to say "No" at
Marburg. Philip was
urging him with
might and main to ac-
knowledge the Zwing-
lians as brothers;
Zwingli was begging
for brotherhood with
tears in his eyes; Lu-
ther's own heart was
burning with desire
for union and frater-
nal fellowship, and
yet he felt bound to
decline Zwingli's
hand.

73

THE CASTLE OF COBURG.

On the third of April, 1530, Luther, Melanchthon, and other Wittenberg theologians set out for Augsburg. On the fifteenth of April, Coburg, 130 miles from Augsburg, was reached. As no safe-conduct for Luther had been furnished, the Elector placed Luther, who was still under the ban of the Empire, in this powerful castle of Coburg, behind walls that, in the Thirty Years' War, were to defy all the efforts of Wallenstein. The Elector Johann, to whom the castle at that time belonged, wished to have Luther out of harm's way during the Augsburg Diet.

MARTIN LUTHER.

Looked at in the flesh, perhaps, no one would have thought of Luther as the chosen instrument of God to grapple with the magnitudinous tyranny by which Europe was enthralled. Rome has never forgotten nor forgiven him. Profited by his labors beyond what she ever could have been without him, she still curses his name and everything that savors of him. Oft-answered and exploded calumnies are revived afresh to throw dishonor on his cause.

SCHMALKALDEN.

During the Christmas season of 1530, the Protestant princes and the representatives of a number of free cities met in this building in the little town of Schmalkalden, to form a defensive league for mutual protection against the Emperor and the Catholic princes. This League of Schmalkalden laid the political foundations of religious liberty for our modern world. Luther was the first effectively to assert the principle of the independence of the State from ecclesiastical control.

JOHANN FRIEDRICH, ELECTOR OF SAXONY.

Johann Friedrich, who succeeded his father, John the Constant, had been brought up in a strongly Lutheran atmosphere by Spalatin. He was an even more ardent disciple of the Reformer than his father, and for his unflinching courage in confessing the faith in peril of his life deserves to be honored as one of the greatest heroes of the Reformation. His wife, Sybilla, also took an active interest in everything pertaining to Luther's cause.

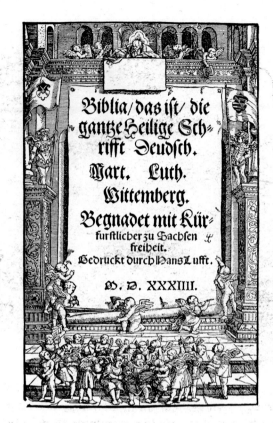

FIRST EDITION OF LUTHER'S TRANSLATION OF THE COMPLETE
BIBLE, 1534.

The importance for the whole of Christendom of Luther's
translation of the Bible can hardly be overestimated. The
German people received in it a treasure which enriched them
for all time. Their language, their literature, their thought,
their life, their schools, and above all, their souls were enriched
thereby. Luther's version has won the highest praise. Idio-
matic, vital in every part, clothed in the racy language of
common life, it created, apart from its religious influence, an
epoch in the literary development of the German nation.

THE CASTLE IN WITTENBERG.

Friedrich, surnamed the Wise, who became Elector of Saxony in 1486, usually resided at Altenburg, in the southern part of his territory, but built this castle at Wittenberg in order to have a residence for his northern dominions also. At this castle occurred the famous meeting of Luther and the papal legate, Cardinal Vergerio, who had come to "that sink of heresy" (Wittenberg) in November, 1535, and invited the banned and outlawed heretic Luther to breakfast with him. He referred to Luther as a "beast" in his report to Rome, but later in life the study of the writings of the "beast" made him a heretic in the eyes of his Church. He died in Tübingen, active to the last as a publicist against the Papacy.

LUTHER BIDDING
FAREWELL
TO HIS FAMILY

The brother counts of Mansfeld, Albert and Gerhard, had asked Luther's good office in settling a dispute of long standing. His first trip in October, 1545, was fruitless, as the counts were suddenly called away. At Christmas Luther was again the guest of the Count Albert, but Melanchthon was taken ill, and Luther hastened to Wittenberg with him, promising that he would return. On January 23d he started for the third time on his errand of peace, taking with him his three sons. His wife, Kate, saw him depart with a sorrowful presentiment that she should never see him again.

80

LUTHER'S DEATH.

Luther suffered an apoplectic stroke on February 18, 1546. The physicians Wild and Ludwig, the Count of Schwarzenburg, Count Albrecht and the Countess were unwearied in their efforts to relieve him, but to no avail. The pastors Jonas and Cölius, who were with him at the end, inquired of him: "Reverend father, do you die in the faith of your Lord Jesus Christ and in the doctrine which you preached in His name?" The answer was a clear and distinct "Yes." It was his last word.

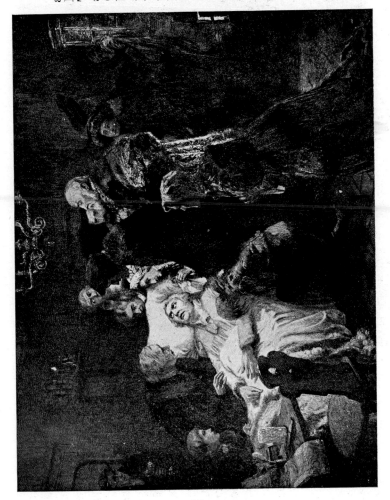

81

FUNERAL ESCORT OF
LUTHER.

The counts of Mansfeld wished to have the Reformer buried in Eisleben, but the Elector of Saxony insisted on having the body sent to Wittenberg. Clothed in a white Suabian gown, the corpse was placed in a leaden coffin. Dr. Jonas delivered a funeral sermon on February 19th, and Pastor Cölius preached a farewell sermon on February 20th. Escorted by the two Mansfeld counts and a great number of horsemen, and greeted en route by mourning thousands, the body reached Wittenberg on Monday, the twenty-second of February, where the largest crowd ever seen in the little town gathered to receive the dead hero.

82

THE EPOCH OF THE REFORMATION.

Next to the Epoch of the Gospel the Reformation period certainly stands out in history as an age of far-reaching influence. The artist is here endeavoring to represent this brilliant age in all its manifold phases and meanings. The revival of Christianity holds the center of the stage. By restoring to fallen Christendom the doctrine and life of apostolic times, Luther's Reformation secured the future development of humanity and prepared for the nations who receive it a reign of intellectual light, liberty, morality, order and achievement.

INDEX

Absolution, 75.
Abuse of Luther, 21, 223.
Address to the Nobility, 112, 114, 117, 263, 313.
Ailly, Pierre d', 71, 73, 87, 180.
A Mighty Fortress, 37.
Amsdorf, 159, 168, 222.
Anabaptists, 17, 34, 229, 267, 307, 318. (See Münzer.)
Angels, 259.
Apocalypse of St. John, 267, 268, 272.
Aristotle, 45, 49, 88, 181.
Asceticism, 279, 292. (See Monasticism.)
Augsburg, 114, 130, 138, 220.
Augsburg, Diet of, 229.
Augustine, 37, 49, 63, 82, 86, 90, 106, 110, 180, 210, 225, 249, 315.
Augustinians, 53, 57, 70, 75, 100, 136, 142, 155, 163, 166, 171.
Aurifaber, 37, 190.
Autobiography of Luther, 59.

Babylonian Captivity, 227, 283.
Ban, 159, 170.
Barge, 20, 26, 147.
Bernard of Clairvaux, 73, 79, 86, 95, 107, 244.
Bible, Interpretation, 46, 182, 249, 265, 291, 303.
Bible, "Modern" Theologians of the Middle Ages and, 93.
Bible, Source of Doctrine, 93.
Biel, 71, 79, 91, 101, 107, 180.
Bigamy in General, 227, 241.
Bigamy of Philip of Hesse, 227.
Bismarck, 20, 69, 244, 268.
Black Cloister, 53, 63, 65, 82, 156,

163, 165, 180, 193, 213, 221, 244.
Blasphemy, 258, 305, 310.
Bonaventura, 73, 74, 102.
Brant, 267, 273.
Bull of Excommunication, 12, 141.

Cajetan, 114, 129, 135, 138, 144, 229, 237.
Calvin, 42, 151, 184, 244, 252.
Canon Law, 50, 127, 181.
Catharine von Bora, 22, 188, 190, 199, 205, 211, 218, 244, 258.
Catholic Background of Luther, 236, 242, 253, 282, 298, 316.
Catholic Biographies of Luther, 21.
Catholic Hierarchy, 92, 286.
Catholic Piety, 276.
Catholic Reformation, 23, 270, 285.
Catholic Religion in Middle Ages, 89, 270, 276, 292.
Celibacy, 152, 166, 273.
Charles the Fifth, 118, 138, 140, 201, 206.
Church a Missionary Institution, 295.
Church and State, 88, 92, 167, 173, 261, 294, 305.
Church of England, 314, 317.
Cochlaeus, 21, 34, 39N, 55, 196, 223, 229.
Colet, 264, 269.
Confessional, 88, 153.
Confessional Advice, 235.
Confessional, Inviolability of, 238.
Congregation, 296, 314.

85